Contents

'Under Tony Blair and then Gordon Brown, Labour invested more money than ever before in our schools, and the results of 13 years of Labour government are there for all to see'

- Rt Hon Ed Balls MP, Secretary of State for Children, Schools and Families, speaking before the 2010 British General Election

'Schoolchildren in the UK fell in an international league table charting standards in reading, maths and science, it emerged today.

'Figures published by the respected Organisation for Economic Co-operation and Development showed the UK fell from 17th to 25th for reading and from 24th to 28th for maths. In science, pupils dropped from 14th when results were last published in 2007 to 16th this year.

'The results will cast a major shadow over Labour's education record and spark claims that a £30 billion rise in spending under the last Government failed to produce decent results.

'Andreas Schleicher, from the OECD's education directorate, said overall scores achieved by UK pupils were "stagnant at best, whereas many other countries have seen quite significant improvements".'

- The Daily Telegraph, December 6, 2010

'The results are based on tests of 15-year-olds carried out in 2009, and follow a disastrous [earlier] set of results for Britain in 2007, when the country was downgraded in literacy, maths and science.'

- The Guardian, December 6, 2010

Foreword

MY NAME is Frank Chalk and this is the story of a year in my working life as a teacher at... well, let's call it St. Jude's School, Downtown, to spare any blushes.

St Jude's is a pretty poor school – not the worst, by any means, but at the lower end of what our old friend Alastair Campbell used to call 'bog-standard comprehensives' – with a working-class catchment area in a middling-sized city. As such, it's typical of a huge number of schools in Britain, which is quite a horrifying thought.

I've taught maths full-time for quite a few years, and have also done supply teaching. In case you are unfamiliar with the modern education system – if, for example, you're an ex-pupil of ours – a supply teacher is someone who fills in for absent full-timers across a range of subjects. This gives me a broader range of experience than most teachers have: I haven't just taught in one bad school, but many. In all, I've got around 10 years in the classroom under my belt.

I'm a normal bloke from an average background in a small northern town. My mum worked part-time as a teacher and my father worked as a project estimator for a local company. I attended my local comprehensive school and went to university, in the days when you didn't leave with £30,000-worth of debts but they *did* expect you to learn something worthwhile in return. (In my case it was maths.) I'm 45 years old and married. I love outdoor stuff, like skiing, mountain-biking and walking in the countryside.

Obviously, my real name isn't Frank Chalk. Again, I've tried to save a few blushes – my wife's a teacher, too, as are some of my friends, and I wouldn't want them to get embarrassed, or worse, if they are identified.

I've also altered the names and other details of the staff who feature in this book and swapped a few of the kids' names around, for obvious reasons.

However, the characters I describe are real and so are the events: every single one of the stories contained within this book is completely and utterly true. It all happened to me and I have deliberately and carefully avoided exaggeration. I've even kept in about 5% of the bad language (though I have used asterisks). I hate swearing but you can't reflect the atmosphere of a modern comprehensive school without it, I'm afraid.

If you're around 30, parts of this book will make your hair curl. If you're around 40, they'll make your hair fall out. If you're 50 or older...well, to be honest, I wouldn't recommend you read this book without paramedics standing by, defibrillator and oxygen tank at the ready. School isn't like it was in your day. (Or mine.)

All that said, I'm quite sure that there are teachers out there who could tell even more shocking tales. I know that many of them share my despair, though they mostly keep quiet about it. It doesn't do to rock the boat too much.

You might get the impression from reading this book that I don't like kids and that I'm flippant about their futures. Actually, I *do* care, very much, about our youngsters; this book has been born out of my frustration and despair at seeing young lives ruined beyond repair in our classrooms, day in, day out.

Ruined by parents, who spend more time watching TV than talking to their children, who serve them reheated junk food instead of fresh meat and vegetables and who fail utterly to encourage them to get the most out of their school days (some actively encourage them to achieve as little as possible, for reasons I can only guess at).

Ruined by junior schools and, as you'll see, later by us at secondary school.

And ruined by 'the system'.

Blair and Brown promised us 'education, education, education' and failed, disastrously. Cameron and Gove don't show much sign – yet – of getting to grips with the problem, either.

But I don't entirely blame our Prime Ministers, or the hapless succession of ministerial blunderers they have overseen. The rot set in many years ago, and a succession of governments, of both political hues, are responsible. So, too, are the hordes of politically-correct educationalists and right-on teachers whose theories and experimentation with what was once the finest education system in the world have conspired to smash the hopes and dreams of millions of young Britons, to the point where many no longer even have hopes or dreams.

I went into the profession, initially, to 'put something back'. I thought I could 'make a difference', too. Perhaps I was naïve.

I've spent years telling my non-teaching friends about what goes on in the mad, mad world of the state education system.

But – fed a constant diet of lies and distortions, by the media, the teaching unions and ministers, about ever-improving exam results, huge investment and shiny new computers in every classroom – they assume I'm joking, or at least exaggerating.

Sadly, I'm not.

Frank Chalk, May 2011

THE AUTUMN TERM

A French farce

I CAN'T always have felt like this.

In fact, I know I didn't. Somewhere in my distant past, I was a nice, liberal bloke who believed in the British education system.

I know I believed in it when I was in my late teens, and why wouldn't I? I'd come through my A levels OK and I was at university, and I couldn't have got there without a decent education.

I know I did in my early 20s because that was when I decided to become a teacher, and I wouldn't have wanted to become a teacher in the first place if I'd known then what I know now.

But, try as I might, I can't recall the *feeling* of believing in it.

I can't even remember when I lost the feeling.

It was probably at the end of a lesson very like today's, when I'm covering Madame Du Pont's French lesson.

Mme Du Pont is about 35, elegant and mysterious. She is herself covering for the regular French teacher who has been away with 'stress' for so long that the kids have long forgotten his name. In fact, come to think of it, so have I. No-one seems to know how she came to be employed here and her English takes a turn for the worse when questioned about her previous teaching experience or qualifications. Her background story has changed several times, too. She is now claiming to be studying at the university, and working here to improve her English.

I find this surprising; I can't think of a worse place to improve your English.

Foreign languages are always a nightmare to cover in our school.

The kids never know anything at all. And I mean *anything*. No matter how bad you think you were at school, struggling to get by with your pidgin Franglais, you will be fluent compared with most kids today. They know about four words but they have no idea how to write them down or even string them together in the right order to make a spoken sentence. Mind you, I'm not much better myself. Quite why I'm covering French I don't know.

So it is with a heavy heart that I turn the doorknob and enter the classroom

It is nothing less than an assault on the senses. Every wall is filled with brightly-coloured posters. Even the windows are partly obscured by them. Mme Du Pont must have used up the entire department's yearly supply of poster paper in the six months she has been here.

I scan her desk for the work. Ah! Here it is.

'Ze children must carry on with ze worksheets!' I find myself reading, in her comically strong accent (the only interest I retain in French lessons these days is in putting on an outrageous foreign voice and reading things out). The 'worksheets' contain lots of pictures and the odd French word thrown in for good measure. The idea is that the kids fill in the blanks.

I can hear the first arrivals shouting and screaming outside, so I venture out and close the classroom door behind me. They are a Year 9 group and lively, to say the least. That's no surprise; it's the last lesson of the day, and they have dosed themselves up with sugary snacks and fizzy drinks at lunchtime. I always make my classes line up and settle down before letting them in. Now that I am a supply teacher, I no longer have my own classroom; every lesson I cover is in a classroom that belongs to somebody else and I am acutely aware of this. I know how heartbreaking it is to have a display of work wrecked, or equipment damaged, by a horde of unruly teenagers.

This lot are deliberately jostling other kids passing by and a couple of minor scuffles erupt, with no signs of quietening down. I stand at the doorway looking to my right, down the corridor. Only four are queuing.

'God, sir. Let us in!'

'No need to call me God, Leon.'

I look at my watch and calmly start counting the time out. 'Two minutes! You know the score… three minutes!'

They'll be going home after this, and they know that I will write down on the board the number of minutes they take to settle and add them on at the end, thus delaying their visits to the local off-licence, or to the bushes in the park. But it's not having that much effect.

The first half dozen are now lined up, quietly asking if they can go in and shouting 'Shhh!' to the others, who are singing and shouting.

I'm sick of this. It's not fair to the decent pupils.

I slowly walk down the line, gently but firmly placing each child behind the one in front.

'Don't touch me!'

'Oi! Watch it!'

'I'll get me dad on you!'

By the time I reach the end of the line, some have pushed in at the front and one boy has kicked open the classroom door. I return to the doorway and close it.

They behave like this because most of the time, in our school anyway, they are allowed to do so. Most staff tend to let them in quickly to get them out of the corridor, so as to avoid unnecessary embarrassment: this way, the chaos is contained in the classroom, where nobody else can witness it. That is a major cause of our problems – so much bad behaviour is simply swept under the carpet and ignored. The kids will only improve if they are forced to.

I don't care if we end up standing out here all lesson, though I regret that more time was not invested in teaching them to stand still and shut up when they were younger. I would not be having to do it now.

I stand, arms folded, by the door. Speaking calmly, I say, 'We are on nine minutes now. You know you have to be quiet before you go in to my lessons. If it gets to ten minutes I will fetch your Head of Year and you will all do a half-hour detention.' (No, they won't, I think to myself.)

'No, we won't!' yells one boy, near the back of the line. 'You can f*ck off!'

Is that kid telepathic?

No, he can't read *books*, let alone minds.

However, just in case, I form a mental image of me strangling him.

It seems to work: there's a moment of quiet.

Right, that'll do. Seize the moment, like a drowning man grasping at a passing branch.

'OK, in we go. Remember, coats on the hooks.' They like to keep their coats on at every opportunity, regardless of the ambient temperature, as they provide useful places to conceal things like crisps, phones and spliffs.

I remain in the doorway so that they can only go in one by one. They push and shove each other, or pull on each other's bags and coats, completely oblivious to my presence.

I glance at my watch. We've wasted over ten minutes already. There is nothing unusual about this. It's a scene that's being repeated all over the school, although usually inside a classroom.

I have told six pupils where I want them to sit, because I know they are potential troublemakers who will wreck the lesson if allowed to. All of them simply ignore me and sit together at the back. They are used to getting their own way, fighting over seats and enjoying the mayhem caused by not being made to sit in a fixed place each lesson. Who can blame them? It's much more fun than learning French vocab. I'd probably do the same thing myself.

But I can't let them run things, so I spend the next few minutes moving them. Once again, I won't rush any of this: the basics have to be sorted out before we try to do any work. This might appear pedantic, but Choice = Chaos at our school.

Five of them eventually do as they're told. Unfortunately, I can't shift Darren, the sixth reprobate. I've tried telling him firmly and I've tried telling him quietly. Both attempts have failed. Instead, he has put his coat back on and entwined his legs, bag and chair. He is now holding on to his desk, theatrically, and hysterically shouting, 'Help! Rape!' at the top of his voice. This may sound bizarre, but sexual innuendo is everywhere in the school. It is disturbing, at first, but it soon becomes just another unnoticed oddity of your working life.

The group around him are laughing loudly and starting to clap rhythmically, while chanting, 'Don't move! Don't move!'

It is immensely frustrating, all of this. Actually, it's more than frustrating: it's heartbreaking. About a dozen of this class are behaving perfectly, now; they have got their worksheets from the front and started them, following the instructions I've written on the board. Some of these kids now want help and are sitting patiently with their hands up, occasionally calling out 'Sir, Sir!'

But Darren won't allow me to help them; he is the centre of attention and he is absolutely loving it.

I am a good actor, if nothing else. I can keep my face impassive and my voice calm, even though inside I am seething. I have seen this situation many times before and it annoys me greatly. I walk slowly back to the front of the class and, looking him in the eye, quietly announce: 'Darren, come on now. Move to the front or I will have to get Mr Phillips to come and he will exclude you.' (No, he won't.)

Mr Phillips is the Deputy Head in Charge of Discipline. His name strikes terror into the heart of every pupil. (I wish.)

'No he won't!' screams Darren. Unfortunately, he's calling my bluff, so I don't have much choice now.

I take out my phone and tap the Duty SMT number (the SMT is the Senior Management Team, of which more later). I get through to the secretary, who says that she will get Mr Phillips to come over. Loud enough for him to hear me, I ask her to text me the contact number for Darren's mother also.

Although some of these kids are extremely thick, by anybody's definition, they are very quick to grasp things like punishment-likelihoods and cost-benefits. They may not be able to spell 'kudos', but they know what it is and they know that it can be gained by destroying a lesson and providing entertainment for their friends. They can also weigh this up against the low probability of any significant punishment.

I glance at Darren and quietly tell him that I will be making a phone call to his mother. (I don't know what his family arrangements are, or who – if anybody – he is scared of, but I will make it my business to find out.)

'Do you think I care?' he screams back. 'Phone me mother! I couldn't give a f*ck.'

That last bit is said with a mocking smirk. I take two quick steps towards him. Through sheer luck, and nothing else, Darren pretends to cower in mock fear and I soften my face and gently say, 'Right, come on, let's get on with your worksheet.'

I put it on his desk and, to my relief, he gets his pencil out.

The others around him have calmed down a little now and get their pens out too. Like many of their tantrums, this one is over as quickly as it began.

I can finally help the poor kids who have had their hands up for ten minutes.

I keep an eye on Darren; he is still sitting with his coat on, but is quiet now.

As I guide a girl through the tasks, I am bubbling with anger and frustration. Darren has completely destroyed the lesson. I'd dearly love to pick him up and throw him bodily out of the room for the sake of the rest of the group, but the prevailing ethos is to pander to every whim of kids like this.

For a few moments, peace reigns.

Then, all of a sudden, the atmosphere is shattered by a screech.

It's Cherelle, and she's furious with Spencer; she's attempting to pull his hair out and cursing him in industrial terms.

Spencer is appealing to me for help, while trying desperately to free himself.

He has thrown Cherelle's bag out of the window and down into the playground below, where it has already attracted the attentions of a group of stray children. Several pupils, including Cherelle, saw Spencer do it but he protests his innocence. The weird thing is, I believe he really *does* think he's innocent; although this all happened less than a minute ago, he has no memory of it. The default position for almost all kids caught out in wrongdoing is denial, and when this ingrained response is combined with a goldfish-like memory, the attention span of a retarded gnat and a lifetime of E numbers, this is what you get.

Cherelle has stormed out, a handful of Spencer's hair in her fist, and I can already hear her angelic tones – 'Gerraway from ma bag, yer f*ckin' tw*t!', etc – drifting up from the yard.

Just then, Mr Phillips arrives and asks me what the problem is with Darren.

I explain that I want him taken away.

He asks the boy to leave with him and Darren refuses.

Mr Phillips keeps on trying, pleading almost, saying that he doesn't want to have to exclude him. After ten minutes of this farce, during which time Darren plays to the group for all he is worth, lapping up the attention whilst everybody else is distracted from their work, he gets up, picks up his bag, waves goodbye to his friends and walks out.

His parting comment of 'I hate him!', with a nod and a gesture at me, gets them laughing again.

Mr Phillips ignores this, and instead just chivvies him along, pretending to be in some sort of control of the situation. I ask him to bring Darren back to see me at the end of the lesson, but I will be surprised if this happens.

This is all miserably predictable. Mr Phillips is a very nice man but is a weak, ineffectual cog in a broken engine, a system that offers him no support. The kids know this and treat him accordingly. His best shot is to try to befriend them – a total waste of time, and inappropriate anyway – when what we really need in charge of discipline is someone like Genghis Khan, with powers to match.

It's time to pack up and then the bell goes. I reckon we did fifteen minutes useful work out of a one-hour lesson. Five or six kids, egged on by a dozen others, destroyed the lesson for the other twelve.

That's bad enough, but bear this in mind: those kids will destroy every lesson this week, this term and this school year, for the simple reason that they enjoy doing so and there is nothing to stop them.

It's no exaggeration to say that we are allowing them to destroy the lives of their fellow pupils.

I keep behind the worst of them and we sit for a while.

They don't keep particularly quiet and they keep reminding me that, by law, I am only allowed to keep them for ten minutes, otherwise they will miss their buses home.

Halfway through this rather pathetic attempt at detention, Mr Phillips returns with Darren and says that Darren is sorry for what he has done and knows that he has let himself down. After some prompting, Darren apologises to me and says he will try harder to behave next time.

I'm not particularly interested in his apology, to be honest. Experience has taught me that many of our pupils will say literally anything that they believe will get them out of trouble. What I really want is to be able to dissuade him from doing this sort of thing again

– I'd rather be teaching him than arguing with him, after all. But we have no real way of doing this so the only other option is to chuck him out of school for a bit, so the other kids have a chance of learning something in his absence, and hope he gets the message. With this in mind, I ask Mr Phillips how long Darren is to be excluded for.

Mr Phillips sidesteps this. Schools are under pressure from the Government not to exclude pupils and many Heads and Deputies lack the courage to stand up to it. He says that he thinks that Darren knows that he has let himself down and is very sorry. He should write a letter of apology to me so that we can put this behind us.

He says this in a final sort of way, making clear that the matter is closed, and leaves.

Later, I go to his office to discuss it further.

I tell him, again, that I want Darren excluded, even though I know I am wasting my breath. He won't budge. I ask if Darren can be taught in isolation for a few days, but I know that we don't have a system in place to do that and it would, doubtless, spark complaints from Darren's mother that we would not be brave enough to ignore. I give him a list of the eleven others that I want put on school detention. No joy there, either: that is 'too many', apparently. Anyway, I must go through the Department and they must be given 24 hours' notice of the punishment. It's almost pointless. I shrug my shoulders and say, 'I give up then, let them do whatever they like.'

Mr Phillips frowns at me and tells me that there are set procedures in place for tackling discipline and that they must be used. I tell him that they clearly do not work (ironically, as I speak we can both hear someone who sounds uncannily like Darren whooping and screaming in the corridor outside; Mr Phillips affects not to notice).

And I end another school day bubbling with frustration and impotent rage.

It's been a day, once again, marked by a total absence of discipline and, as a result, effective teaching.

If you are not familiar with modern, inner city schools near the bottom of the pile, you may be tempted to believe that I am exaggerating some of the above (and some of what follows) to make a better story. If you work in one of these schools, however, you will know that such scenes are a daily occurrence.

Labels, glue and blood pressure

AFTER SOME years spent teaching full-time, I have switched to supply work.

Although I still teach pretty much full-time, I do, in theory, have the freedom to do other things as well. Psychologically, I'm no longer tied to St Jude's by an umbilical cord, and this fact is important because it has prevented me from going bonkers.

Supply work also gives you a bit more variety. The way it works is this: the phone rings, it's school asking if you can come in because a given teacher is off for a week or so (stress, nervous trouble, broken nose etc). They offer you money, and you say yes. Later, you wonder why you didn't say no, because there is a downside: as a supply teacher, you tend to get the worst classes. This is because their teachers tend to be away more often and, in my case, also because Mrs Borrowdale once heard me call her a witch. Mrs Borrowdale is in charge of organising Cover. Sometimes, I am booked well in advance to cover an arranged absence – to fill in for Mr Blunt while he goes on his Anger Management Course, for example. Other times, I am woken by a phone call from The Witch at 7.15am, saying cheerfully, 'Come on in, we've got lots of teachers away'.

On days like those, my first challenge is to find out what lessons I'm covering (since I have been at the school for years now, most of the kids think I am a normal teacher who just can't make up his mind which subject to do).

Sometimes my timetable actually changes during the day: someone may have to leave unexpectedly, or an emergency might arise. I just accept whatever I'm given.

Knowing which lessons I am to cover is only half the story; then I have to track down the work that has been left for the kids to get on with. This often requires the skills of Sherlock Holmes. It can be Sellotaped to the teacher's desk, from where it will often have been removed by a naughty pupil. It might be left in my pigeonhole. It might be left in some random other person's pigeonhole. Or it might not be left at all.

I love the element of surprise.

Today, I am covering for another teacher who seems to be permanently off with stress (the school cannot replace her as she is still officially employed).

It's a red letter day, too: the new set of science textbooks has finally arrived.

This may not seem much to you but I feel like bringing in champagne to celebrate or asking the Head for a half day's holiday. In the past, we have shared one dirty, dog-eared textbook between two or even three children and it's a book which doesn't even cover the right topics for our syllabus.

These new ones are written by the people who set the exam, so they must cover the relevant stuff.

The Head of Department arrives carrying the books and hands them out to the kids, handling them with great reverence.

'These books are brand new,' he intones solemnly, placing one neatly on my desk. 'They must be treated with great respect and care so that others may use them in the future.'

It's a Year 7 class, so they are listening intently. For many of them, these will be the first books they have ever seen that are not covered in graffiti. (For readers who left school a while ago, the year numbering system has changed. We are a secondary school, so when kids reluctantly come to us at the age of 11 they go into Year 7. Confusingly, it is actually their eighth year of schooling – reception year, when they started at age four, was their first. At the end of Year 11 they take their GCSEs. Sixth Form is Years 12 and 13. But we don't have one of those).

As he drones on, I examine one of the books. It has that pleasant smell of newly-printed paper and, like all modern textbooks, is a masterpiece of political correctness. It is chock-full of bright pictures of children from ethnic minority backgrounds doing science experiments and photographs of every kind of phenomena. Even the teachers are in wheelchairs. Any wrongdoing is illustrated by a white boy; here is one, foolishly sticking his fork into an electrical socket and being electrocuted. Here's another, drinking from a test tube.

What I cannot find, to my mounting horror as I flip through the book, are any questions.

Oh, bloody hell!

Why are all modern textbooks in every subject full of photographs but devoid of questions?

I also notice that, actually, it doesn't quite seem to cover the syllabus to which we have recently changed after the head of department assured us that it was 'the easiest one yet'.

He hands me a pile of rectangular labels and half a dozen glue sticks.

'Get them to fill these in and stick them in the books. It'll only take two minutes. I'll pop back later to pick up the glue.' Off he goes.

I am in good spirits because this task ought to be a breeze.

I glance at the labels. They look absolutely ancient; someone's dug them up from the back of a stock cupboard. The typeface and print are from another era. They must be decades old.

Each label has four headings.

'Do not touch these yet!' I say, giving them out and quickly drawing one on the board so I can fill it in for the kids to see.

SCHOOL: St. Jude's
NAME: Julius Caesar
TEACHER: Miss Barrow
FORM: 7A

'Put them down!' Dale has been unable to resist writing his name next to 'SCHOOL' and has to be given another one.

'Now, listen carefully while I explain what we are going to... put them down!' Brett has dropped his on the floor and it has got dirty. Another label is given out.

'Right, listen! Do not touch these labels *until I say so!* OK? All I want to see on your desk is the text book, label and your pen.'

Pause, while we look at our desks and make any necessary adjustments.

'Don't touch that glue!'

I rescue a glue stick from an over-eager hand and place it safely out of reach on my desk. There's something about glue sticks; everybody wants one. The kids love sticking things in their books. In fact, they love most activities that don't involve learning something or answering questions.

Now, let's make sure we do this nice and steadily: 'Right. First of all, at the top is the school name, which we all know?'

Nods all round.

'Next there is your name. *YOUR* name, OK? I've put in 'Julius Caesar' to show you where. Underneath that we have your teacher's name – Miss Barrow.'

'OK?'

More nods. Now for the tricky bit; the class is made up of kids from four different Registration groups.

'Finally, it says 'Form', which is your *REGISTRATION* form, not 7T, which is your *science group*. OK? I have put 7A, which is an *EXAMPLE*! You will write in your own.'

They seem to have got it.

'Now, first of all, you will fill the forms out and then I will come round and check them all, then we will stick them in. Do not stick them in before I have said that you can. OK?'

Nods. We can't *wait* to use those glue sticks.

I watch them like a hawk: 'No, Stella, don't use a pencil, use your pen… Oh, OK, here's one.'

Thirty seconds into the exercise, the first label is destroyed as Stella (it's amazing how many kids are named after alcoholic drinks) attempts to rub out her pencil marks and clumsily causes the label to fold in half. It is no longer good enough for her, so she scrunches it up instantly and throws it in the general direction of the bin. Under my glare she then gets up and puts it into the bin. Fortunately we have a generous number of spares, so we carry on.

Less than one minute later, Kat (seriously, that's what her parents called her) scrunches up her label, too.

'Stop!' I shout.

Everyone looks at me.

'What is wrong with that label?'

I immediately see that she is using Stella's pencil and has repeated her mistake. It's interesting that the lower the kid's own standards are the less likely they are to accept anything other than the most perfect handouts. Any slight fault, such as an insufficiently sharp pencil or a slightly creased piece of paper, will not be tolerated. Even if they have forgotten their own pen, they won't accept a pencil or a Biro with a chewed end. The amount of waste is truly astronomical. Any

A4 paper that is not perfect will be scrunched up and rejected.

'Right. From now on, we have another rule. Nobody scrunches up labels and nobody uses a pencil. Oh, and nobody tries to rub anything out. Yes, Dale, I know that is three rules, thank you for telling me. We do not have an endless supply of these labels.'

For God's sake, these kids are twelve years old.

I rub out my example answers on the board to a chorus of moans and groans.

'What's wrong? I'm going to write the answers in with you, OK?'

Nods of understanding all around. I glance at my watch. Bloody hell, we're twenty minutes into the lesson already.

'OK, all together now. School: St. Jude's, right?'

I write in 'St. Jude's'.

'No problems?'

Oh God, please don't let there be.

But there is somebody who has spelt the school name wrongly and is on the point of scrunching up the label.

'No!' I scream. 'It doesn't matter if you make a mistake.'

Downcast looks.

'Oh, all right. But this is the very last time.'

Another label ends up in the bin. This is doing my head in.

A hand rises slowly from the back of the class accompanied by a shameful look and a chorus of accusing 'ahs' from all around.

'What?'

Stella has written the name of her previous school by mistake and has started to cry.

'OK, OK, here's another label.' If there's one thing I can't cope with it's crying kids.

I notice that the pile of spare labels doesn't look quite as big as it once did.

Keep the momentum up: 'Right we've all got the school name, good. Let's move on. Next is your name, *YOUR NAME*!'

Now it is my turn to mess up. Forgetting their natural inclination to copy, exactly, whatever I do, I write my name on the board next to 'NAME' and – aaargh! – by the time I turn round, half a dozen of them have copied 'Mr Chalk' into the space next to 'Name' on their labels.

'Stop!'

I cover my face with my hands. I need a drink.

Calm down, Chalk. I tell myself. Think tropical islands, warm beaches and palm trees.

That's better.

Let's try again. Slowly, slowly.

'OK. Put your hand up if you've written 'Mr Chalk' next to 'Name.'

Six hands go up.

'Alright, no problem.'

Six more labels given out. I sit on my desk at the front, voice still calm.

Let's try a different idea.

'I'm not going to write anything on the board any more in case it causes confusion. In fact, let's roll the board round.' I give the board a mighty heave and it rolls round.

'There. All gone now.'

My troubles seem to disappear.

'Now, has everyone written their name next to 'Name'?'

Nods and a few hands raised.

'What? Yes, *both* names.'

Several groans.

'OK, OK, your surname is fine. Just put your initial... WHAT THE... *What are you doing?*'

Dale has just ripped up his label.

'Look,' I say, in an icy voice, 'it doesn't matter if you've put your initial first, your surname first, your first name first or even somebody else's name first. Whatever you have written is fine.'

I am approaching the end of my tether and the pile of remaining labels is getting very low now.

We manage to get past 'Teacher' with only two putting their form teacher by mistake, Chesney copying the word 'Teacher' and Dale writing in the name of his favourite teacher. (That wasn't me, I can assure you.)

Now the final hurdle: 'OK. Only one more to do now.'

Glance at watch again.

Christ, there's only ten minutes of the lesson left!

'Now, remember: 'Form' is your *REGISTRATION FORM*, the one you register in.'

Eyes down, pens moving. We're nearly done, and thank God because there is only one spare label left.

A commotion has broken out at the back. I walk over and pick up Chesney's label to see that he has written 'G22' next to Form.

'That is not your form group, Chesney, is it?'

'That's the room I register in, Sir.'

A chorus of nods and then the accusations fly. 'You said the room number we register in.'

A quick look around… no, surely not? Yes, yes, they have. They've all got it wrong.

This is the straw that breaks Mr Chalk's back.

'Look!' I bellow. 'All you had to do was fill in four simple things and it's taken all bloody lesson and you've still got it wrong. How can it possibly be that difficult?'

I snatch the textbook off my desk and, to my horror, manage to pull the front cover off. I stand there, holding the severed parts of the book, one in each hand. I am frozen in shock and all is suddenly silent.

The Head of Department chooses this moment to return.

The rules of teaching

IF YOU are considering seeking work as a Teacher, the following tips, learned painfully over many years, will help smooth your path in the classroom.

Do judge by appearance.
It has become an article of faith in our politically correct world that you should never judge a book by its cover. This is completely wrong. Just as an airport penny dreadful announces itself by its appearance, so will problem kids. You can spot them a mile off, whatever anyone

says. Earrings, tattoos and outlandish hairstyles mean only on thing: sit them at the front, on their own, before they've even had a chance to muck about.

Use sarcasm.

This is a favourite weapon of mine ever since my PGCE (teacher training) days when, naturally, we were expressly forbidden to use it. The key, as with most things, is the manner of delivery. Practise until you can deliver the remarks with the utmost sincerity.

'My *word*, Dwayne, that's a nice tattoo on the back of your neck. I might get one done myself.'

'Yes, Keeley, I think it's *terrible* that Mr Blunt could have put you in detention for throwing that ruler at Tracey when it wasn't really you at all.'

Use mystery and unpredictability to your advantage.

Practise a slightly lopsided, serial killer's smile for when you first meet them. Keep on grinning and they will soon think that you are insane. This works hugely to your advantage as they are always slightly worried about what you might do next, rather than the other way round. Another good tip is to carry round something incongruous, like a Geiger counter. They will spend the entire lesson asking what it is for. Just say that you're ever so sorry but you can't tell them.

Do not be gullible.

If you are covering for someone else, with a strange class, please do not bring the honourable profession of Teaching into disrepute by falling for any of the following:

i) You are teaching a group whom you do not know and a boy knocks on your door halfway through the lesson and says, 'Mrs Stout would like to see Callum, please.' (If you let Callum out, five minutes later I promise that they will both be knocking on some other poor Supply Teacher's door saying 'Mrs Stout would like to see Dwayne, please', and so on.

ii) Two boys knock on your door and say, 'Mr Jones wants to see Mike Hunt'.

Please do not announce 'Is Mike Hunt in here?' to the room; you will regret it, particularly if you are female.

iii) If you hand out a piece of A4 for all the children to write their names on because you have not been given a register, please do not accept that Ben Dover, Phil McCavity, Harry Hardcock, Roger Rubshaft or anyone else with a dubious name is a member of this class. Just keep them all back at the end to do it again.

Get a list of all the 'Frighteners' (the teachers they are scared of).
Casually drop one into the conversation early on in the lesson. Something along the lines of, 'Mr Blunt is popping round later; don't forget to remind me to give him your books.'

Know your enemy.
With a new class, always get the troublemakers' names off another teacher, with descriptions. You can really freak them out by looking at them in a funny way and saying, 'Dwayne, isn't it?' This astounds them and they will pester you for the rest of the lesson, asking you how you knew their name. Just say mysteriously that you have a 'Certain Gift.'

Add that your mother was a gypsy. (This helps, as they will immediately put away mobile phones and other valuables.)

The Prison Hint.
Occasionally I 'accidentally' drop into the conversation a hint that I may have served time in prison and then quickly change the subject, refusing to discuss it further. This gains tremendous respect, especially if you repeatedly deny it. Carefully select another teacher who can act and get them to half-suggest the same on your behalf in one or two of their lessons.

Never raise your voice.
They hear lots of shouting all the time at home, in school and on the TV, so it doesn't impress them much. Always speak very slowly and clearly, adopting a very deliberate, controlled, and slightly menacing tone. Practise this for hours until you have it perfect. It will help put the seed in the pupils' minds that you might be an axe murderer.

Likewise, make all your body movements slow, calm and precise. (One unexpected side-effect of this is that it can send them all to sleep, if you're lucky).

Remember that you are God and repeat this to yourself regularly.
You own the classroom, the school buildings, every aspect of their lives between 9am and 3pm and your Word is Law. It is essential to demonstrate absolute control from the very start, or you will be eaten alive. Line them up outside and do not let them in to trash the classroom until they are silent. To hell with whether that's official school policy or not. It works. If you haven't been given a seating plan, just sit them boy, girl, boy, girl. Never get into arguments, just say everything calmly as if you all know it's the best thing to do. If anybody refuses just quietly throw them out. If they won't go, chuck their stuff out into the corridor and they will follow. Do not listen to any nonsense about 'Mr Jones lets us listen to the radio, sit where we like, chew gum, drink whisky, smoke marijuana and so on.' He is not here, so sod him.

Train every class to stand up when you come into the room.
This is great fun, and makes other teachers green with envy. After a while, the kids even start to get a bit of pride at all standing up at the same time. Insist that everyone is wearing every item of his or her school uniform correctly.

Use the kids to your advantage.
If you're doing supply work, and if by any chance you take a dislike to the teacher you are covering for (for example, if they have left crap work), extract revenge by stealing their board rubber, or giving it to one of the children as a prize for doing good work. Don't forget that it is traditional for supply teachers to give out all the pencils, rulers and felt tips that they can find in the stock cupboard and not collect them in at the end. Just let the kids go when the bell rings and leave everything scattered over the floor.

Punish collectively.
Don't hesitate to make the whole class suffer if somebody won't

admit something. Collective punishment is a great idea. Keep them all back for two minutes at the end, in silence, and make it clear that they should sort it out amongst themselves afterwards.

This tactic is another which falls into the 'PGCE No-Nos that work' category.

People will say things like, 'How would you like it if you were punished for things that others have done?'

By way of reply, just point out that quite obviously we all are – our taxes would be far lower if 90% of the population didn't have to pay for the crime and vandalism committed by the other 10%.

Always carry out your threats.
Do what you say you will do. Track down the little swines and turn up in their lesson. They absolutely hate that. Never, ever, let anyone get away with anything, no matter how tired you feel. Who cares if you didn't quite hear that muttered comment? Teach them not to mutter again. Speaking up is very important.

Dress smartly.
This shocks the pupils, as they are used to seeing teachers who look like their main job is standing motionless is a field of barley. Sometimes, I hint that I am a school inspector. Forget this modern 'we're all the same' nonsense and 'dressing down.' Get smart, and get respect. To most people, appearance is far more important than whatever you might have to say.

Affect an accent that is posher than the pupils' (Not difficult).
This will worry them because you are obviously 'Not From Round Here.'

As most will never venture more than half a mile from the Cherry Tree Estate (once a fortnight to sign on, plus Court appearances or burglary outings) they find this quite disturbing.

Keep your private life private.
I never, ever tell them anything true about my life outside St. Jude's. Just make up the first thing that comes into your head when questioned about marital status, whether you drink, smoke, have sex

with animals, or whatever. It is a foolish teacher who lets slip anything about his private life: as with prisoners of war, it will all be used against you at some stage.

There is an exception to this, which we will discuss later.

Copying out with the bottom set

I ALWAYS try to get to the classroom before the kids.

There are two reasons for this.

Firstly, to keep them out as there seems to be a rule that doors only get locked when you do not have a key for them.

Secondly, to see if any work has been left if I've not already got it.

Unfortunately, today I am teaching on the other side of the school for the previous lesson and I arrive to be greeted by the sight of Liam leaning out of the window shouting at someone in another room opposite, Sean doing his impression of a rap star dancing about on a desk while Jordan tries to tip him off, Dawn and Keeley on their mobile phones to boys in other lessons and Tracey applying makeup to her hideous face.

Yes, it's Year 11 maths with the Bottom Set – set 6, in fact, which is about as low as even we go.

Jade greets me: 'I ain't goin' to do no work this lesson, so don't even ask me, I've had it up to here with teachers today!'

This is accompanied by various gesticulations to emphasise her point.

I show no interest whatsoever in any of them and – resisting the strong temptation to push Liam out of the window – merely straighten out a few desks. I am immensely relieved to see that I only have eight pupils to deal with. There should be another seven but they never come in any more. Frankly I don't blame them.

I write a title and the date on the board, glance at the work left, place their exercise books neatly on their desks, along with a textbook

(Jade promptly throws hers on the floor) and, slowly but surely, they all sit down in two rows.

It has taken only ten minutes.

After I have made sure that we all have something to write with, which takes a mere five more minutes, we are ready not to do any work. (I must add that after 15 minutes I still haven't spoken a word to any of them – I'm a great believer in non-verbal communication.)

Most of my lessons are simply attempts to get them to behave in a civilised manner. If they bring their own pens it's a major achievement.

Jade informs me again, just in case I had forgotten, that she still, 'Ain't doin' nothin!' and crosses her arms to emphasise the fact.

'Quite right, Jade,' I reply. 'Don't copy this title down.'

Liam joins in: 'If she doesn't have to do no work, then I'm not neither!'

'Excellent, Liam!' I say, idly trying to work out the true meaning of all those negatives.

I start to write the page number and the exercise on the board. We are doing simple area calculations with different rectangles.

Jade is now fighting with Liam over control of the textbook. I find her another one. It never ceases to amaze me how many groups have to share the books.

I simply start with the first question and do it on the board for them. I carefully draw the rectangle with my board ruler, mark in its length and width, multiply them together, writing down all the working out and go through it out loud, finally writing down the answer in square centimetres.

They copy it all (including Jade).

I move on to the next question, repeating the whole procedure. After I've done six of them I just draw the rectangles and then, after three of these, I just write down the question numbers up to the end of the exercise.

It isn't long before we witness the amazing effects of copying out. It must be the greatest teaching method ever invented; I can't understand why it wasn't emphasised more in Teacher Training.

There is an atmosphere of tranquillity now. I speak in a relaxing voice and soon they are completely hypnotised by its soporific effect.

I move gently and slowly away from the board and sit down while they continue writing.

I win about 15 minutes' peace and then the spell is suddenly broken as a buzzing noise causes them all to run to the window. I don't waste my breath telling them to return to their places; instead, I simply push Kyle gently out of the way (a bit more non-verbal communication) so that I can get a better view myself.

It appears that two of our former pupils, Ryan and Shane, have decided to pay us a visit in order to show off their new motorbike (though your concept of ownership might be different from theirs.)

Ryan is riding round the playground with Shane on pillion. Neither of them appears to have made a great deal of progress since leaving us. Ah! Now Mr Phillips has gone outside to welcome them.

They are both making a finger gesture to him that I can only assume means that they think he is their number one teacher. And although I cannot hear all that they are shouting, they also appear to be suggesting that he was born out of wedlock.

Pot and kettle spring to mind, as they say.

At home with Mrs Chalk, and Anthony crops up

MRS CHALK is a teacher, too (though not at St. Jude's), and she's a far better one than I ever could be.

She's no pushover, and she's not naïve, but she has a knack of getting the best out of her kids which is only to be envied by donkeys like me.

She's a great cook, too – tonight, we've had a delicious lamb hotpot and she's sitting at the table with a glass of wine as I clear away the dishes.

We're talking about one of the Year 10 boys at St Jude's, Anthony.

He's a bright kid, very witty – some of his quips and gags in class have me turning away and pretending to write something on the board as I stifle the laughter.

The trouble is, because he's bright, he's bored out of his brain in most of the lessons and I think he's on the verge of going off the rails. He's been hanging around with some of the real undesirables and today he didn't turn up to school at all.

'It's such a waste when decent kids make the wrong choices,' I say. 'They see the naughty kids getting away with it time and time again and they think that it's really cool to behave like that.'

'It is,' says Mrs C.

'What… cool?' I ask, mildly surprised.

'No, it's such a waste,' she says, looking at me as though I'm simple.

'Ah,' I say.

'I'd have a bit of a talk with him,' suggests Mrs C. 'Keep him behind and give it to him straight – tell him he has two choices: University and a decent life…'

'Maybe he could become a teacher like me,' I interrupt, grinning.

She gives me a withering look and continues: '… or a life of petty crime and prison, with no chance of ever having a decent job or lifestyle. Sometimes you can get through to them.' She puts her head on one side, reflectively. 'Ask him how he wants *his* children to grow up.'

'Actually, he's one of the few who don't have any yet,' I say. 'As far as I know.'

A wander around St Jude's

IF YOU send your kids to our school you are either desperately unlucky in life, or plain stupid, or you just hate them. This is not one of England's finest educational establishments.

On the plus side, this means each day throws up interesting situations – in short, the material for this book.

St Jude's is a set of crumbling, Victorian red brick buildings which must have looked first rate when they were built in the late Victorian era. The intricate quality of the brickwork, and the skill and attention to detail employed by the craftsmen involved in its construction, is still visible. Unfortunately, this is in stark contrast to most of the work currently being done by the pupils inside.

I say 'crumbling': the buildings are desperately in need of attention. The school is damp and draughty, with a liberal covering of graffiti being their only modern aspect.

In front of the main buildings is a grey, concreted playground. Here, bullying and extortion can take place under the watchful eye of the unfortunate teachers (note the plural: nobody ventures out here on their own) whose turn it is to patrol the area at break.

The amount of litter left lying inside and outside the school has to be seen to be believed. Crisp packets, sweet wrappers, empty fizzy drink cans, bits of food from the canteen and empty plastic bottles are everywhere. Many teachers are afraid to ask a pupil to pick rubbish up. To do so is to invite indignation, even anger. 'F*ck off! I ain't a cleaner!' is a typical response. Mind you, in the past, I have actually been stopped by the Head from making the kids pick up litter on the basis of 'Health and Safety'. I found this hard to understand, but the result is that the school is drowning in a sea of waste. The kids, and their parents, throw away litter without a thought because they either don't care about or understand the environmental consequences, because they have no concept of neatness, order and aesthetics and because there is no punishment, whatsoever, for doing so.

Behind the school is the playing field, where football, cricket and rugby could be played safely were the grass not strewn with broken glass, dog mess and hypodermic needles. There are also two tennis courts, surrounded by a wobbling wire fence which is full of holes and curls up at every edge. The nets sag dejectedly, even comically, and the surface of the courts is so uneven that a game is reduced to one of sheer chance. Future Tim Henmans will not be produced here, I can assure you.

Half-a-dozen 'temporary' (erected 1975) Portakabins scattered around the school grounds serve as extra classrooms. Their windows are covered with wire mesh to protect them from stray footballs and other missiles; this does not help their drab appearance. They are in a sorry state, with endless bits of wood nailed to them in half-hearted repairs over the years. Freezing in winter, baking in summer, noisy all year round. You know you've upset somebody higher up if you end up teaching in here.

Let's venture inside the main school building.

High double doors admit us into the entrance hall, which is usually filled with a motley crowd of good-for-nothings who have nothing better to do than complain to the Head. Just to clarify, these are the *parents*, not the kids: it may surprise you to know that there is a constant stream of visiting mums and dads, all day, every day. They're not supposed to turn up without an appointment, of course, but that's no deterrent. If their son or daughter is asked to leave a class, five minutes later – thanks to the wonders of modern mobile telephony – they are at school, demanding to know why Declan's mp3 player has been confiscated or why Mr Chalk is always picking on Liam or Shazney when they 'weren't doing nothing wrong'.

Some parents have actually been banned from the school premises. Never having obeyed any instruction in their lives before, you can imagine how diligently they observe this prohibition. Many of them, of course, are ex-pupils of the school, and the funny thing – I say 'funny', but I suppose it's actually quite a bitter irony – is that we see far more of some of them now than we did when they were supposed to be here. Often, a shouting match will break out, as they debate the relative faults of each other's offspring or re-open the classroom rivalries and tensions of yesteryear. When this happens, the old crone, Mrs Borrowdale, puts on her glasses, shuffles out from her Deputy Head's office, sizes them up for her cauldron and mutters something or other. She must have some residual power over them because they invariably shut up.

The Headmaster's Office is next to hers, on the left-hand side of the Entrance Hall, and every few minutes his door opens to disgorge a disgruntled complainer so that the next one can take his or her place. He ought to stick a revolving door in.

Opposite the main entrance is the School Hall where each morning an Assembly is held for a different year group. Every second Friday, the whole school gathers in there for an hour of mayhem.

A long corridor runs off the entrance hall leading in one direction to the gymnasium and in the opposite direction to a set of stone stairs which have been worn into smooth slopes by the patter of many tens of thousands of feet over the decades, from hob-nailed boots to leather shoes to counterfeit trainers in four or five generations. The original green and brown tiles cover the walls of every corridor to waist height.

Halfway to the gym lies the Staff Room, with its faded wooden door for children to knock on and run away. Inside, there are groups of shabby, unmatched, padded chairs surrounding low, Formica-topped tables which are covered in mugs and piles of exercise books and A4 paper. Many of the chairs are leaking foam and a few make disconcerting creaks when sat on.

There is a row of tables against the longest wall, covered in more A4 paper and piles of exercise books, many of which are spilling onto the floor. The room is populated with teachers talking rubbish or marking work furiously (often in both senses of the word).

Along one wall are pigeonholes for all the staff, where they can pick up condescending notes from the SMT. Next to the pigeon-holes is a huge notice board covered with out-of-date memos, urgent reminders, demands to keep the room tidy and desperate pleas for the return of missing exercise books. Next to this is the dreaded Cover Board, with its details of lessons to be covered, which room they are in, where the work is and who Mrs Borrowdale has decided is going to cover them. All full-time teachers dread seeing their name on the Cover Board. It means that a free lesson, which could be used for marking books or chasing up miscreants, has suddenly turned into an hour-long headache of screaming mayhem. Every member of staff is firmly convinced that they are given more than their fair share of cover and bitter arguments frequently break out.

The fourth wall is a huge window that looks out over the play-ground. This would be a depressing sight indeed but it is difficult to approach the window due to the vast number of plastic boxes full of coursework and old books piled up against the wall below it.

In the corner is a gigantic sink, full of dirty water and overflowing with mugs, teapots and vast amounts of cutlery. A sorry-looking sign above this disease hotspot announces that dirty cups must be washed immediately after use.

The entire room appears to have been furnished during World War Two, although by the look of some of the occupants there's certainly no rationing.

Leaving the Staff Room, we head for the canteen, where additive-ridden blobs of salt, sugar and fat are served under the laughable description of lunch, to be washed down with fizzy drinks of various unnatural colours, usually lurid blues or vivid greens. Afterwards, a visit to the vending machine for the purchase and consumption of a wide variety of chocolates and other comestibles neatly sets the kids up for an afternoon of sugar-spiked chaos.

Behind the canteen are the computer rooms. These are by far the nicest rooms in the place and are chock-full of expensive PCs, printers and all sorts of electronic wizardry to enable the kids, effectively, to type. There is also a computer technician, who makes sure that he is not around and it is locked whenever you arrive. He also ensures that the machines mysteriously crash halfway through every lesson losing all the 'work'. This is great if you are covering because it means that you can simply repeat the same lesson a few times.

Everything is connected to the internet, of course.

Good news! Those parents who care can relax in the knowledge that there is some sort of watchdog program in place to prevent the kids accessing pornographic sites.

Bad news! They're not foolproof and the kids soon find ways to circumnavigate them; some of the sights they see would trouble all but the most broadminded.

The printers have lives of their own, occasionally sparking up without warning and at random times of the day, to churn out endless pages of slightly smudged A4, while the teacher frantically stabs at buttons begging them to stop. Naturally, if you actually do want to print something, they ignore your request. This is frustrating, but then if they had deigned to burst into life they would have run out of ink.

Up those worn old stairs to the first floor, now, where the science labs are situated. Next to each is a prep room, where the lab technicians rule over vast stores of test tubes, Bunsen burners and measuring devices. In the corner is the Forbidden Cupboard, which is crammed full of ancient jars labelled with the skull-and-crossbones. These are all the chemicals that are not allowed to be used in schools anymore, for Health and Safety reasons. I recognise about half of them from my own school days.

Above the science labs, on the third floor is the strange territory known as The Library, which houses odd things called 'books'. It is a place where the pupils can be taken for a lesson, which will involve them scrawling their names on new desks and, perhaps, looking at the covers of some of these 'books'.

Head of Year offices are dotted around the second and third floors, usually with a gaggle of pupils outside, awaiting their turn to protest their innocence and explain how the teachers all pick on them. When teachers get fed up of pupils persistently being abusive or refusing to do as they are told, they pass them up the chain of command. First, they are sent to the Head of Department, to whom they are also abusive and whose instructions they also disobey. Next, they are sent to the Head of Year where the process is repeated.

Finally, they are sent to The Deputy Head in Charge of Discipline, who has a meeting with the pupil, along with his or her parents, or at least some adult who may be vaguely related to the child, and forgives them everything over a nice cup of tea.

It never seems to strike anyone that this is a serious betrayal of these children and of our duty as teachers, *in loco parentis* as we are, to instil discipline and some sense of responsibility into them. Equally, no-one in authority ever seems to make the obvious connection between the lack of discipline in schools (or, indeed, in any area of many of these kids' lives) and their subsequent failure to achieve their potential because of their inability to fit into society. Certainly, we educators are too busy being nice and understanding and bickering amongst ourselves to notice: the higher echelons complain that teachers often send them problems they should deal with themselves (which is occasionally true) and the teachers complain that those higher up do nothing (which is invariably true). I'd like to meet an educational theorist, one day, to explain why I think this is a cruel and neglectful con-trick which lets down kids who start life with little chance in the first place.

But enough hobby-horsing (for a moment or two, at least!).

Most of the school's remaining space is taken up by classrooms which, for reasons beyond me, all have internal windows looking back out into the corridor. These are conveniently low and large enough to allow banter to take place between pupils in the classroom and those passing by. You can imagine how this assists the smooth running of the lesson. Wise teachers cover the windows with examples of the kids' 'work'; in turn, the kids scribble on the work and make peep-holes in it.

Due to the sorry state of the buildings, staff will do anything for a bucket. The more buckets you have, the higher up the pecking order you are. Buckets bring security and peace of mind under a threatening sky. When it rains, we all panic and madly scrabble to catch drops from the leaking roof and windows. Buckets are regularly stolen or borrowed from rival classrooms. Hordes of the most innocent-looking children (we have a few) are released to patrol the corridors and target the newest and most gullible teachers, knocking on their doors and asking 'Please could Mr Chalk borrow a bucket just for this lesson?' Only the most credulous and naïve fall for this ploy.

Cleaning does not appear to take place in our school. I am told this is because our cleaning budget is insufficient to get the job done properly. Dirt fills every corner and is ingrained into the floors. In fact, the entire place is filthy.

The very worst parts of the building have actually been abandoned. Rooms are locked and windows boarded up, like some sort of gothic mansion in a 1950s horror film.

The antique heating system, with its massive iron pipes, is a tribute to the high-engineering standards of our ancestors but, as it has scarcely been maintained over the last century, I would advise that you bring a jacket should you visit us in winter. In summer, however, as tangles of wire and tape adorn most windows to prevent them from opening, staff and pupils alike are slowly cooked.

The sign outside the school gates saying, apparently without irony, 'SLOW CHILDREN CROSSING' leads us neatly on to a look at our customers.

Meet the pupils

THE KIDS at St Jude's are typical of those at many inner city comprehensives. Teachers at work in the thousands of places in the below-average to failing-completely bracket will recognise our cast.

The level of ability of the children when they arrive at our Secondary School is shocking.

It isn't much better when they leave, mind you.

They are supposed to be our guests for five years but often decide to cut short their stay in order to devote more time to selling counterfeit goods on the market or starting a career in house burglary.

In mathematics, many of our pupils cannot do even the simplest sum without the aid of a calculator. Some cannot do the simplest sum even *with* the aid of a calculator: for example, you will ask the question 'What is 9 x 7?' They will tap it in wrongly as '9 x 77' and claim that the answer is 693. They have no idea of the relative size of numbers and do not sense instinctively that this cannot be right. Instead, they accept whatever the display says. It is useless to argue with them; they simply wave the calculator at you as if it is some sort of talisman to ward off evil answers. It is trusted far more than the teacher.

After seven years of Primary schooling, much of their written and verbal output is gibberish, and in many cases it does not improve significantly during their stay at St Jude's. Half are unable to read, write or spell properly when they leave. They cannot punctuate or structure a sentence – they just ramble on, misusing words they don't understand and mis-spelling most of those with more than two or three syllables. Maybe it's no surprise, given that you can say this of a few of the teachers, too. (This desperately poor grasp of our language isn't just a problem at St Jude's, by the way. Numerous Ofsted reports, including one in January 2006, show it's a wide-ranging problem across the country. Meanwhile, the Assessment and Qualifications Alliance, the country's biggest exam board, has reported that pupils use 'text-speak' like 'm8' [for 'mate'], 'u' [for 'you'] and '2' [for 'too' or 'to'] in GCSE papers which are also littered with swearing and slang contractions such as 'gonna', 'wanna' and 'shoulda'. Ya dunno whthr 2 laff or cry.)

The ability level is low and getting steadily lower, whatever the Government or the teachers' unions or the league tables or the exam results say, but this pales into insignificance when compared with our main problem which is – as I hinted earlier – the behaviour of our children.

Discipline, manners and respect are almost unheard of. There are a variety of reasons for this – poor home life, poor schooling in early years and a collective and creeping failure of will to impose rules and standards by teachers in schools for the last 30 years or so.

When our pupils arrive at the age of eleven, their attention span is often very short. Many, perhaps most, are unable to sit still and keep quiet for more than a few seconds at a time when these are the basic prerequisites, surely, of successful learning. I am no anthropologist but I suspect that sitting still and listening are not innate human traits; they need to be taught and, by extension, learned, and the earlier the better. Thus, this inability is not the fault of our pupils: it's simply that nobody, at home or in their early schooling, has ever bothered to insist they behave in this way.

When we try to introduce them to the concept it is a whole new skill to learn. This may sound unbelievable but it is absolutely true.

Many straightforward tasks become impossible. They cannot listen to a set of instructions or tackle a problem that has more than one stage. Instead of persevering with a question, if the answer is not obvious, they will immediately shout out 'I don't geddit!' or 'Can't do it!'

Teachers rush over to help, providing instant gratification, which simply encourages the child not to try to puzzle it out for himself next time. This is madness: it's no use complaining that kids have short attention spans if we don't try to lengthen them.

If you *can* actually get them to listen to and understand your instructions, that's only half the battle; it's quite another matter getting them to obey them. Older readers will understand the concept of 'having to do what the teacher tells you'. This has quite gone out of the window, along with an exercise book or two, Shazney's new pencil case and the whiteboard marker.

Kids will question anything they do not want to do. They have no hesitation in answering back or just shouting out, 'I'm not doing that!'

Often, they'll lob a profanity or two at you at the same time. At one time, swearing directly at a teacher would have been extremely rare and would have been dealt with harshly. Now it is an everyday occurrence, and one that is often ignored by many staff members (myself included much of the time, I'm afraid), along with so many other faults. Many of the children swear loudly throughout a lesson, partly to shock, partly because they hear these words so often that they have no idea that there is anything wrong with them and partly because they have never been taught any self-control.

Ah! Self-control. Many of our kids have virtually none. They respond to stimuli as a plant does, without any conscious thought. They react instinctively, by shouting or striking out at the source of an irritation. It's important to realise that these are reflex actions; there is no malice involved. In fact, generally there has been no thought going on in their minds at all.

Just as they lack the ability to sit still and listen, they lack the ability to think before acting, or to pause in order to decide the best course of action.

If, after a given event, you have the time to go through it, stage-by-stage, with a pupil, to find out why he did what he did, invariably he will not be able to explain his actions. The most commonly-used explanation is: 'I don't know why I did it. I just did.'

Often, they regret their actions, apparently deeply so, especially when the consequences for themselves and for others are explained slowly and carefully. They can get quite upset. This won't stop them doing exactly the same thing in the next lesson however; they find it almost impossible to control their impulses.

Again, it's no surprise that they act as they do: their parents are usually little different, as demonstrated by the speed with which they race up to school at the slightest whim.

Even the basics are ignored. The idea of punctuality is a joke with a late punchline. The kids turn up when they feel like it, with a whole host of excuses. They are rarely punished, so lateness is not seen as a problem. Truancy is rife (in 2005, figures from Truancy Watch showed that 50,000 children skip school each day), often with the full knowledge and even connivance of the parents. Parents are occasionally prosecuted for this, but it's rare and it is a long, drawn-out process which has to be undertaken by the Local Education Authority. You can imagine how effective it is.

We have a school uniform which the pupils are supposed to wear, but a visitor would be hard-pressed to say what it is. The Deputy Head in Charge of Discipline is reluctant to enforce it as he thinks it's a good idea to allow the pupils to 'express themselves in a way that reflects their different outlooks and cultures.' As a result, they all look pretty much the same anyway and Assembly resembles a Rap Awards convention. Maybe one day I will 'express myself' a bit more and turn up dressed as an astronaut, or a Roman soldier, or in a loincloth.

It's not just the fact that the behaviour of the average child has declined, however. We are now teaching a much broader spectrum of kids than was once the case.

The reason for this is the Government's policy of 'Inclusion' (basically, this means that we have to take everybody, whether they are suitable for mainstream education or not; Inclusion policy also makes it extremely difficult to expel naughty kids). Inclusion, combined with the closing down of Special Schools, has resulted in us being flooded with the two types of pupils that we are simply not able to deal with.

The first type are the Special Needs children, those whose mental or learning ability is below that of their peers, through natural low intelligence or a genuine handicap. These youngsters are absolutely stuffed; all teachers, at least those with any compassion left in their souls, feel for them tremendously. They get some assistance in some lessons but nothing compared with what they could receive in Special Schools.

The second group of kids we cannot deal with are the nutters and psychopaths, whose behaviour we cannot control because we lack the appropriate resources – namely straitjackets, guns and watchtowers. Often, their behaviour is diagnosed as being the result of one of the ever-growing number of 'learning difficulties', Attention Deficit Disorder, Attention Deficit Hyperactivity Disorder, Oppositional Defiant Disorder etc, of which more later, which means more and more of them are sliding, artificially, into the Special Needs bracket. The majority of them, in my opinion, are just badly-behaved children who have never been properly disciplined. Many have already been expelled from other schools, often more than once. When a kid is expelled, the LEA noses around the other schools in its area to see who it can force to take them. Once returned to education, the child simply resumes where he left off. The only way to escape this is to be able to claim that you are full. Needless to say, every school with any sense claims to be full to avoid having to take them. Unfortunately, it is well known that St Jude's is not full.

Both groups leave our care unable to read, write or do simple sums properly after a total of twelve years of full-time education at massive cost to the taxpayer.

Of course, both groups also hold back everyone else. Teachers (against their will and better judgment, in the majority of cases) spend half their lessons dealing with the kids with Special Needs and the kids who can't behave, while having to ignore the pleasant, well-behaved ones, who actually want to learn but who sit there quietly being ignored, with their hands up, as their life-chances slowly ebb away.

At St Jude's, these kids stand out because there are relatively few of them. They rapidly get bored with the work, which is far too easy for them. They spend lessons helping the slower ones along, reluctantly (and I don't blame them: why should they do my job... they're not being paid, and there's no state pension at the end of it all for them, is there?). And, of course, they face the pressures of conformity: few children, if any, are strong enough to resist for long, so you watch them change over time until they are just like the rest of the mob.

Jenny is one of these, a Year 7 pupil just started at the school. She does not come from a particularly good home, but in a better school she could do well. It moves me almost to tears to see her, bravely struggling with a bag of neat exercise books, against the tide of ignorance coming the other way. I worry that her sharp, inquisitive mind will be dulled by our school, a small light in the darkness being snuffed out. Nowadays, there is no escape for bright kids from poor areas. They must go to the local crap school and fail miserably. Forty years ago, Jenny would have passed the eleven-plus, gone to a grammar school and possibly university.

So much for our modern, fairer society.

Anyway, let's introduce a few of our customers.

Take Liam, for example. (In fact, please take Liam full stop, and don't bring him back.) A scrawny, weaselly character, he is 15 years old and was expelled from his previous school for kicking and punching a female teacher. I once read his behaviour file; it was like an encyclopaedia of crime. Procrastination may be the thief of time, but Liam appears to be the thief of just about everything else. We are proud to have him as our guest.

Jordan and Sean have reading ages of eight. That is not particularly good, considering that they are also both 15. Like Liam, they are in Year 11. Liam has miraculously avoided arrest but Jordan and Sean have both been in trouble with the police for what is known in the trade as 'petty crime.' (You may not find it quite so petty if you own the car whose wing mirrors they have kicked off, or whose paintwork they have customised with a key.) We are all grateful that this is their final year with us.

Poor old Bradley from Year 10 burnt both hands quite badly when he set fire to a mobile classroom at his last school. Strictly on the QT, I have encouraged him to do the same to ours so that we can get some new ones that don't leak.

Connor was thrown out of his last school for persistent truancy. At least he doesn't bother us too much. When we see him, he's in Year 10.

Wayne is also Year 10 and was also expelled from his previous school, in his case for the theft of a teacher's handbag. He sold her house keys to a burglar. He is well known as a local drug dealer so is one of the few with a grasp of fractions. Lovely lad. Glad to have him on board.

Kerryann is in Year 9. She is hyperactive, 14 years old and cannot sit still nor do any written work. She's not at all malicious, but single-handedly destroys lessons simply by getting up and running round the classroom. She will not stop because she loves the attention this gains her. Her mother regards her as a little angel and cannot understand why we complain.

Lewis is also in Year 9. He has set off the fire alarm at least twice and openly boasts of the windows he has broken in the school. Given the exorbitant cost of having any work done by anyone in the public sector, including the replacement of windows, his vandalism runs into thousands of pounds. He is, apparently, on his 'Final Warning.' That will certainly teach him a lesson.

Tyler is in Year 8 and spends most of the day dancing around jabbing his finger into the air. I am not entirely sure why.

Like Kerryann, Dale is not malicious, just completely wild. In fact, he is as mad as a fish, to use the description which earned me a stern rebuke from one of the Special Needs Assistants, who accused me of stereotyping people with learning difficulties. All I could think of in reply, at the time, was: 'But he's nuts!' This probably didn't help. He is in Year 7.

Stacey (also Year 7) spends virtually all her time in the Emergency Room as she refuses to work with most of the teachers. Every now and then she sees the Educational Psychologist, who helpfully tops her head up with more nonsense and reinforces her delusions.

Ryan and Shane are ex-pupils of ours who spend more time on the premises than they ever did when they should have been here. I have occasionally bumped into them in town and they are perfectly pleasant to exchange a few words with. As pupils, however, they were the stuff of nightmares.

The list goes on and on: these are just the first handful that spring to mind. We have hundreds more kids who are simply 'naughty'. In a better school, they might well cause no serious problems as they would, perhaps, adapt to the better behaviour of the majority. Here though, they *are* the majority. The problem for teachers at our school is that, after a while, the behaviour of the naughty ones seems quite normal and the nice, quiet kids begin to seem a bit odd.

The LEA (Local Education Authority) provides a few support staff who help some kids in some lessons. Unfortunately, this help is usually dependent on their parents filling in the forms to request it and they very often cannot be bothered to do this. (Sometimes, to be honest, they can't read the forms.) After all, it's only school and playing truant and messing about never did them any harm, did it?

The behavioural problems take up so much time that there isn't much left for actual teaching. Lessons are constantly disrupted by groups of kids arriving late for no real reason, not to mention the hordes of ne'er-do-wells who skip lessons and roam the school in packs, looking for trouble.

Many non-teaching friends of mine cannot understand why it is so difficult to teach a simple lesson to the kids. They say, 'Why don't you just do this…' or 'Well, I'd just do that…'

In reply I just open and close my mouth like a goldfish. I don't know where to begin.

TV seems to have a lot of answers at the moment. The box is full of programmes showing some educational guru or other demonstrating how Dwayne and Ashley can be transformed, by constant attention and small group tuition, into effective pupils who are beginning to realise their potential.

You don't say!

Even *I* could do something with these toe-rags if I had them on their own all day with a free reign over what they do (never mind all the threats and bribes you don't see off-camera.) I'd like to see a few of these so-called experts deal with an awful class day in, day out, on the terms under which we have to work. Now *that* would be worth watching.

The simple answer is that most of what goes on in some of our schools nowadays is beyond the comprehension of most civilised people, especially those older than, say, 35.

I want to try to illustrate this in the various lessons that I describe (in gruesome detail), to give you some idea of what goes on in an average (very average) teacher's life on a daily basis. It covers the few highs and the many lows of my recent teaching career. The highs aren't exactly Everest, and the lows… well, they're subterranean.

Oh, I nearly forgot; there are two final groups inhabiting our school, known to staff as 'Ghosts' and 'Waifs'.

Some pupils pass on from school but return in the afterlife, unable to enter the next world (ie that of work). Our powers are too weak to vanquish them. These Ghosts haunt the school gates, rattling their (fake gold) chains, wailing in anguish at any staff brave enough to approach them and generally making a nuisance of themselves.

Sometimes, they grow bold and venture deeper into the school premises. If not cast out they can make unattended objects levitate and disappear.

They often interact with Waifs, children who wander the school and its grounds like, well, like waifs. Some of these are beginner truants, who haven't quite got the hang of it yet. But, mostly, they have been thrown out of their lessons by teachers who cannot stand them any longer. Occasionally, though, they are simply kids who have been sent on errands or foolishly entrusted to deliver messages and have decided instead to wander the corridors. Some Waifs fear the Ghosts; others seek them out to learn more of the ways of the Dark Side.

My pigeonhole (1)

ONCE A week, I check my pigeonhole in the Staff Room to see what nonsense has landed in it.

Ah, an early invitation to the end-of-term do.

Visions of last year swim through my mind; Mrs Borrowdale got completely drunk and turned into a lecherous old witch (as opposed to being merely an old witch).

Here is a letter about truancy. This is a major problem for the SMT because there is a government initiative to reduce absenteeism and they want to be able to tick that box. The irony is that most teachers love it when some little wretch doesn't turn up; there are more than a few I actively encourage to stay away.

(Incidentally, our standard punishment for truancy is an hour's detention. 'So, Ashley… would you trade an hour sitting on that bench for six hours spent lounging around in the park smoking a few joints and drinking cans of lager?'

Mumble, mumble.

'Correct! Get yourself off to the bench straight away!')

Next to it is a letter about something called 'Attachment

Disorder' (I might start a 'Disorder of the Week' competition, I muse) with references to Asperger's Syndrome and autism generally. Things like Asperger's are real conditions that some kids really do have. Those kids need help. But this medical complaints business, generally, drives me mad, and not only because many of the new conditions being 'discovered' can be applied to just about any youngster. If a child is just naughty or lazy, deal with it. If he has a genuine problem, educate him in a school designed to meet his needs. Experts are always banging on about 'rights' but the one right they never seem to acknowledge is that of the average child to get a half-decent education instead of being ignored while the teacher spends all her time trying to deal with kids who should be in Special Needs Schools. If I'd wanted to teach Special Needs kids (and some teachers do, and do it very well), I'd have gone into Special Needs education. Ah... I forgot. Most Special Needs Schools have been closed and these children are (almost) all dumped in Mainstream nowadays. I wonder which genius thought that was a good idea.

Here is another note: what madness is this? We are going to have a School Council, to give the kids a say in how the school is run. Hmmm... what might they come up with, I wonder to myself? Lessons about rap music? Body-piercing classes? No homework? No rules? No *teachers*? You think I'm joking, but does anybody *seriously* want any of our kids running the school? Why, that's the job of the SMT! Mind you, come to think of it, what difference would it make?

There is a round-robin note from the Head informing us that Wayne's mother has telephoned the school to complain that one of the teachers has referred to her son as a 'little moron'. The Head's letter asks that the teacher in question desist from using this epithet. I am not the guilty party and I bin the note, with all the other irrelevant bumf. I reflect further on it as I make myself a quick cuppa. On the one hand, calling a kid a 'moron' probably isn't the best way forward. But on the other hand, you can be driven to this sort of remark against all your instincts. And in Wayne's case, it is undeniably a very accurate description of the boy. This sort of honesty is not popular in teaching where, each year, we enthusiastically embrace an endless selection of new words to replace old ones which have fallen out of favour.

Finally, there is the latest magazine from the General Teaching Council. This is a body which state-employed teachers are required to join and for which privilege we must pay an annual fee of £33. (By the way, this cash is later reimbursed in our pay packets in a sort of bureaucratic monetary merry-go-round. Why they do this, and how much the whole thing costs the taxpayer, I don't know. It's all quite beyond me.) As far as I can tell, the GTC seems to be another way of employing people to talk about things. Maths being my strong(est) suit, I quickly tot up £33 x 420,000 in my head. It's... er... well, it's quite a lot. Where's that calculator?

I love to read the GTC magazine. I have applied for several posts on the Council, as the idea of being unelected and unaccountable appeals to me greatly. I would love to lecture teachers on their professionalism, preferably by email from some pleasant study trip to check out education in the Bahamas. We could go location-hunting, me and a couple of attractive young female teachers frolicking along some far-flung beach, to find the perfect spot to film adverts to attract new blood into the profession. (Incidentally, a recent survey by the NASUWT found that 95% of teachers didn't believe that the GTC reflected their views on teaching. I wonder whose views it *does* reflect? Maybe those of Leon, Darren and Shane?)

Draining my cup of tea, I pick up a stray copy of *The Guardian*. Steeling myself to leave the womb-like safety of the Staff Room, I scan the jobs pages. Those teachers who are no longer in love with teaching are always looking for ways out and *The Guardian* is like a Colditz escape manual, full of TEACHING-TYPE JOBS IF YOU CAN'T COPE WITH ACTUALLY TEACHING.

Why put up with filthy classrooms, awful children, obnoxious parents, endless reports and forms when you can have a much easier time telling teachers how to do their job properly?

What I really want to do is to go around schools telling the staff how to teach (obviously you won't catch me demonstrating my own skills) and explaining wonderful new ways of 'communicating ideas' and so on.

The Guardian and your own LEA website are overflowing with jobs like this, all with salaries that kick off at around the £35,000 p.a. mark and include huge bonuses, holidays, index-linked state pensions and guaranteed leave for stress every third week. Look for positions that contain the following words and phrases:

> Behaviour
> Specialist
> Learning
> Develop
> Advisor
> Support
> Set targets for
> Facilitator
> Research
> Best practice
> Co-ordinator
> Administrator
> Trans-gender
> Diversity
> Community
> Liaison
> Traveller
> Outreach

If the job you consider yourself best-qualified for isn't there, just make one up, using a random combination of the above words, and apply for it anyway. There are so many positions up for grabs that the chances are that nobody will realise what you have done and before you know it you'll be Advising with the best of them. How does 'Traveller Liaison Outreach Project Facilitator' sound?

Or 'Trans-Gender Learning Research Co-ordinator'?

No, I think 'Diversity Best-Practice Support Advisor' fits the bill.

Mr Jones and the wasted lesson

MR JONES teaches (or, more correctly, doesn't teach) mathematics.

He is tall, thin and in his late forties. He wears a faded, mottled-brown sports jacket with those traditional leather patches on the elbows.

He is, no doubt, an expert in his subject but I think it is unlikely that, in the 25 years that he has taught at St Jude's, he has managed to impart one single fact of mathematical significance to the 10,000 or so pupils who have passed through his hands.

His results are terrible, even by our low standards, and have been during all the time he has been here.

Thanks to the teaching unions, however, he will never be sacked; he will simply go on being bad and not teaching maths until he retires.

I could forgive him all the above were it not for the fact that he also wears a beard. I have always gone by the maxim 'never trust a man with a beard' and it has never let me down. He also wears Personality Substitutes, another terrible crime in my eyes. Ties that depict Homer Simpson, socks with Disney characters on them or, Heaven forbid, badges. These are not, and have never been, amusing. Certainly, they have no place in the Staff Room. If you wish to dress to amuse then head for the big top. (I urge any teacher reading this to go immediately to the corner of the Staff Room where all the mugs are kept and carefully check each one. Any that bear 'comical' phrases such as 'Teachers never grow old... they just so-and-so' or 'You don't have to be mad to teach here but etc etc' should be thrown away forthwith.

Remember, you are doing the noble profession of teaching a favour.

Covering for Mr Jones is a nightmare.

This is because the pupils expect to behave in the same way as they do when he is there (ie appallingly). His lessons are utter chaos and the shouting tennis match between him and the children can be heard along the corridor.

His classroom is a terrible mess. Piles of books, graph paper and bits of equipment are strewn everywhere and all the work from his different classes is mixed up. He is always the last teacher to produce his class reports and loses anything that is given to him. A couple of years ago the builders had to come in and do some repairs to the wall at the back of the class; a couple of kids had spent weeks digging away at the plaster and brickwork, like prisoners in Alcatraz. They had made a hole in the wall almost big enough to crawl through and hidden it with a filing cabinet. Mr Jones had not noticed a thing.

Today, I am covering his Year 11 lesson as he has been sent on an Assertiveness Course. As he is such a disaster, he gets to go on all sorts of courses at vast expense to the taxpayer. He has been going on them for 25 years, to no visible effect, and will continue to go on them for another 15 until he retires. I kid you not: he was due to go on an Organisational Skills Course last month but forgot to send off the application form.

It is Set 6 – the same group that I had a couple of weeks ago, when I nearly managed to hypnotise them. Mr Jones used to be given only the bottom sets, in order to limit the damage he could cause, but he complained to his union and they insisted that he be given a full range of abilities in order that he could ruin a wider selection of children's futures.

Once again, the eight regulars have turned up. I have no idea why, but I'm certainly relieved that at least some of the nightmare characters are 'away'.

Six out of the eight pupils have left a green 'Report Card' on my desk, issued to each one after Mr Phillips has received a given number of complaints about them. This must be handed to the teacher at the start of every lesson; at the end of the lesson, you use the card to comment on each child's behaviour and work. If, after the week is up, a pupil has accumulated too many negative comments he is given an amber report card. Finally, he receives a red one. If that, too, is littered with marks of disapproval the child is supposed to be excluded for three days. Needless to say, this rarely happens (though most of our clients could not care less either way) and the report card system is therefore at best a farce and at worst an encouragement to misbehave: the kids see a report card as a badge of pride.

In fact, it is a prime example of an idea that looks good on paper (and enables the SMT to claim that it has a discipline policy) whilst being completely ineffective in practice. Schools are totally removed from real life, where only tangible, measurable results matter. Businesses go bust without selling their products, patients die if they're left untreated and it's no good drawing up an action plan to clean your dirty car. In the public sector, however, it's all about ticking boxes, producing policies and attending meetings. Whether the countless 'strategies' work or not is an irrelevance.

The weekly School Detention, held by the SMT for an hour after school each Friday, is another case in point. Only Heads of Department can put pupils into detention, which means mere teachers have to justify a request, filling in a form identifying the child's wrong-doing and outlining what other measures have already been tried and have failed. The Head of Department then has to fill in another form showing, in turn, what measures the department as a whole has taken and why they have failed. The pupil's parents then have to be given 24 hours' notice of the detention. At the end of that endless stream of paperwork, the kid then produces a letter from his mother. The letter will say that it is too dangerous for the child to get home on his own and he can't be picked up from school later than normal. Or it will claim that the parent simply didn't receive the letter or message informing them of the detention in the first place. That's if you get a response; quite often, the errant pupil simply never turns up for the detention and the matter is forgotten. Is it any wonder that teachers simply give up?

But I digress.

Jordan, Liam, Sean and Kyle are sitting in the front row not listening to me explain how to calculate the value of x, given that $x + 4 = 10$.

I haven't a clue why we are doing this, as they are not even entered for the GCSE exam. Even if they were entered, it is obvious that they will never be able to calculate 'x' in a million years (or need to). Now they are drawing pictures of men armed with guns, daggers and chainsaws. Perhaps they will find careers with Walt Disney's famous animation studios. Or perhaps they won't.

I've confiscated a soft porn magazine from one of them and a bottle of Coca Cola topped up with a healthy supply of rum from another.

'What's the point in us doing this?' asks Jordan, porn boy, busily not doing it anyway.

'No point whatsoever,' I reassure him, cheerfully. I carry on with the next example.

Behind them sit Dawn, Keeley, Jade and Tracey, who are also not showing the slightest interest in my sums. Dawn and Keeley are writing a note to a boy in another class. Occasionally, they even ask me how to spell something. I help them out, struggling bravely to keep a straight face. Jade and Tracey are discreetly playing noughts and crosses.

I must say, teaching algebra is so much easier when nobody is paying the slightest attention.

I'm quite enjoying it, so I move on to more complicated examples such as $2x + 5 = 11$. I even get Jade to wipe the board for me when it is full.

I glance at my watch: only ten minutes left of another successful lesson.

I notice that Dawn is using the pen she was awarded at Presentation Evening for having the best attendance in the year. We like to reward achievement. Her exercise book is virtually empty, however, as she would never dream of doing any work. Instead, she is using the pen to write on her desk.

My despair reaches no greater depths than Presentation Evening, where prizes are liberally distributed for good attendance (ie not absolutely appalling attendance) and other classics such as 'Most improved pupil.' I mean, it's not exactly difficult for some of these kids to improve; just keeping quiet for five minutes would do.

Maths cover isn't actually too bad if you're covering for anyone other than Mr Jones. The textbooks still have lots of questions for the kids, ostensibly, to get on with and there are always plenty of opportunities for colouring. Graphs and shapes should always be coloured in and graph paper provides hours of pattern-making fun for the average 15-year-old.

In fact, thinking about it, it can be quite relaxing.

Frank Chalk

Miss Simpson: Making a crisis out of drama

THE STEREOTYPE of the badly-dressed teacher is alive and well at St Jude's.

Casting my eye around the Staff Room, I cannot see anything that looks like it has been purchased in the last twenty years. Outfits that would be ridiculed elsewhere are worn with pride. I spot a velvet smoking jacket, plenty of leather elbow patches, some brown nylon trousers, ties that can only have been Christmas presents (in the 1970s) – and that's just the stuff that isn't obviously homemade. We really could use Trinny and Suzannah's help.

Miss Simpson stands out, even in this sartorial desert. Mr Blunt is convinced she is doing it for Comic Relief. Today, in stripy leggings plastered with cat hair and a strange, multicoloured jumper which she has (badly) knitted herself, she is a sight to behold. Mr Green recently bet me £20 that she is colour blind; we have been trying for weeks casually to persuade her to try to read the charts, but without success.

She teaches English and drama. The kids quite like her (maybe she reminds them of their own mothers). She keeps dozens of cats and dogs and (funnily enough) lives alone.

I would rather visit the dentist than cover Miss Simpson's drama lessons. In fact I would rather extract my own teeth with a pair of rusty pliers. Her lessons are always a nightmare.

Today, my timetable makes depressing reading; it says quite clearly that, from eleven until twelve noon, I am responsible for Year 10 drama. It is a tradition that any teacher forced to cover drama after break or lunchtime gets their cup of tea made for them in the Staff Room. This is a bit like the condemned man's final breakfast, except that you can't order deep-fried peanut butter and Jell-O sandwiches and, sadly, they won't shoot you after you've drunk it.

I make my way to the drama studio, a large room where the lesson will take place. There are no desks so even if the kids are horrendous (which they will be) I cannot sit them down and make them do written work. Last time I was given a drama cover, I had a brainwave and typed out an instruction to do some maths problems from a textbook, signed it with Miss Simpson's name and showed it to the class. I had a much more relaxing lesson than usual, but she complained.

As always, the room is unlocked and the kids are in there, racing around and playing games. They are shrieking and stealing each other's bags and generally causing mayhem. I chuck them all out and line them up outside. I am resigned to my fate.

I look at the scrap of paper on which the work is written, hoping against all odds that it will say something like, 'Go to room B34 where the pupils will sit in silence and do Exercises 1 to 10 in their books'.

But, no, it is the usual: 'Pupils are to carry on with their drama projects.'

Loosely translated, this means they have a licence to do whatever they want.

I try to gain some information.

'So what are you doing in drama, then?'

'Our projects!'

'And what are your projects, exactly?'

'Miss says we can do whatever we want!'

Oh, good.

I give them the usual warnings about not shrieking, not running around and so on, but this goes out of the window and for the next 30 minutes it is absolute pandemonium. The girls are pretending to use their mobile phones as part of a 'Play' ('Miss lets us!') and the boys are fighting ('Miss said we've got to practise this scene!').

The noise is driving me mad, as is the fact that they have the perfect excuse for messing about all lesson. I feel sorry for whoever is teaching them next as they are all completely manic now.

As for me… well, I seriously think I am about to explode.

All of a sudden, the girls go quiet. One of them walks over to me and hands me the phone. The boys see this and stop their gang warfare scene. I put the phone to my ear and now that it is quiet I hear the unmistakable voice of Mr Blunt. After confirming that he is speaking to me, he makes it extremely clear that if any more of my kids make phone calls to pupils in his lesson he will come down and shove the phone up my backside.

I decide that it would be best if we spent the last ten minutes of the lesson doing some silent mimes.

Nathan, and school-phobia

IT'S YEAR 8 geography, and Nathan has to leave half way through the lesson to see the Educational Psychologist.

He regularly plays truant and his parents claim that he is 'school-phobic'.

No doubt the psychologist will enthusiastically support this nonsense and suggest that we go out of our way to accommodate his every whim. After all, without educational problems with a psychological element to them, there'd be no need for educational psychologists, would there?

Maybe I'm just a cynic. But, to hell with it, I never listen to anything an educational psychologist says. It is invariably nonsense.

Anyway, right on cue, Nathan picks up his bag.

'It's time for me to go to the Ed Psych,' he announces, coming to the front to get his coat. After reminding him of the unfamiliar word 'please', my curiosity gets the better of me.

'What does 'school-phobic' mean, Nathan?'

I'm always fascinated by what the kids think of these things.

'It means that I can't come to school,' he replies helpfully.

Then he considers where he is at this moment and adds, helpfully, 'Well, not all the time.'

He then ponders further still. 'Well, just not for some lessons that I don't like 'cos the teachers pick on me.'

'Why do they pick on you Nathan?'

'They just do, every time I do anything wrong.'

See what I mean? Complete and utter lunacy, and all at the tax payer's expense. I am sure the experts are left with a lovely, warm feeling inside after indulging this silly boy's daft ideas. But I would like to have five minutes with one of them, just to ask what they think the end result will be? I mean, what sort of education do they imagine Nathan will end up with? And what will happen to him afterwards?

A further thought strikes me. 'Nathan, do I pick on you?'

'Yeah, sometimes.'

That's good; I wouldn't want to feel left out.

Kylie, a quiet little girl, is struggling with an aspect of the work. This is unusual, as she is a very bright kid with an aptitude for schoolwork that's incredible, given her background. She is from one of the roughest families in the area. Her father is in prison for attempted murder and both of her half-brothers, ex-pupils of ours, are in and out of jail about as often as the warders. Her mother, an alcoholic, is like a human revolving door, constantly spinning and bringing fresh squads of unsuitable men into her life as she ejects the rejects. She has four other children younger than Kylie by three different blokes. I've been to their house; it's filthy, it smells and the noise from the TV, the stereo, the crying toddlers and babies and her mother's loud and foul mouth has to be heard to be believed. With all this against her, this poor little mite is fighting and battling to succeed. She's polite and attentive, she doesn't mix with the rougher gangs of girls in school and she tries ever so hard. Her homework is done on time, and is always among the best in the class. She seems to have grasped that she has one shot in life, and that this is it. We talk about her in the Staff Room; we are determined to do whatever we can to help her. I spend a few minutes crouching by her desk, going through the questions that have been set, and get a tremendous kick out of watching her little face light up as she unravels the problems and begins to understand.

'What are you going to do when you grow up, Kylie?' I ask her, fairly *sotto voce*.

'I'm not sure, Sir,' she says. 'I'd like to be a doctor but I probably won't be able to do that.'

I grin at her. 'Of course you can be a doctor, Kylie. You're a clever girl. You just need to keep working hard, that's all, and keep on trying and believing in yourself. After all, if I can be a teacher…'

She smiles shyly and blushes.

If she can just keep her head above water I really think she'll make something of her life.

I have my fingers crossed so hard they're going white.

Top set, bottom set:
A game for all the family

WITH THE renewed interest among our political classes in the once-derided practice of setting, this is a tremendous and topical game for two or more players, requiring one teacher and a class register.

The teacher selects a top and bottom set but does not tell the other players which is which.

He calls out ten first names from the first group and then ten from the second.

The players have 30 seconds to write down which group they think is the top set and which group is the bottom set, without ever having met or heard of the kids before. When time is up the teacher announces the answer.

The game is traditionally played over five rounds and the player with the most correct sets wins. Here's the first round, to get you started.

Unknown Set A: Wayne, Tracey, Shazney, Dwayne, Liam, Sherry, Coyne, Ashley, Kyle, Jordan.

Unknown Set B: Mary, Joseph, Jonathan, Philip, Stephen, Michael, Jane, Andrew, David, Rosemary.

Now, how easy was that?

More advanced players simply ask for the register's hyphen count (for example, Kerry-Ann and Bobby-Jo will be giveaways).

Watch out for any child whose name should end in 'Y' but actually ends in 'I' – insofar as they are proper names at all, Sherri and Geri are your friends here.

One more tip – good players never make their minds up until all ten names have been called out. Don't be swayed by the odd case of a Kylie sneaking into the top set by mistake. You'll be right far more often than you're wrong.

What the game demonstrates, of course, is that simple-minded people tend to name their children after the fashion of the day (a good tactic, if you know the age of the group, is to cast your mind back to see which pop singers, soap actors or football stars were well-known just before they were born).

It also illustrates how names which were considered the height of fashion when your child was born can come back to haunt you in later years. Imagine being born in, say, the 1920s to parents with an interest in foreign affairs. How exotic and classy Adolf or Benito would have sounded at the time.

I once spent a free lesson on my first day in a new school putting an entire year group into sets based only on their names. I gave it to one of their teachers and she was horrified to see how accurate it was.

With this in mind, I have written to the Education Secretary advising the abolition of testing and suggesting, instead, that sets, GCSE results and, indeed, careers should simply be decided on the applicant's name. To date, I have had no reply.

Incidentally, I am thinking of copyrighting *Top Set, Bottom Set*, so you may see it on the shelves in time for Christmas. In the meantime, find a teacher and try it for yourself.

The disastrous lesson

TODAY I performed one of my best-known comedies, 'The Disastrous Lesson'. This is a popular production which never fails to amuse the other staff no matter how many times they see it.

Scene 1
The Room Change.
This is a traditional farce, well-known territory to any supply teacher.

Lulled into a false sense of security by his instructions on the Cover Board, our hero arrives to confront the horror of his Year 8 science group. Unfortunately, due to a timetabling error, the room is already occupied by another class. An argument follows and the group is cast out, leading neatly into...

Scene 2
The Long March.
This is where the motley crowd journeys to the Promised Land (Room LC 53, which we have been promised is empty). They face many challenges and dangers on their route, including the Classroom with the Low Windows, which can only be passed by hurling abuse at its occupants, then fleeing the wrath of its Ruler, King Blunt.

Scene 3
The Locked Classroom.
On arrival at LC53, another traditional scene familiar to all supply teachers awaits us, involving a 15-minute delay while the correct key is located.

Scene 4
The Missing Textbooks.
Nail-biting stuff, where the treachery of another teacher is revealed...

Scene 5
The Lost Pupils.
Where Mr Chalk discovers that not all survived the long March. Some have fallen by the wayside and become Waifs; others have paused to consult the Oracle of The Vending Machine. The purpose of this sinister device is to ensure that the kids are completely hyper on E numbers, additives etc. They absolutely worship this machine; some of them even talk to it.

Scene 6
The Off-The-Cuff Lesson.
The science work that has been set for this lesson is now of little use, since the textbooks that it refers to have disappeared. 'Do the

questions on p78 and then the diagram opposite' is not of much use to us now.

There are no teachers in the vicinity who teach this subject; the vague promise of 'I'll send someone to find the Head of Department, oh no, he's away – maybe the Deputy then… ?' does not reassure me, followed as it is by the swift exit, stage left, of the speaker.

Therefore, an off-the-cuff lesson is called for.

This is made slightly trickier by the fact that all the available science material in the room is for a year 11 Set.

We are marooned far from home. Still, it could be worse; at least it's not drama.

We also have Mr Chalk's Emergency Survival Kit, without which he rarely leaves home. It contains the essential equipment for this situation: a dozen cheap Biros and a dozen pencils, 160 coloured pencils, 120 sheets A4 blank, 120 sheets A4 lined, 240 assorted felt-tip pens, 60 sheets of graph paper, two pencil sharpeners and a dozen rubbers.

This enables me to dream up work with varying success for any subject you care to name.

Off we go then: I've established (via the class snitch) that we are doing 'plants and animals', so let's kick off by making a list of our favourite ten plants and ten animals. We can then draw a picture of them and maybe even decide whether the animals have a backbone or not.

I encourage them with the possibility of a Merit Mark. Kids have to be bribed outrageously to do even the most mundane of tasks. This is known as 'Rewarding Achievement' and enables the SMT to tick another government box. (The Merit Mark scheme is a new idea. Merit marks are recorded and the children with the most will get prizes and be allowed on the School Trip to the seaside. Unfortunately, like everything else, there is no coherent policy about them, specifically as to what they should be dished out for. In the absence of this it is left to the teacher's judgment. The inevitable result is that the worst teachers give them out like confetti in an attempt to bribe the worst kids to behave. It looks like this year's school trip is going to be full of naughty kids, while the children who have worked hard and are in the middle of the ability range get nothing.)

Two of them are busy chattering while I'm explaining what we're going to do. I simply move towards them without altering my tone or doing anything else. Sometimes the proximity of a teacher is enough to make them behave. This only works with kids who aren't too bad, but it helps reinforce the strength of your presence. Having a powerful presence is a vital aspect of teaching, though its development is often neglected. Experts would probably label it as 'bullying' so it must be a good thing.

'Callum, stop drawing a cannabis leaf. Yes, I can see you... look through these textbooks to find some examples of plants. Yes, I know it's a plant but can't you think of another one?'

Billie-Jo has a great sense of propriety: they are in Year 8, so only a Year 8 textbook will suffice. She will not open a Year 11 textbook. Only the most pristine piece of A4 is good enough for her and no, Mr Chalk, your selection of cheap Biros will not do.

We are running low on vital supplies – for once in my life, the felt tips have been left at home, typical, and I only have 75 sheets of blank paper left.

Tyler is starting to be a nuisance so I make him responsible for sharpening all the coloured pencils, with the possibility of a Merit Mark should he do it well (he won't). He does his job quite diligently but soon starts to get carried away, snatching pencils off other children to feed into the mechanical sharpener. I sense that we are starting the inexorable decline into chaos that I have witnessed so many times but I am distracted by a letter on school notepaper that Nathan has in front of him.

'What's that Nathan?'

He hands me the letter, which is from SMT. It explains that since his visit to the Educational Psychologist it has been decided that he will start off by going to the lessons 'he feels he can cope with best.' It then lists the ones he will be attending. I look at this list (all of three) and I am puzzled.

'Nathan, science isn't on your list of subjects – what are you doing here?'

'I like science.'

'But you're not ready for science yet! It says so here.' I wave the letter at him, and he consults it.

'Oh, yeah. Sorry, I forgot.' And he goes back to his place and starts to pack up!

'Hang on a minute, where are you off to?'

'I have to go home. I'm only allowed to go to English, drama and geography.'

God, I can't handle this madness any more.

'Nathan, you've been here for 45 minutes and you seem absolutely fine to me and I'm a proper psychologist so I should know.'

'Are you really, sir?'

'Oh yes, Nathan. I have had a lot of experience with every kind of…'

A loud and continuous clanging bell rudely interrupts this bizarre exchange. We move into:

Scene 7
The Rescue.

Just as the lesson is running out of steam, the fire alarm suddenly goes off.

SAVED!

All race out of school, disregarding all commands to walk.

We line up in form groups outside on the field.

There is much jeering by Ghosts and Waifs; registers are taken, the head teacher Mr Morris confirms that there's no fire and we head back inside just in time for the final bell.

There is no happy ending for this play, alas; it has just become apparent that it was one of the lost boys from my lesson who set the alarm off.

The Head would like to see Mr Chalk in his office for a coffee-less chat.

The End

Dozing in the staff room

WE PASS a milestone as I am sitting in the Staff Room with my feet up, half-dozing, half-listening to the various conversations around me. Over on the other side of the room, the first teacher has said, 'It's been a long term.'

Well, it *is* almost five weeks since the summer holiday and we must battle on for another 12 working days until half-term.

The unions are being discussed to my left. There are several different teaching unions, with differing views and methods, so they are a very disjointed force. My own opinion of them is pretty low. They talk a good game, but they don't do much for individual teachers. There are certainly plenty of things that they *could* be doing. I'd like to see them insisting on police prosecutions for all pupils and parents who are involved in violence, drugs or any other illegal activities in schools. Every day, around the UK, teachers are getting assaulted; I've been threatened myself and plenty of my colleagues have been attacked. You can't move in hospitals for lurid signs advising you that abuse of, and assaults on, staff are not tolerated. You only have to look mildly irritable on a plane and the pilot is diverting to the nearest police state. And imagine if people kept beating up tube train drivers: the whole London Underground would be out on strike, sharpish, until something was done about it.

Why are schools any different?

To my right, Miss Wade is giving the new student teacher some pearls of advice. She is telling her how to get a pupil to move if they do not want to. This is a fairly classic problem in the classroom.

'You should always try to avoid a confrontation,' she babbles. 'So what I do is I move someone else at the same time so they don't think that you are just picking on them, or I say something like, 'If you move, I'll let you use the coloured pens.'

This business of negotiating with the kids, or bribing them, bothers me deeply. I can't deny that I've done it myself, occasionally, but I don't think it really achieves anything. All you've done is surrender control of the situation to the pupil. They will remember that: they may not know what 11x8 is, but they are smart enough to realise that if they refuse next time you ask them to do something you may cut them some sort of deal. It's all part of a big thing I have about the tail wagging the dog. We're told to change our ways of teaching to suit the kids. Shouldn't it be the other way round? As teachers and parents, we try far too hard to please children. They sense this and play up to it at every opportunity.

As I listen to Miss Wade talk rubbish, I reflect that the people in charge of teacher training have a lot to answer for. Basic skills and sound advice have been replaced by woolly 'concepts and ideas.'

And I smile thinly to myself: just last week, in this very room, I heard her telling a different student teacher that if a pupil refuses to move you should take the whole class outside the room and leave the malefactor there alone. The student seemed impressed by this. I remember the PGCE 'experts' telling us the same thing; while I could not be bothered to argue with Miss Wade, the nonsense of it is obvious.

What if the rest of the group refuses to move (as they may well do)?

If they do agree to move, how will you find an unlocked, empty classroom in the vicinity? Are you supposed to lead this rabble through the school, causing havoc, in search of a free room? How long will all this take? I mean, aren't you supposed to be using this time for teaching?

If you do find a room, what do you do when the next kid plays up? Decamp again?

And what about the original hooligan? Will he be sitting and studying, quiet as a mouse, in the seat where you left him? Or will he be wrecking the joint?

Opposite me, they are discussing ASBOs. I'm all in favour of anything that makes life difficult for yobs and, while I certainly don't expect them to work perfectly, they will definitely work better than doing nothing at all, which seems to be the only other option we have recently tried.

Next to them, the conversation is about teenage pregnancies. There are always pregnant girls at school, as young as 12 or 13. The kids are sex-mad and very open about it. You hear tales of them doing it at school, but Mrs Chalk says it's mainly in the bushes in the park, though I'm not sure how she knows. We've got a couple of Year 9s pregnant at the moment. (Sorry, I've phrased that rather badly, but I'm only a maths teacher. *'A couple of our Year 9s have got themselves pregnant.'* Is that better? Er, no. Oh, I give up: you know what I mean.) The UK has the highest rate of teenage pregnancy in Europe simply because we do nothing to discourage it. Nobody should have children if they cannot afford to pay for them, and certainly not at 12 or 13. But there is not enough downside to make our children terrified of themselves having children. There are no adverse consequences, not even the guilt or shame of old: quite the reverse. They're the centre of attention, they're handed the keys to a council flat and a load of benefits. We should be sending the message: 'Don't do that, because you will end up with a dreadful life.' Last week, Shayla, a Year 11 girl, came back into school after 'maternity leave' and brought her baby in to show her friends. What a great idea! Everybody, teachers included, gathers round and coos and makes clucking noises at the little bundle while Shayla basks in the attention. Now they will *all* want one!

The group on the next table are discussing one of the 'Please make me famous, I'm desperate'-type programmes that seem to be on the telly every night these days. When I first started teaching, and we're not talking in the Dark Ages, most staff were reasonably serious-minded people who wouldn't have given a moment's thought to this tripe. Now the Staff Room is littered with dog-eared copies of *Heat*, *OK* and *Garbage* (OK, I made the last one up). The group chatting about the show seem quite fascinated by it; at least, they demonstrate a working knowledge of the various characters and their moronic machinations. I must admit I can't really understand this mad desire to be famous, though I know it inhabits almost every single one of my pupils. I can understand people wanting to be rich, because it increases the options available to you and should, in theory, take away financial worries (although no doubt it brings its own problems). But the desire to be known by everyone strikes me as plain weird. All I care about is being known by my friends; I'm certainly not interested in what someone I will never meet thinks of me. As I slump lower in my chair, I wonder to myself if this strange urge replaces the old neighbourliness we seem to have lost, at least in our cities? A hundred years ago, and even more recently, most people would have been known to all the inhabitants of their village, which might have numbered a couple of hundred people, or their immediate neighbours in their town. This familiarity has disappeared for many of us. Perhaps these wannabes are unconsciously crying out against the anonymity of modern life? Or perhaps they're just lazy and thick? Who knows?

The conversation on the table on the far wall centres on a complaint made about Mr Blunt by another teacher. Teachers are forever writing letters to the Head with formal complaints about each other. I don't understand why they can't air their grievances like adults, calmly and openly. The job is supposed to be about communication skills, after all. It reminds me of a recent conversation with a barrister friend of mine who has handled a dozen or so court cases involving teachers over recent years (and he is not a specialist in the area by any means). He says that, invariably, one of the witnesses for the prosecution is another teacher from the same school. Whatever happened to team spirit?

Another teacher is complaining that the parents of a kid in her form have asked the Head for two weeks' holiday during term time and that he has granted them permission. That's because, he knows the whole 'permission' thing is a charade; if he says 'no' they'll go anyway, and it will spoil our figures under the new Government initiative to reduce unauthorised absences. This is another tremendous example of how things can so easily be improved simply by totting numbers up in a different column. Astonishingly, by the way, parents sometimes ask the Head for permission to take their kids away on holiday during SATS tests. Though, thinking about it, the results don't count for anything so why bother doing them?

Good teachers, and the privilege of watching them

MR BLUNT and Mr Green are brilliant teachers.

Mr Blunt is tall, strongly-built and exudes an air of authority like few others can. A no-nonsense disciplinarian, he has that indefinable presence that is essential in a successful teacher.

He is in his late forties and has taught here for the last twelve years, having come into teaching late after becoming bored with his previous job managing an insurance company. He has a vast knowledge and interest in his subject, which is history.

Although he does not live very near to the school, he has made a tremendous effort to get to know most of the parents, to get involved in the community and to win its respect. This gives him a huge advantage when dealing with naughty kids. He often attends local meetings and does a couple of historical walks around the area each year, which are surprisingly popular.

Mr Blunt is such a good teacher that it is a privilege to watch him in action and his lessons should be compulsory viewing for all the other staff at our school.

He is aware of everything that is going on in the classroom and exerts control constantly but effortlessly. He can impart an enthusiasm for learning that puts my puny efforts to shame. His control of the kids is first rate. He has zero tolerance for every form of poor behaviour and relentlessly pursues miscreants. His classroom is a shrine to cleanliness (it is rumoured that he tips the cleaners to do a better job on his room).

He will arrange meetings with parents at their own houses to discuss their offspring. He always pushes the idea that the parents and the school are a team and that without each other both will lose.

He can put the fear of God into the toughest pupil, stretch the brightest brain and encourage the slowest. He tries constantly to open the kids' minds to how much better they can become.

Such an aura has built up surrounding him that even the casual mention of his name, along the lines of 'Oh, don't forget to remind me at twenty past that Mr Blunt is coming to borrow some exercise books', is enough to quieten a class.

Like Miss Wade, Mr Green teaches science. Unlike Miss Wade, he is awe-inspiringly good.

Once a week, in the last lesson on a Wednesday, I support Callum, a dense element in Mr Green's Year 8 science class. I sit next to the boy, making encouraging noises and helping him with what he calls 'work'. When he behaves well, I draw him a picture of a machine gun and he draws a knife. All harmless stuff and we get on fine.

Today, there is another teacher in the room helping Fatima, who doesn't speak much English. I don't know the teacher that well, as she doesn't speak much English either.

Mr Green reminds me very much of the television presenter Johnny Ball (*Think of A Number?*). He can demonstrate a tremendous enthusiasm for absolutely anything to the point where I am convinced that he is on drugs; surely nobody can be *that* interested in The Periodic Table of the Elements.

The kids are all sat bolt upright doing weird things like asking questions and listening. We are having a roller coaster tour of the Elements which seems largely to involve destroying them. We are all absolutely gripped. Some kids have written nearly half a page of notes! Mr Green has no interactive whiteboard, no handouts, no obvious plan to the lesson and his ideas on Health and Safety are shocking. However, we have seen some amazing bangs and flashes, and at one stage the lab was filled with choking gas, which the kids loved.

Mr Green's almost manic enthusiasm is infectious and sweeps across the room in waves of madness. It simply cannot be resisted. Although 30 minutes previously I could not have given two hoots about which element lives under sodium, I'm now gripped as though by a first-rate Hollywood thriller... now I cannot wait to find out. He is asking the class and they are all searching frantically for the Table. Completely carried away, I wrench the textbook out of Callum's hands and greedily run my finger down the column to see which element is next. A forest of hands is all around me and some pupils are erroneously shouting out 'Lithium!'

I have to force myself not to shout them down, for I have found the correct answer.

Callum tries to take the textbook back and a tug-of-war develops: at this point, I realise that the other support teacher is looking at me rather oddly. I manage to smile and scratch my ear.

'Go on, Callum… tell them!' I say, loudly, adding through my teeth, 'It's potassium, halfwit!'

'Gimme my friggin' book!' mutters Callum, taking the book from my now relaxed grip (we have come to an accommodation in respect of swearing out of the earshot of others).

Mr Green really is this good, I'm not exaggerating. If he asked the class to leap out of the window, they would do so without question (so would I, probably).

When the kids leave, they are chanting Group One of the Elements with a religious fervour.

I am too shallow to understand why a man of his undoubted ability (he graduated with a first class degree from Cambridge over thirty years ago) should choose to devote his life to what seems like a thankless task, when it would have been very easy for him to have gained much more money and status elsewhere. I think, from talking to him, that it's because he didn't expect to end his working life like this; who could have predicted how far education has fallen in three decades?

Away from the children, he is quieter and more contemplative. We often talk after the lesson, tidying up stray books, scrap paper and bottles of chemicals lying around with price labels saying 1s 6d on them. Both of us are completely out of touch with modern teaching, to an extent that is comical.

Sometimes we test each other.

'Any idea what a B.I.P. is?'

'None whatsoever. Do you know what T.L.R are? I heard the new student teacher mention them.'

'No, sorry, can't help you there.'

Sadly, and to my surprise, he admits that he is now thinking of leaving teaching entirely. He feels that he cannot control the disruptive kids as he used to and he can't bear to see the bright ones suffering as a result. (I point out that he ought to get out more, and see what goes on in the rest of the school.)

Whereas it will be no great loss when I finally hang up my gown, it will be a real blow to the profession, and to the next generation, if people of Mr Green's calibre are put off teaching by the current behavioural problems.

Teachers like him and Mr Blunt hold a school together.

Every school has a few of them.

They should have their salaries increased, immediately, to something more commensurate with their ability and the effect that they can have on kids.

I suggest a special tax on Premiership footballers. Many of them wouldn't miss a million or two; that would be a start.

I know it's unfashionable, but I happen to think that good teachers are more important to children, and to the country, than people who can kick a ball between some sticks.

Nothing is too simple for us

MISS WADE only joined us this year.

She's relatively new to the profession but gamely refuses to allow her lack of knowledge or experience to hold her back from pontificating on any and every topic of discussion. At first, I thought she must be some kind of teaching genius as she offered constant advice to all who would listen. After covering one or two lessons for her whilst she attends various courses, however, I am beginning to have my doubts. In fact, along with Mr Jones, she is one of the five per cent of all teachers (my estimate) who are absolutely useless.

Miss Wade is similar to Mr Jones in a number of ways: principally, that she is well-meaning, irritating and naïve and completely unable to control a class of children.

Unlike Mr Jones, however, she knows next to nothing about the subject she is supposed to teach. It is distressing to watch her in action; each one of her lessons destroys a tiny piece of the potential of 30 children.

Like Mr Jones, she could stay on for decades as it is next to impossible to be sacked from teaching. My only hope is that she will be promoted to the SMT, where she won't be able to do as much damage and where incompetence does not stand out as much.

Naturally, she resolutely refuses to admit to any problems. I'm sure she could be improved by simply taking some honest down to earth advice from one of the genuinely expert teachers that every school has. But that's not going to happen because she thinks she's brilliant, and they all hate her.

She is in her early twenties, and wears the sort of outfits for school that would look stunning on a woman two stones lighter venturing out on a Saturday night. Nevertheless, to Wayne and Lee's eager Year 10 eyes, she is a gift from Heaven and, compared with the horrors strutting round the Cherry Tree Estate, I can understand why. Wayne has even drawn a picture of himself enthusiastically coupling with her on the cover of his exercise book. How touching. (By the way, even Year 7 pupils will make suggestive comments if you draw anything dodgy on the board, like a funny-shaped graph or a test tube. Often, they'll do it without any provocation at all. They grow up a lot quicker than we did in my day, that's for sure.)

Teachers like Miss Wade are an absolute nightmare to cover for. The kids expect to run riot and rarely disappoint me. The work left is always vague and often at the wrong level for the group.

Today, she has gone on a Leadership Course.

I arrive in the science lab to find the kids already milling about in there.

Oh, bloody hell.

I am late because the lesson is not in the room that my cover sheet says it is and I have spent ten minutes running around like a lunatic being directed this way and that by well-meaning staff. This happens all the time.

Because I am flustered, I make the fatal mistake of rushing the start of the lesson. Instead of throwing them all out and lining them up, thus buying me valuable time to find out what the hell we are supposed to be doing, I just stand in the doorway, glare at them and wait for them to sit down.

Most don't know me at all but they sense I may be important

because I wear a suit, carry a briefcase and am not smiling or moving. Unfortunately, this will only work for a short while; they soon realise that you cannot actually pull out a Colt .45 and shoot them.

I keep it going for as long as possible though.

I move a couple of kids and tell them to watch the board very carefully, even though there's nothing on it. This is a great one: nobody ever asks why.

I desperately scan through the numerous A4 pages she has carefully Sellotaped to her desk and eventually locate the work she has left for the Year 8 group to do. Physics, chemistry and biology have been replaced by 'science' in many schools, nowadays. That's just as well: it would be nigh-on impossible for us to recruit a physics graduate to teach physics, anyway. Fewer and fewer people study the subject at University (because it is much harder than media studies or psychology, and seems to carry no more weight) and, for those that do, there is no shortage of well-paid jobs elsewhere.

I write the following work on the blackboard (making the chalk screech horribly): 'Make notes on the elements mentioned on pages 26 and 27. Answer 'What Do You Know' questions on page 28'.

I have barely finished writing this when pandemonium breaks out.

Every hand is up and almost every child is shouting one of the following:

'What do you do?'

'I don't geddit!'

'Help me!'

'This is sh*t!'

'I can't do this!'

I say 'almost every child', because half-a-dozen are shouting 'I need a pen!' or 'I haven't got a book!' and two or three are actually turning to the correct pages in their books.

I fold my arms, realising that we need to change tack.

'OK. Pens down, everybody. Yes, Ashley I know you don't have one. Put your hands down and shut up. Look at me! Fold your arms! Now… nobody say a word!'

I should have done all this to begin with, but after all these years I still overestimate kids constantly.

Hang on a minute, what is Nathan the partial school phobic doing here?

'Nathan wha…'

But before I can say any more he rushes out to show me his letter, which now has 'science' added to the list of subjects he can 'cope with'. I idly wonder whether I could get a similar letter for myself, only with 'drama' crossed off it.

Right, let's try again, but a bit slower.

'Put your right hand up if you do not have a pen.' The fewer choices you can introduce into the equation, the better.

Four hands shoot up. Tyler is changing rapidly from right hand to left, looking at the other hand-raisers for clues.

'Borrow one off a friend now. You have ten seconds. Nine, eight, seven…'

A flurry of activity.

Billie-Jo is still gesticulating wildly so I give her a pencil. She screws up her nose at it and holds it as if it has the plague. She then finds a pen and drops the pencil on the floor, completely forgotten, all within 30 seconds. I glare at her with my most outraged expression and she picks it up.

'Put your right hand up if you do not have your exercise book.'

Eight hands go up.

I place a piece of A4 neatly on each desk.

They hate writing on A4 and start to moan that they 'have nothing to write on'. Two of them mysteriously locate their exercise books immediately.

'OK, put the title, 'The Elements.'

Oh, you fool Chalk! A flurry of hands and shouted questions starts.

'Stop it!'

Of course they can't spell the word 'elements': you have to write everything on the board.

I write the title and the date on the board (for some reason, younger pupils are often obsessive about writing the date; they don't bother to remember what it is but they always want to write it in).

'Now, I'm going to read the notes to you and then we are going to copy them out.'

Smiles, everyone is much happier now. They will not have to use their brains.

'If we can do this quietly then we will draw the equipment seen on page 28.' (I wave the coloured pencils and felt tips enticingly.)

It is absolutely shocking, I know. Children of thirteen years of age should be working out questions, solving multi-stage problems and learning how to summarise information in note form. Instead, because they cannot do any of this, or even spell 'elements', we are reduced to copying work and pictures. This is work that could be done perfectly easily by a bright seven-year-old.

When the clock on the wall indicates that there are only ten minutes of the lesson left, everyone starts putting coats on and closing books.

'Oi! Get back to work. We will pack up two minutes before the end of the lesson.'

There is uproar. They always pack up ten minutes before. Bearing in mind each lesson is 60 minutes long, and that the first and the final 10 minutes are wasted, this is depressing in the extreme.

'The clock is slow.'

It isn't.

'We need at least ten minutes!'

'To do what, precisely?' I enquire. Half of them haven't brought anything to pack away!

They are all anxiously looking at the clock as it approaches five minutes to go. Some are starting to fret.

'Oh, all right, all right! Start packing up.' The relief is palpable, even though I can see perfectly well that at least half of them have already started to put their arms through their coat sleeves surreptitiously. I go round and take their books (asking them to pass them to the front is like asking for book-throwing mayhem).

I recover my pencil before it disappears into Davina's pencil case. She is a thieving toe-rag, I'm afraid. Many pupils will pinch anything that is not nailed down; if you should be so foolish as to leave a nice pen lying around, it will disappear quicker than you can say 'David Blaine'.

Two minutes to go, and everyone is frantically buttoning-up coats, putting on baseball caps and woolly hats and then taking them off again under my irate glare. Their next lesson is all of one flight of stairs and a corridor away, yet some are dressed for the Arctic. It shows what a life of TV, central heating and no exercise does for your body's thermostat.

'This room will be spotless before we go anywhere!' I announce. They all look around but their confused faces suggest they have managed somehow to miss the mass of litter strewn about the floor.

'Come on! Pick it up!' They all look outraged. Cries of 'It wasn't me' fill the air but they bend down and start collecting odds and sods of rubbish.

Several are announcing that the class next door is leaving. Their eyes are bright with panic.

'For God's sake, we'll go when the bell goes!'

Which it immediately does.

'No! Row by row. This row first.'

This is all new and terrifying to them; they all try to move forward at once, like a herd of curious bullocks, before melting back nervously. Drib by drab, they leave, all breaking into a sprint once they have cleared the classroom door, like a rabble charging the Pound Shop counter in the January sales.

It is as though they are desperately eager to get to their next lesson; I know full well, however, that most of them will manage, somehow, to be late for it.

Cooking with Mr Chalk

MRS O'BRIEN is a short, stout lady of around 50 who teaches cooking.

Though, hang on, didn't they change the name? To home economics?

That's right. Oh, but then they changed it again, didn't they? To domestic science?

Yes. But wait a sec, wasn't it... didn't they... ?

That's it. Mrs O'Brien now teaches 'food technology'.

A tremendous example of how changing the name of something is supposed, somehow, to equal 'progress'.

Well, Mrs O'Brien is a straight-talking woman from Belfast and it's 'cookery' as far as she's concerned, and 'none of yer modern nonsense.'

Good on her.

Today she's off sick – a most unusual occurrence where she's concerned – so Chalk's in charge.

For some reason, I am not allowed to let the children do any actual cooking in food technology. I suppose it follows a general principle – after all, we don't do a lot of maths in maths either – but I think it's actually something to do with the Health and Safety people. Though what on earth they think I'm likely to do I don't know. They can't imagine I'll attempt to poison the kids, can they? *Can* they?

We line up outside and, as usual, I do my best to appear totally calm, both with my voice and movements, in the hope that it will somehow rub off on the kids. There's method in my madness: children really do sense your confidence unconsciously and adjust their behaviour accordingly. This is called 'non-verbal communication' by people who lecture other people about teaching. It doesn't always work, mind; sometimes I go too far and the kids think I'm drugged up.

As they aren't cooking, Mrs O'Brien has left her Year 10 group the task of 'Designing a Pizza'. I've never felt that there was a shortage of pizza designs at my local Italian restaurant, or in the freezer cabinet at the local supermarket for that matter, but the kids happily get on with drawing one, topped, most originally, with chocolate and beans. It doesn't sound like education to me, but that's probably why they take to it so enthusiastically.

Food technology is one of a choice of three subjects our kids can choose, the others being 'Design Technology' and 'Materials Technology'. In theory, they choose the one they are most interested in. In practice, most choose whatever their friends are doing.

Whatever their reasoning, on average they tend to be slightly better-behaved than in subjects they *have* to do such as maths, English and science. I suppose it's a lot more fun making a bookshelf or drawing a cake than dry-as-dust work such as puzzling out the value of 'x'. I must say, though, that I'm slightly dubious about the usefulness of constantly asking them to *design* things. Last week, some of them were tasked to produce drawings for a CD rack. Why waste time designing one of those when you can buy a perfectly good one in Argos for a tenner? The kids don't seem to be taught that mass-produced things are cheap whereas one-offs are expensive, and why this should be: facts, that is to say, worth the learning.

There are not so many of them in the lesson today as there is a trip to McDonald's, organised by the Support Team to reward the really naughty kids who have managed to improve and behave reasonably for about ten minutes (I'm not inventing this, honestly; I cannot understand how the Support Team do not know that McDonalds is not the best place for young people to eat). Meanwhile, the kids who have been good all year get nothing. This is a recurring theme in schools: if you are quiet, well-behaved and fairly bright you will be ignored, whereas if you are a lunatic who shuts up for five minutes you will be handsomely rewarded. As soon as they have received said reward, of course, these children immediately and invariably revert to their former behaviour.

So, yes, it's easy in here today. The room itself has been recently refitted and it's still quite smart as Mrs O'Brien is very strict.

It's nice and warm, too, thanks to the heat from the ovens and... hang on a minute. Why are the ovens on? And what's that smell of burning paper?

Cutting-edge typing

COVER TODAY for Mr Burton, our resident Dungeons-and-Dragons expert and Head of Information Technology.

Mr Burton is a skinny little chap in his mid-twenties, with little round glasses and a greasy ponytail. He dresses entirely in black, with only the occasional heavy metal t-shirt under his funny-looking jacket to provide colour. I find shoes are usually a giveaway when judging character; Mr Burton's are wide and black, with built-up heels and metal buckles. Perhaps the kids regard him as extremely fashionable, and maybe that's important to him. I think he looks like a clown.

Certainly, no-one can argue that his IT rooms are not a sorry sight.

They were refurbished just a couple of years ago, at huge cost and at the same time as the cookery (sorry, food technology) rooms.

However, whereas Mrs O'Brien watches over her domain like a hawk, and notices the slightest blemish, Mr Burton watches over his like a slob who couldn't care less. Consequently, it has deteriorated rapidly. Thousands of pounds'-worth of mindless vandalism has been done, with obscenities scratched into desks, computers damaged and letters prised out of keyboards (for some reason, 'F', 'U', 'K' and 'C' seem to be the most popular trophies).

In my opinion, Mr Burton needs sitting down and being told to get a grip. As far as I know, this has not happened.

The work done in the IT suite looks, to a non-expert outsider like myself, like a mixture of typing and that exercise you used to do aged six, in junior school; the one where you would cut pictures out of magazines and stick them on a large piece of coloured paper to make a collage.

Cutting and pasting, we used to call it.

Nowadays it is still called cutting and pasting but it is much easier: there's no messy glue to worry about, and the participants are all 15 years old.

What progress we have made!

The Year 10 group arrive in dribs and drabs, some claiming half-heartedly that their previous teacher kept them behind. I get them to sit down at the computers and most of them manage to retrieve their work and get started.

Lee, Bradley and Coyne (this is a name, apparently) cannot find theirs and claim that it has disappeared off the computer system. I have no means of knowing whether this is true as the technician is, as usual, unavailable. There is little else for them to do and I have that annoying feeling of helplessness. I let them draw pictures on the computer for the time being, checking from time to time to make sure they aren't trawling the Internet for hard-core pornography.

Fifteen minutes into the lesson, the last half-dozen of the group appear. They have some stupid excuse for being late, which I know is nonsense. Employers are desperate, not just for skilled workers but for ones who can turn up on time, who will be polite to customers and clean up after themselves. In short, for people who will behave in a civilised manner. Very few of our kids can do any of these things, for the simple reason that they have never been forced to. They are late for school, time and time again, without any real punishment. As we so often do, we are taking the easy option but selling them short: punctuality is so important in the workplace and our touchy-feely slackness will count against them in a few short years. Mind you, their parents hardly set them a good example. They turn up late to meetings that have been arranged for them, offer some transparent excuse and expect the school to bend over backwards to accommodate them. Sometimes, they don't turn up at all and, naturally, they don't trouble themselves to offer an explanation as to why. Their kids inherit this benefits culture attitude, that society owes them something and must look after them.

Wayne then walks in, striding straight into the room in a deliberately dramatic entrance. He is brandishing his report card and playing up to the rest of the group, most of whom find his antics highly amusing. I walk over to the door and open it with a flourish, showing that I can do drama too. I jerk my head, indicating that he should come outside so I can sign his card. Actually, I just want to get him into the corridor where we can't be overheard by the others. I take his report and then give him some serious verbal abuse, about how he is a jumped-up waste of space.

He replies: 'You can't say that, I'll get me dad in.'

I cast doubt on his father's ability even to find his way to the school unaided, write on his report that he has been a disgrace and put it in my pocket, telling him he can't have it back (they often 'lose' reports that have negative comments on them) and tell him to wait outside the Deputy Head's office (fat chance).

'Get a f*cking life!' he shouts, disappearing round the corner.

It never ceases to amaze me how often this particular piece of advice is offered, quite without irony, by our kids. It can only be that they genuinely have no perception of how their own lives will probably pan out unless they knuckle down and get an education.

I return to the chaos in the computer room. Lee has pulled the plug on somebody else's computer and now they are wrestling on the floor. I separate them and throw Lee out almost before he has even got back on his feet.

A couple of the kids ask me the same question about how to do something simple on the computers. I take out my marker pen and write down the procedure, step-by-step, on the electronic whiteboard at the front of the classroom. Standing back, I see that I have mis-spelled a word. Seeing no board rubber, I try to rub it out with a bit of tissue but this proves impossible.

It dawns on me that something is horribly wrong; the sniggers of the pupils don't help.

It only takes a few days to have the whiteboard treated so that it can be used again, though this time with the special electronic pen only.

I still don't see what all the fuss was about. This incident did nothing whatsoever to restore my faith in the importance of high technology in low education.

The Head, and the rest of the SMT

THE SMT (Senior Management Team) runs the school. It consists of The Head, the Deputy Heads, the Assistant Head, the Deputy Assistant Head and a few hangers-on.

They all teach a few lessons a week and each has a little office with his or her name on the door.

This is about as good as it gets in modern teaching, I'm afraid.

There is a daily rota set up so that, at any time during the week, one of them is the Duty SMT Person. This means that if there is a major incident in your lesson (for example, a fight or a kid who refuses to work or move) you can phone them and not get any answer, or send a message and they will not turn up.

Mr Morris, The Head, is not long for this world. He is about 55, but looks nearer 90. He is quite small and skinny and wears a very old-fashioned but smart suit. He has been here for years and it shows. He is thoroughly fed up with the place and is counting the days until he can retire. He is always happy to listen to other people's problems before putting them instantly out of his mind; he has enough of his own. His blood pressure is apparently rather high and the doctor has told him to avoid stress. Leading St Jude's is not really the ideal job.

Despite this, he always has a faint smile on his face. He will always say hello to any member of staff and attempt a jovial reference to an incident or happening; he will invariably get their name wrong and the incident will have happened years ago to someone long retired.

Mr Morris has a remarkable ability: that of not noticing that about which he would rather not know. He can walk straight past groups of fighting pupils and carry on a conversation whilst torrents of foul abuse are being shouted from all directions. He has perfected this art after years of practice and is known to Staff as 'The Ostrich' for this reason.

He teaches a few lessons of maths each week and the kids think he is Mr Jones's dad.

I reckon Mrs Borrowdale, The Witch and first Deputy Head, would cheerfully finish him off given half a chance. She is about 50 and in the good old days would have been burned at the stake, after a good session on the ducking stool. She is a spiteful old bat who doesn't have a good word for anybody. She teaches English and is good at keeping her own classes in order. The kids are worried that she might turn them into frogs.

She has only contempt for the difficulties of others, however, and delights in revealing the atrocious behaviour of the children in other teachers' lessons (mine, for example).

Mr Phillips, the second Deputy Head, is a complete contrast. He is about the same age but is one of the nicest people I have ever met. I have never heard him say a harsh word to anyone, which makes him completely useless at his job as Deputy Head in Charge of Discipline. He will invariably cave in under pressure from parents. Sometimes he will phone up parents when their offspring have committed some heinous crime, and end up praising them.

The kids respond to his pleasant manner by running rings round him. Last year his car was stolen and driven across the school field whilst he looked on helplessly from his office.

He teaches economics occasionally.

The SMT is regarded by the rest of the staff as a bunch of buffoons.

The phrase 'Lions led by Donkeys' was used to describe the phenomenon of mulish generals being placed in charge of British troops during World War I, but it applies equally to modern teaching. The lack of ability of those in charge to get a grip on a situation, and to take immediate, decisive action rather than simply debate everything endlessly, is one of the major problems in the State education system.

A regular source of bitter mockery is the group's grandiose nomenclature, on the grounds that: 'Senior' implies that its constituents have some sort of special skill and authority lacked by ordinary mortals, and they don't; 'Management' suggests that they effectively manage the staff, the school's resources, the pupils and parents, and they don't; and 'Team' gives the impression that they are working together to create some sort of unified response to problems such as persistently naughty pupils, threats from parents to teachers, school uniform policy, standards of pupil and staff conduct and a host of other things. And they aren't.

They are known collectively to the rest of us as the Smallminds.

The school always reminds me a bit of the Titanic, with the SMT sipping champagne in their room, assuring each other that all is going splendidly, whilst we sail straight towards an enormous iceberg.

Far too many incidents are simply brushed under the carpet, as it is much easier to hold meetings and presentations than support those teachers below them who are trying to improve discipline.

The best thing the SMT could do (apart from commit mass hara-kiri in the playground) would be for each of them to pin a simple notice on their door saying *The Buck Stops Here*. Meaning, *'If you've done everything you can and had no success, come to us; we promise that it will be sorted out, with no arguments or excuses. We lay our reputations, and our careers, on the line with this simple promise'.*

I can't see that happening any day soon. I do know, however, that if most businesses managed their customers like many schools manage their staff, they would go bust within six months.

Saint Goodboy's school

I HAVE gained admittance to the Promised Land!

For the six weeks leading up to Christmas, I shall be doing one day a week at St John's, a school on the opposite side of Downtown which has a very nice, middle-class catchment area.

I like to think of it as St Goodboy's.

It's still a comprehensive, so you don't pay to go there, but it has an excellent reputation and parents will do anything to get their child a place, including lying about their address, claiming the child lives with relatives because they are getting divorced, even attempting to bribe the Head.

I don't blame them. Anybody who doesn't send their kid to the best possible school they can pay for, or con their way into, is a fool. The saddest thing is when I hear parents (usually middle-class, and often teachers, believe it or not) say: 'I think that a bright child will always do well wherever they go.'

Let me assure you, dear reader, that this is not true.

Most days, I ride my bicycle to St Jude's, as several cars have been vandalised in the car park recently, but I decide to drive to St Goodboy's. I notice several differences between this school and ours almost as soon as I pass through the wrought iron school gates.

For a start there *are* school gates.

Ours were stolen years ago by a local scrap metal dealer.

What is missing from the gates, however, is the gang of dubious-looking youths hanging around, looking for trouble.

Trundling slowly up the school drive, trying to avoid the kids spilling out in front of me, I take in two more differences. One is that they are all wearing the same outfit. I believe this is known as a uniform. Secondly, a couple of groups have shouted 'sorry' when they moved back onto the footpath as I steered around them. I notice that the pupils are also noticeably bigger than ours and, on average, without wishing to sound like Mr Griffin (a rather dubious ex-teacher at St Jude's), far less ugly. None of the boys appears to have a skinhead and I don't notice any girls that have trowelled foundation all over their faces or pulled all their hair back in a knot so that their head looks like a sprout. Everyone is carrying a bag over their shoulder, and most of them look pretty full. At our school the kids often just roll books up and stuff them down the back of their trousers.

This is all so new to me and I've not even reached the door yet.

Unconsciously, I still behave as if I am at St Jude's. As I walk in through the school doors, a little uncertain where to go, a child comes up to me and says 'Can I help you?' I instantly suspect a trick and check that my mobile phone is still in my pocket, glancing around for his accomplice. Then I remember where I am and it becomes apparent that this child that I am glaring at really does want to help me, rather than mug me. I try to soften my expression and explain who I am. He takes me to the Staff Room, pointing out things along the way. He is more grown up than I am, and he can't be more than 13.

We pass displays of work that have not been vandalised and which I can only assume have been done by the teachers or bought in; they are in a different league to anything I've ever seen before.

Once inside the Staff Room, I introduce myself, pick up my cover timetable and sit down with a cup of coffee to take in my surroundings. It's just like our Staff Room, but slightly newer. I relax as I go through a mental checklist; the pigeonholes for depressing messages from SMT, notice board full of demands, the grubby padded chairs around low Formica tables, endless plastic boxes full of books and piles of exercise books spilling over everywhere. Yes, it's all here, even the sink in the corner with its traditional sign above the carnage. I note that there are even a few 'comedy' mugs lying around and make a mental note to dispose of these later when the room is quieter.

Lots of teachers are walking around with bits of paper, looking for other teachers and asking, 'Have you seen so and so? I need his SAT marks'. It is all so familiar; only the faces are different. Mind you, they do seem to be a bit better dressed than our lot. I haven't seen any home-made clothes yet.

Looking round, I can see the same teacher groups as we have in St Jude's. The old fuddy duddies, dressed in ancient cardigans and worn-out jackets, the young crowd discussing some indiscretion from the previous weekend and laughing amongst themselves, the ambitious ones with dark suits and earnest expressions. I have already identified at least three potential Odd Teachers and a possible alcoholic. I'm starting to feel at home.

Off to my first lesson, following another teacher who points me in the right direction. I can't help noticing again that the kids all say 'sorry' when they brush past you and 'excuse me' when they need to go in front of you. What's all that about? I've been in our school too long and am struggling to get my head around this strange place.

More display work claiming to be done by Year 7. Christ, it's better than anything I've ever seen. Year 7, my eye. They don't fool me. We pass a picture board covered with photos of children on a school skiing trip, with the obligatory unnecessary comments written next to them by the teacher (*'The Hotel'* next to a building with a sign on it saying 'Hotel', *'The bowling evening'* next to a kid bowling a ball. Even the odd humorous one, with half a dozen exclamation marks in case you didn't realise it was funny: *'Ellen falls over!!!!!'*)

Mind you, I have to say it's a cut above our selection of Mr Duncan's out-of-focus shots of the trip to the industrial museum, taken before he collapsed and had to go home in a taxi. Or the worryingly large numbers of pictures of the kids taken by Mr Griffin which still adorn the notice board.

We find the right room and the helpful teacher next door unlocks it for me. Work is Sellotaped to the desk in the traditional manner. Unusually, however, it is still there. I sit down and read through it.

This is strange; the teacher appears to have left her entire day's work for this one lesson. I check my timetable and, yes, I am only covering her first lesson and it is only one hour long.

She must have been confused.

I locate the text books and check my briefcase for the emergency supplies. Yep, with 200 sheets A4 blank and 160 felt tips, I can cope with anything.

I look around the classroom and see more examples of amazing art work and come to the conclusion that every teacher must have been told by the Head to spend hours making a dozen examples and put it up in their classroom with 'Year 7' or 'Year 8' written underneath it.

I start writing the work on the board. It's a good, old-fashioned blackboard, none of this new-fangled stuff here.

God, there really is loads and loads of work.

I feel a bit daft writing all of it up there, but it will save the teachers who cover the rest of the day a bit of effort.

I push the board round and keep on writing.

They certainly get plenty done in a day here.

After a while I check my watch; where are they? It's five minutes past the start of the lesson and everything's gone quiet outside now. I can hear the next-door teacher through the wall, starting her lesson. Oh hell, I bet it's a mistake on the timetable, I'd better go and ask.

Opening my classroom door I am astounded to see a line of 30 kids standing in a silent line, staring at me. It's actually quite spooky and I nearly jump out of my skin.

I am completely out of sync with this place. Why aren't they shouting, fighting, pushing, kicking the walls and screaming at each other? In St Jude's you can hear them coming from half way down the corridor.

I am completely thrown; normally I would be able to spend a few minutes lining them all up, getting rid of chewing gum, putting out cigarettes and removing offensive weapons. But I let them in, mumbling something about sitting down quietly. They completely ignore me, sit down and get their books out.

And they keep getting more things out: pens, rulers, felt tips, pencil sharpeners, geometry sets and calculators. Soon every desk is covered with equipment. My plaintive, 'Hands up if you need a pen!' is simply ignored.

Finally, they stop unloading industrial quantities of stationery and are all sat up straight looking at the board.

Nobody is speaking except for a few whispers.

It's downright eerie.

I begin to feel like the Wicker Man.

One of the possessed children puts her hand up and offers to give the textbooks out. I nod, struck dumb. I'm used to giving the textbooks out myself; asking a child to do it is normally asking for trouble. You're met with, 'I'm not your f*cking skivvy!', or 'Gizzem 'ere' followed by the swift dispatch of the textbooks, aerially, to all points of the room at high speed.

But none of this happens here, and within 60 seconds all are working hard. They really do not need me at all. I open the textbook (the girl put one neatly on my desk that has 'Teacher' written on it). The work involves writing an account of a siege through the eyes of one of the foot soldiers and then doing the same for one of the people in the besieged town.

Bloody hell; there's hardly anybody in our school that could do this, including half the staff.

They then have to answer a load of questions about the action.

I relax a bit and read through the chapter in the textbook. After a few minutes, I look up. It's incredible, they are all working away. Why has nobody stolen anybody's bag? Why is nobody pushing or prodding anybody else? Why isn't anybody asking me how to do the work (thank goodness, because I would struggle)? Why have I not heard the sound of scrunched up A4 paper? They must be planning something.

After 15 minutes, I'm getting a bit bored. I really am a spare part here. I look out of the window gormlessly, but I can't settle. The silence is getting to me. I start humming a tune and rapidly turn it into a cough as they all start to look at me.

This is really weird.

I want someone to do something wrong so I have something to do. Certainly nobody needs my help.

Forty-five minutes into the lesson, a hand goes up. This is more like it; she's stuck.

'Yes?' I say eagerly.

'Sir, what do we do when we've finished?'

Finished! There's half-a-term's work on the blackboard, for Christ's sake.

I go over and look at her book. Sure enough, she has written two accounts of the siege. There are full stops and commas galore. I even spot a semi-colon! What the hell is going on?

'How about drawing a picture of the castle?'

I brandish the magic A4 blank paper and some of my felt tip pens.

She takes the A4 but turns down the felt tips as she has a far superior set of her own. Within minutes, several more have put their hand up, brought their work out for my approval and started drawing castles.

When we are about five minutes from the end, one of them puts up his hand to remind me of the time and they all start to pack away. They do actually need the full five minutes to pack away all their stuff again.

When the bell goes, they troop out, row by row, and thank me for the lesson. I am dumbfounded and still wonder if the whole thing is some sort of wind up. Perhaps I am being secretly filmed?

The following lesson is in the next corridor and is French. Once again, there is a ton of work left for them, but that's not a problem: everyone is virtually fluent. I can barely write it up on the blackboard before they've finished. They all have dictionaries to look up words, which they flip through with alarming speed, noting new ones down in their vocabulary books without having to be told.

After taking a couple of registers, I have noticed that the names of the pupils are very different to ours. Traditional names dominate; there are plenty of Matthews, Stephens, Andrews, Sarahs and Janes. The more adventurous parents have plumped for things like 'Josh' and, among the girls, there are a few Annabelles, an Aramella or two and even an Araminta, which is going a bit far. If you're going to give your child a ridiculously posh name, the least you should do is send them to a private school.

For the last lesson of the morning I am down to cover Year 8 maths in Room RF14. I let the kids in, tell them to get their maths books out and write down the work on the board. It strikes me again how much bigger these kids are than ours. They're huge, in fact.

After about 20 minutes, the reason for this becomes apparent, and it's not superior diet or genetic engineering. Their geography teacher walks in and apologises profusely to the class for being held up.

It's actually a Year 10 group; I'm in the wrong room, teaching the wrong subject. Mind you, they have happily done my simple maths questions without any complaint.

When I eventually find my correct class, they are busy getting on with the work that has been written on the board.

A different world, almost literally.

Of course, St Goodboy's has its own set of problems. Although most of the kids are pleasant and well-behaved, the naughty ones, because of their greater intelligence, have a level of deviousness that St Jude's kids do not have.

I fall for something that could never have happened back home. In the afternoon lesson, I arrive at the IT room to find the pupils already lined up quietly outside. Lulled into a false sense of security, I let them in and sit them all down at the computers. They switch them on and get their disks from the box on my desk. I already have the word processing work that the teacher has left for me, but Sellotaped to her desk is a typed note explaining that, due to a change of plan, the class should just be allowed to use the Internet this lesson. It is signed at the bottom. It looks perfect: too perfect, in retrospect.

Like the fool that I am, I go along with this and the kids enjoy a pleasant half hour until their teacher arrives back unexpectedly and wants to know why they aren't doing the work on spreadsheets that she has left them. I grin, weakly.

And some of these kids are spoilt and arrogant, too. Many of their parents have high-powered jobs and much nicer houses and cars than those of their teachers; the modern, materialistic tendency, to look down on those less well-off, filters through. You're 'just a teacher' to some of them, which is a shame. I wish I could take a class back to our school to make them realise how incredibly lucky they are to go to a school like this and have decent parents who don't brawl with each other in the street. Mind you, these mums and dads can be a pain as well. Although they are unlikely to turn up at the school and start swearing and fighting, they do phone up constantly to ask why their little darling Tristan is not in the top set and why you only gave him 'good' for his homework. They are even more defensive than our parents about their kids' behaviour and are obsessed with new middle class ideas about bullying and attainment. It's amazing how often they complain when detentions are given. For God's sake, we're only keeping them behind for an hour, not bloody executing them, Mrs De Monteforte.

The teachers are kind of unreal, too. They all feel under tremendous pressure to maintain the school's position near the top of the league tables for our area and talk constantly about results (they mean exams; at our place they would mean football). And they are absolutely horrified at behaviour that would be seen as nothing out of the ordinary back at St Jude's. They really struggle to deal with badly-behaved kids because they are a rarity.

But, while there are cons as well as pros, if you are confident in your knowledge of the subject you teach (the kids can ask some pretty difficult questions) and actually enjoy teaching as opposed to overseeing colouring-in, then St John's is a much more satisfying place to be.

Back at St Jude's, the staff listen with a mixture of envy, disdain and disbelief when I recount my experiences.

Eventually, one says, 'I'd hate to work there, though.'

And there are nods and murmurs of agreement, though no-one looks too sure.

Mrs Borrowdale, bottom set English

MRS BORROWDALE'S Year 11 Bottom set English group are the stuff of nightmares.

They hate her, and she hates them.

That is not to say that they like me any better. I have just ejected

Sean into the corridor, with one of my favourite lines (which I can't remember being taught on PGCE): 'Get out of my classroom, you toe-rag!'

Often, when a kid is told to get outside, he will refuse, become gobby and look for an argument. It is considered great sport to wind up the teacher. If this happens, I immediately insult them as much as possible, which usually provokes them into storming out anyway.

I have no qualms about chucking naughty kids out of the classroom so they can play in the corridor and rattle the door handle like the ghost of Marley. Out of sight, out of mind (and if it saves me from going out of my mind then it's going to be done).

Sometimes they wander off to pull faces at kids in other class-rooms or disturb somebody else's lesson. Other times they just clear off and disappear. I don't lose any sleep worrying about whether they have been run over, or are holding up the local off licence. It's every man for himself in my game.

There is a place called the Emergency Room where naughty kids can be sent. They usually return with notes saying that they cannot be accepted because I have not filled out a Student Behaviour Form. I refuse to waste my time with these forms – if I say a child needs to go to the Emergency Room, he needs to go to the Emergency Room and I'm damned if I'm going to spend time negotiating the point with some petty bureaucrat hiding behind a mountain of waste paper. I simply send them back again and an amusing game of long-distance ping pong develops, until the kid eventually vanishes without trace.

With Sean out of the way, the remainder of the group are sup-posed to be writing stories about how they would cope if they were marooned on a desert island (even the thought of this cheers me up).

Gordon brings his out to ask what I think of it.

I read through it twice but cannot make any sense of it at all. It is absolute gibberish. Apart from all the spelling mistakes and lack of punctuation – it is one, long two-page sentence – it simply doesn't mean anything. The story jumps around from one thought to another without any continuity.

This boy is 15 but his effort is worse than that which a decent nine-year-old would be expected to produce. I'm quite pedantic about grammar, punctuation and spelling (so feel free to email me at frankchalk@mondaybooks.com with those errors you've helpfully spotted in this book) but after years of looking at wrongly-spelled words in the kids' books I have great difficulty in remembering the correct ones.

This particular story contains many of the usual horrors.

'Dose' instead of 'does'.

'Is'nt' instead of 'isn't'.

'Their', 'there' and 'they're' all hopelessly intermingled.

Text messaging words like 'l8er' and 'gr8' litter the rest of the scribble.

Frankly, it's a cmplt ld of bllcks.

By the time Gordon leaves next year, to go to the nearby Downtown College to do Catering Management or something, he will have had (in theory) about 12,000 hours of full-time education and we have not even managed to teach him to write a story. There's something very sad about the waste of so many years of potential learning. You only get one chance at this and it is such a shame when it is frittered away.

As peace descends for a moment, I mentally go over my system of five easy rules for working with kids in the bottom set; they're like a touchstone.

1) Immediately lower any standards or expectations you might foolishly maintain. Then lower them again. Twice.

2) Remember, the felt tips and coloured pencils are your friends. There is nothing that cannot be drawn. Draw, draw, draw! Use A4 plain paper like it grows on trees.

3) Praise everyone, for anything. Grit your teeth and pretend even the most trivial achievement is worth an Olympic Medal.

'Excellent, Tracey! You have sat down!'

'Well done, Kyle! A brilliant drawing of a cannabis leaf! Let's see how well you can colour it in.'

4) No exercise is too childish. There is no shame in 15-year-olds working through a set of Wordsearches with 'Suitable for ages 8 and above' Tippex-ed out. Remember, we are striving to achieve mediocrity.

5) When you have finished, dispose of all work in the nearest bin.

It's important to remember that none of the kids in this group, not one, have any academic ability whatsoever. For the last five years, we have been wasting their time and ours, attempting to teach them nine different academic subjects including a foreign language.

Is it any wonder that they are disillusioned with school? I know I would be if I were in their trainers.

As I come to, I realise I am also facing another problem familiar to all supply teachers. I am certain that several pupils from another class have decided to grace us with their presence. As I have not been given any register for this group, and I do not know them, I have absolutely no idea who should and who should not be here.

Even the class snitch is being uncooperative, under pressure from the various unpleasant characters dotted around the room.

My policy is simple. Inconvenience them all as much as possible and hope that those in the wrong get their comeuppance at the hands of those who are innocent. I keep them all in at the end and get them writing lines: 'I will not try to disrupt the smooth running of Mr Chalk's lesson.'

And I employ the latest weapon in my fight against poor behaviour: the digital camera on my new-fangled phone. I quickly take a few pictures of the whole group and, with a cheerful grin, announce that we will meet again. Which we will, once I've had another teacher look at these pictures. I intend to return the favour by turning up uninvited into one or two lessons tomorrow. (It later turned out, by the way, that one of the kids was not even from our school; he had been excluded from another school for a few days, had rapidly become bored and had borrowed a friend's uniform and turned up here. Shows how useful these short exclusions are.)

Anthony in year 10, again

MRS CHALK and I have gone away for the weekend, walking in the Lake District. It's a long old drive but it's worth every moment when you get there: the views, the fresh air, the tranquillity... it all seems a million miles away from the mayhem of St Jude's.

We leave our b&b at 6am as we've decided to climb the Old Man of Coniston, a 2,000-odd-foot mountain, and it will take a good six to eight hours to get up and back down, allowing for stops to take in the stunning scenery.

At the top, as we sit on a pile of old stones and share some sandwiches, the conversation turns to Anthony in Year 10. Last week he attacked another boy, leaving him badly bruised, and he threatened one of the teachers when he intervened.

'It's a real shame,' I say, munching my ploughman's. 'He's got potential. His older brother is at University and there's no reason Anthony couldn't go either. But it's not going to happen.'

'What about his parents?' asks Mrs Chalk.

'His mum's been on the phone to us this week about him, she and his dad are at the end of their tethers. There's nothing they can do, either.'

'What about in class?' she asks.

I take a swig of water. 'Since he got involved with these other lads, he's got steadily worse, he's becoming more disruptive, more disrespectful,' I say. 'But there's nothing we can do. The system won't allow us to force him to work hard so we have to leave him to his own devices.'

'Well, you can lead a horse to water,' says Mrs Chalk, getting up.

'Hmm,' I say, standing and brushing crumbs off my jacket. 'I'm getting fed up of trying, to be honest.'

And we start the long walk downhill.

The canteen

VERY FOOLISHLY, I have allowed myself to be tricked into doing a duty in the canteen. As a reward for this, I will be allowed a free meal. I will not be taking advantage of this offer; I am looking forward, instead, to eating my packed lunch in the calm and serenity of the prep room, with the added satisfaction of breaking a number of Health and Safety guidelines as I do so.

This pleasure lies half an hour in the future, however, and for now I must put up with the chaos, disorder and ear-splitting racket that is feeding time at St Jude's. The canteen is a complete mess; the floor is a mushy carpet of bits of food and drink and the odd recognisable item like a squashed sausage roll. Every table is covered in piles of unreturned trays. The noise is deafening, as crockery and cutlery spills hither and thither. It really is complete and utter anarchy.

There's a heaving, pushing, jostling semi-queue, formed by those kids who haven't wandered into town for chips or called at the burger van which parks outside the school gates. I am trying to keep the behaviour at a level which is merely bad rather than absolutely appalling. Up at the front there is a problem; somebody is trying to pay for his dinner. This is so unusual – because virtually all of them are on free school meals – that the dinner lady struggles to remember the procedure.

As I try to straighten out the rabble into something resembling a line, I notice that Ashley from Year 8 is trying to hide. This strikes me as odd, until I remember that I have been doing the Year 8 register all week and marking him absent. I suddenly realise what he has been doing.

'Ashley! You're supposed to be playing truant! What are you doing here?'

He knows the game is up and makes a run for it, disappearing round the back of the queue and out of the canteen door. The little scamp has been off for over a week but has obviously been sneaking in for his free meal!

Quite why he should wish to do this is a mystery. The food on offer is absolute muck. Well, it looks and smells like muck: I have never actually eaten anything from the canteen, because it is all reheated, processed, synthetic rubbish.

I'm not breaking new ground in saying this, of course. Jamie Oliver stole my thunder with his excellent exposé on the fiasco that is school dinners.

This is a shame; it's one of my best rants.

Disgusting combinations of additives, preservatives, fat, sugar and salt are formed into dinosaur-shaped lumps in a factory 50 miles away and delivered, frozen, to be fried to a crisp by canteen staff who appear blithely unacquainted with anything resembling a recipe. These are then served daily to our children. The whole set-up really is a national disgrace.

Along with their lunch, pupils are encouraged to swig brightly-coloured drinks containing goodness-knows-what (did human beings really evolve to drink anything bright, cobalt blue?) or to select more fizzy pop from the vending machine. We (or at least, some of us) then wonder why they are completely hyper in the afternoon.

The well-known phrase 'You are what you eat' is, like many such truisms, true. We should be setting them a good example in healthy eating and to hell with whether they want it or not. Hunger works: people marooned on desert islands will eat whatever is available and presumably the same applies to hungry kids. If it is meat, vegetables and water, so much the better. Instead, they go from one sugar rush to another. We have allowed and even encouraged this for years.

As with so many child-related problems, I blame the parents. Many, I'm afraid, are simply too lazy, too stupid or too uncaring to cook properly; it's much easier to shovel sugary, salty 'convenience food' into your kids from an early age. Food habits are built early in life and a poor start is impossible, or at least extremely difficult, to correct, once an addiction has set in.

Today I taught Health and Social Education and followed this by doing duty at the Tuck Shop. (I'm honestly not making this up.) The last thing these nutters need is a vending machine and tuck shop full of Mars bars and crisps.

Half of the behavioural problems, mood swings, hyperactivity disorders, call them what you like, could be cured simply by making children eat a sensible diet and do a bit of exercise.

Instead, kids with ADHD or ADD, or whatever it will be called next week, are prescribed drugs to calm them down.

It's easier to turn them into zombies, you see.

The Cherry Tree estate

WHY ARE so many of our kids so awful?

Could it be anything to do with where they live?

For more than a third of them, home is on the grey, sprawling Cherry Tree Estate which is a mere petrol bomb's throw away from our gates.

Let's go for a little walk through this town planner's dream creation. No, don't be nervous; as with all journeys to foreign lands, as long as we respect the local customs and sensitivities of the inhabitants we should be fine.

Appropriate dress is important, both to blend in and to enable a fast getaway on foot should the need arise. Some sort of loose-fitting tracksuit and white trainers combination would be ideal, although I would recommend that the laces be securely tied as walking aimlessly around with them half-undone in the native fashion is a skill that takes many years of practice. We'll just finish off your outfit with a nice baseball cap and a touch of bling: some gold earrings, a couple of chunky chains and some bangles will go nicely, with half-a-dozen gold sovereign rings on assorted fingers and thumbs. Yes, even Jimmy Saville or 'P Diddy' would feel positively underdressed here. This hooded top, pulled over your cap, should protect your privacy from any CCTV that is still working.

The locals consider books with great suspicion, so please leave them at home. A mobile phone might seem like a good idea in order to summon the Police should a misunderstanding arise, but keep it well hidden lest it be interpreted as a gift. In any case, the Police will probably be here already, dealing with one of the many daily con-frontational, emotional, or matrimonial situations which form the script for the reality TV soap opera in which this area exists.

Now we are ready to venture into the Social Workers' paradise that is the Cherry Tree Estate. Connoisseurs of urban decay will find much to study, but do be careful – should you return after dark – not to tread on a syringe (so many people must be on medication in these parts). Of course, since treading on a syringe is probably the least of the problems you will encounter if you do come here after dark, we shall make our journey in broad daylight.

The sign that welcomes us to the estate has been modified by some thoughtful resident, though – doubtless inadvertently – he has produced an altogether less friendly initial impression. However, undaunted, we press on.

Walking up the road, we can see some fine examples of modern council dwellings on both sides. In the last few years, the local council has, at great expense, demolished a couple of blocks of flats and replaced them with modern, brick-built homes. They may not be the last word in elegance, but they are perfectly well-made, with new central heating and double-glazing. Most have a small garden at the rear, containing a huge volume of rubbish and an assortment of brightly-coloured, plastic toys. Often there is an old fridge, waiting to make its final journey to some unlucky farmer's field.

A satellite dish sprouts from every rooftop, providing the essential, non-stop television which is the life blood of the estate.

Most tribal societies have a central building which serves as a focal point, where everyone can gather for collective acts of worship and celebration, and this community is no different: in front of us, a delightful neon sign proclaims that we have reached the 'Cherry Tree Social Club'. Every police officer for miles around is familiar with this establishment. A list of future events can be seen pinned up on the door. If only we had timed our visit to coincide with the (second) wedding of Dwayne and Shazney.

A service of sorts appears to be taking place inside; we can see the tribal elders gathered round the high altar – a large screen, upon which moving images of their gods can be seen. All the worshippers are wearing special robes, brightly-coloured and with a number and a name on the back denoting their chosen deity. Many have tattooed themselves to indicate their love of Tracey, football, fighting or a mixture of all three. Despite the early hour, some have already achieved a trance-like state of devotion, staring glassy-eyed at either the altar or one of the other religious icons, such as the Carlsberg pump.

The High Priest guides the ceremony from his solemn position behind the bar.

As a slight altercation has broken out, we shall now leave this place and see more of the unspoilt, traditional community that is the Cherry Tree. To our left, just a stone's throw away (as young Wayne is thoughtfully demonstrating for us), the latest newcomers are moving in to their new home, carrying boxes of electrical home entertainment equipment and brightly-coloured childrens' toys with which to fill the garden. This family (or, more accurately, this loose collection of vaguely-related and socially-transient people) has been relocated from their previous house at the request of their neighbours (on both sides). Wayne and his friends are providing them with a traditional welcome, with the aid of a few of those stones. Perhaps nagging doubts about Darwin's theory of evolution are bubbling up in your mind, as they often do in mine after a visit to the Cherry Tree? Or could we suddenly have travelled back a million years in time?

Over to our right, we can see Mr Koshushko's Convenience Store. He is from Lithuania, I believe, and the story of how he ended up here involves various branches of the eastern European Mafia, some loans and his forgetfulness in the matter of their repayment. He focuses on essentials, such as high-strength lager and spirits (which judging by the foreign words on the labels, appear to be imported), pornographic magazines, ready-made meals and violent family films on DVD. For some reason, most of his deliveries arrive in the dead of night in the unmarked, white Transit van parked outside the shop.

Next door is the Yum Yum takeaway which, believe it or not, specialises in pizzas, kebabs, burgers, Chinese food and curry. The chef must truly be an expert. The fruits of his labour can be seen all around the estate, either regurgitated onto the road or in remnant form poking out of various cartons cast onto the grass verges. Combined with discarded crisp packets, tin cans and chewing gum, this forms a deep layer that will provide endless fascination for the archaeologists of the future.

Walking along the glass-strewn pavement, we come across a traditional family group (single mother, three kids who look nothing like each other). If we listen carefully, and we are within 200 yards, we can hear Mother's dulcet tones: 'Gerramoovon, arr Tèquila!'

Ah! How sweet! The little girl was named after the Mum's

favourite drink. Let's follow them discreetly for a few minutes. Perhaps we'll discover a son called Boddington.

Ah, here come Ryan and Shane, driving along in a typical Cherry Tree car ie not registered to either of them. (There seem to be two types of car on this estate – those that have been stolen and burned out, and those that have been stolen and will later be burned out. The stealing and burning of cars is a pastime which unites young and old, part of the social glue of the estate. It's fascinating.) We can only admire the splendour of the various spoilers and aerodynamic accessories which adorn the vehicle, though some might consider them more suited to the track at Le Mans than to an N-reg Ford Fiesta. Not for these two the outdated traditions of the tax disc or motor insurance. Judging by the noises coming from the vehicle it would appear that they have attached the speakers to the outside of the car by mistake; they are making various gestures from the windows, desperate pleas for help in turning down the stereo, maybe?

Everyone needs to relax, and the inhabitants of Cherry Tree are no different. Mr Koshushko has thoughtfully started selling fireworks (all-year round) in permanent preparation for the Bonfire night extravaganza. A few cans of Hi-Strength Lager and a dozen industrial rockets make for a great night out in anybody's book.

Another well-loved pastime is a variant of Pass the Parcel, where various automobile enhancements, plasma screen TV's and stereo equipment are stolen from other inhabitants of the estate and passed around in a giant circle of crime. The French Anarchist, Proudhon, clearly had the Cherry Tree estate in mind when he coined the phrase: 'Property is theft'. I always argue, contrarily, that *property* is property and *theft* is theft. But then I'm not a philosopher.

Ah, here comes the mobile library. This is sent out by the Council as an excellent service to those who find it difficult to get into town (ie the elderly and Dwayne's brother, Lee, who finds it difficult to get out of bed despite his youth). It is the only time you ever spot the Cherry Tree's population of old people; they all come out together in a group on a Tuesday afternoon at 1pm precisely, all dressed up for their weekly outing. Each has his or her books in a plastic bag, in case it rains, and the driver knows each by name. Perhaps this is because they are the only people in the area who would have the slightest use for a library.

Over there is old Jack, a former paratrooper, a brave man who fought at Arnhem in the Second World War. Now elderly and frail, he is, regrettably, afraid to leave his home in the evenings. It's the young people... they don't know what he and his comrades went through to ensure them a future in a land flowing with lager and burgers. And they don't care, frankly.

And look... there is young Liam, playfully attempting to let down the library's tyres. We'll not chide him; it is time for us to bid farewell to the Cherry Tree, for now at least.

And as we leave, are you visited by the same emotion as me? That is to say, overwhelming relief that you do not have to live here?

For anyone born on the Cherry Tree, the future is grim.

Very few ever leave, other than in the back of a police car.

Worst of all, almost no-one expects, or even hopes, to leave.

This is one of the saddest discoveries I have ever made.

School assembly

WE HAVE one of these a couple of times each week, mainly because the law says we have to, but also because they sound like a good idea anyway. Get everyone together and talk to them, that sort of thing.

The reality is that they are a nightmare.

Sometimes the Head will attempt to tell a story illustrating a moral.

Unfortunately, few of the kids round here seem to have been introduced to morals on any level. They have, by traditional standards, a very eccentric view of what's right and wrong so it's no good expecting them to identify a message, even a simple one, hidden (and not particularly well-hidden) in a childishly simple story. Thus, the Head's efforts usually go straight over the heads of the intended audience.

It can be extremely entertaining for the staff, however, and never more so than when he gets confused and mixes up a few different ones. Today, for example, we are hearing about the Good Samaritan who wins the Lottery, then goes off to live a wild life of debauchery but gets mugged, loses most of his money and gives away the rest, before returning, penniless, to the bosom of his family, where he is welcomed with open arms.

I suppose there is some sort of message there for us all, but it matters not: the kids just seem to accept whatever babble he comes out with.

Around Christmas we attempt to sing a few hymns, which is absolutely hilarious. Mrs Borrowdale bangs away at the ancient school piano and snarls through the first couple of verses. The teachers dutifully accompany her while trying to encourage the kids, with threats of 'louder, or detention!'

The only good assemblies were the ones PC Pimblett used to do.

PC Pimblett was the school policeman. He was a traditional copper, a huge, burly man who knew the area and its families. He used to come in to school all the time to give talks about crime, as a sort of antidote to the TV glamorisation of guns, drugs and easy money with which children are bombarded. His gruesome pictures of heroin addicts lying dead in their own urine and the victims of knife or gunshot wounds were as shocking as his vivid descriptions of the unpleasant characters to be found in prisons. He was superb: half an hour of him was worth 10,000 words by a well-meaning but naïve member of the SMT.

Needless to say, his funding was axed.

Apparently, certain groups felt 'intimidated' by having a police presence in the school.

If that was the case we should have had a few more of them, is all I can say.

The head has just announced that the purpose of school is to prepare its pupils for the life they will lead after they leave. I am tempted to suggest that this means that we should put up bars on all our windows and doors and rename the classrooms 'cells'.

But I don't. I'm not sure the Warden would see the funny side.

A glossary of teaching terms

LIKE ALL professions, especially those in the public sector, teaching has its own set of special words and phrases. These are designed to avoid straight-talking and to baffle outsiders. Somebody, no doubt, has a comfortable office, with a fan and a chair that tilts and swivels, where they sit and think up new terms such as 'Learners' and 'Line Managers' to replace perfectly good old ones.

Here are a few that we encounter; I have translated them into English (where possible).

A Levels: Exams taken by children from other schools.

ADD (Attention Deficit Disorder): Has been fed loads of sugar and additives from an early age and never been taught to sit still or made to do any exercise.

ADHD (Attention Deficit and Hyperactivity Disorder): Same as above, but mother has discovered that she may be able to claim disability allowance for a child with ADHD.

Behaviour Management: The science of getting kids to do as they're told. (Incidentally, as a rule of thumb, any term or phrase with the word 'Management' in it has been dreamed up by someone who could not manage anything.)

Behavioural difficulties: A pain in the backside. Hasn't been brought up properly.

Bullying: Between kids, this runs the spectrum from petty name-calling to stabbing. We try not to get involved in this where possible. However, bullying also occurs between adults – usually where a *line manager* (see below) tells you to do something you can't be bothered to do. Also means normal banter between teachers, where one party (the 'victim') has no sense of humour.

Cane, The: Marvellous instrument of discipline, abolished in 1987.

Careers Officer: Raving optimist.

Challenging pupil: Child who needs a thick ear.

Classroom assistant: Poorly-paid teacher's helper, often with no qualifications.

College: A place where our pupils go to fail more exams after they have failed the ones they did at school.

Coursework: Schoolwork that is done by middle-class parents or private tutors.

Deferred Success: Used to be known as 'failure', as in 'Shane had a deferred success in his French GCSE'.

Depression (as in 'Miss Jones is now off with depression'): The doctor isn't falling for *stress* again. (See Stress below).

Detention: On the odd occasions when pupils turn up, a chance to annoy the supervising teacher who is not being paid for his time.

Differentiation: The amusing idea that a teacher has nothing better to do of an evening than dream up six different lessons for the same class. (See Mixed Ability below.)

Disaffected Pupils: The latest fashionable term to excuse pain in the backside kids.

Drama projects: A licence for pupils to do whatever they want.

Dyslexic: Useful excuse for kids who can't be bothered to remember spellings. Mother has pestered doctor to diagnose dyslexia.

Exclusion: A few days off to play *Grand Theft Auto* on your Play-Station. Or roam the streets playing it for real.

Expulsion, Expelled: A very unlikely event, in which the school and Wayne finally part company after he has behaved appallingly for years.

GCSE: Exam that more and more children pass with flying colours each year. This is either because pupils are becoming steadily cleverer, but hiding their lights under very large bushels, or the exam is getting steadily easier.

Ghosts: Ex-Pupils who are unable truly to leave. They must haunt the school grounds forever.

Gifted child: In our school, a child who would be average anywhere else and who leaves St Jude's believing he or she is a genius (at least until the GCSE results come out).

Headteacher: PC word for Headmistress or Headmaster.

Inclusion: A policy of ignoring bad behaviour.

Individual Education Plan (IEP): Loads of time, money and effort wasted on a kid who would be better off in a special school.

Invertebrate: Creature lacking backbone. (See *SMT* below).

Learners: PC word meaning 'kids'.

Learning difficulties: Thick.

Learning impaired: Really thick.

Line Manager: Boss.

Mixed Ability Teaching: A method of boring the clever pupils whilst baffling the dim ones by having a huge range of abilities not learning together in the same room. (See *Setting* below.)

ODD (Oppositional Defiant Disorder): Condition in which a kid will not do as he is told, and needs a thick ear or six of the best with the *cane* (see above) to encourage him.

Offensive Behaviour: Calling a black or Asian pupil, or a girl, rude names. If you are white and a boy, tough luck buddy.

Ontological Objectives: God knows.

Pedagogical Perspectives: See above.

Permanent Exclusion: I've heard tales of this, like I've heard tales of the Wild Man of Borneo and the Yeti. A mythical punishment that teachers can only dream of (see *Inclusion*). I *think* it means expelled.

School-phobic: Kids who don't like coming to school, and would rather hang around in bus stops smoking, groping each other and drinking cider. I swear I'm not making this up, it's a real term. Has there ever been a kid who didn't have 'school-phobia'?

Setting: An obvious, tried-and-tested concept. Setting means dividing your pupils into 'sets' according to their ability so that you can teach a class made up of kids with a small range of similar abilities, rather than a class made up of kids with a large range of very different abilities. This has been proven to benefit children whatever their ability but is considered un-PC for reasons I cannot fathom.

Sick Building Syndrome: I'm not sure what this refers to but our school building looks pretty unwell to me. Possible staff excuse for non-attendance ie 'The doctor says I've got Sick Building Syndrome', which really means 'The doctor is sick of the sight of me.'

SMT (Senior Management Team): A bunch of incompetent buffoons who would last five minutes in the private sector, if they were lucky.

Special Educational Needs (SEN) (as in 'he has SEN'): Yet another way of avoiding using the word 'thick'.

Stress (as in 'Miss Jones is off with stress'): A preference for taking extended holidays rather than dealing with everyday problems.

Students: Another PC word for the kids and one which I find quite strange: surely the word 'student' implies something to do with studying?

Study Leave: The practice of allowing your kids to wander round the streets or hang round school premises causing trouble the week before GCSEs.

Supply Teacher: A teacher who is either too bad to get a regular job, or who cannot cope with real teaching, or is bone idle. They are often very well read as they have plenty of time to be.

University: Not applicable.

Waifs: Groups of wandering pupils who should be in lessons but for various reasons are not. They are drawn together by mysterious forces and sometimes interact with the *Ghosts* (see above).

Of course, these are just a few of the abbreviations, acronyms and obfuscations which litter school life.

The kids (sorry, 'learners') themselves have developed a very rich vocabulary and syntax, aimed at explaining away unfortunate failures on their parts. They can be amazingly creative. Here are a few stock phrases of theirs, again translated into common English.

'I don't geddit!' (invariably heard when instructions are written clearly on the board in front of them): 'I only do copying out.'

'I ain't got a pen': 'I never bring a pen and I know you will give me one.'

'My pen broke last lesson': 'I never bring a pen, but you're a stricter teacher.'

'My bus was late': 'I simply could not be bothered to get up this morning.'

'I had to see Mr Baxter': 'I prefer to wander aimlessly around school than sit in your lesson.'

'You don't need GCSE's to do what I want to do': 'I want to be a Premiership footballer, a pop star or a model, or perhaps all three.'

'Me dad ain't got no exams and he's alright': 'My father is a petty thief and I am keen to follow in his footsteps.'

'I'm going to see Miss Smith!' (shouted as irate child storms out of room): 'I'm off to see Miss Smith because she is the only teacher gullible enough to believe my accusations that you pick on me.'

'Me mum says teachers just want you to work so they get more money': 'My mother does not have the faintest clue about how teachers are paid, but did not enjoy school herself and is determined to pass on her hatred and suspicion of education to me.'

'Me mum's coming up to school': 'My parents are on benefits and there's nothing on the telly.'

'I'm gonna tell me mum and she'll sort you out': 'A fat fishwife will be here in three minutes.'

'I'm gonna tell me dad and he'll batter you': Same as above, except some skinny, tattooed ne'er-do-well, possibly genetically-related to the child, will turn up instead. And it will take longer than three minutes if he is in the pub or the bookies.

'I'm going to work for me dad so I don't need no exams': 'Nobody else would ever employ me. My father feels vaguely guilty because he has only seen me twice in my whole life. By way of compensation for his lifelong parental absence, he will give me a labouring job which I will be too lazy to do in his dodgy building company.'

The parents, and step-parents, live-in-lovers and 'uncles', being themselves long-schooled in the art of deception (almost the only thing they are long-schooled in; this has been going on for at least two generations in our schools, now), are also very adept with their excuses for little Chardonnay's non-attendance, poor performance or violent behaviour.

So, to conclude, here is a brief guide to the translation of chav parent excuses.

'Ashley's scool gumper is in the Washer so he has to wair his other on today' (written note): 'I was *really* drunk last night.'

'My Tyrone always admits it if he's done something wrong. That's how he's been brought up!' (On the phone to school): 'My Tyrone

is a lying toe-rag and I'm hoping that if he gives the phone back quietly we won't have to involve the police.'

'*She had to look after the babby*': 'She may only be thirteen, but she's got to look after her baby ie *her own baby*. I know I almost encouraged her to have the thing, but there's no way I'm looking after it. I'm going down the club.'

'*We didn't wake up in time for the bus and there's not much point in him coming in now it's past 11 is there?*': 'We are all on benefits and we have no discipline, of any kind, whatsoever. What do you expect?'

'*All the teachers pick on my Liam!*': 'I am too stupid, literally, to grasp the fact that if all the teachers pick on Liam it is more likely to be his fault than the collective failings of all 65 teachers in the school.'

'*We'd got the days mixed up 'cos our Ashley put the papers out last night and we forgot about school!*': 'Do not bother questioning me further; you will simply come up against the brick wall of my astounding stupidity.'

My personal all-time favourite was a written note we received from a woman who had skived off work herself and taken her brat out of school to go shopping. In the process, while out and about, gormlessly admiring cheap, gaudy tat in shop windows, she had been nabbed (amazingly) by a Police Truancy Patrol. Her explanation read (verbatim): 'I had to teke Wayne shopping four his new shoose. Pleese don't tell my work of this becose I coud not tell them ether.'

Christmas time

A TRADITIONAL festival, celebrated enthusiastically on the Cherry Tree Estate.

The festival starts with the cooling of the embers from buildings set alight on Guy Fawkes Night, usually some time around November 12th.

Mr Koshushko's shop opens a Christmas section and the whole estate is rapidly transformed into a glowing vision of hell.

Look over here at Shazney's house, decorated tastefully with Bart Simpson, dressed as Santa, amid a forest of lights. She will have little need for interior lighting with that display. Her mother's current partner Gary is obviously proud of his skills as an electrician; he beams as he surveys the cable leading from the nearest streetlight. This will minimise the cost of this visual extravaganza and leave more money for lager. I have no doubt that it will also result in a visit from the fire brigade.

Giant inflatable Santas are everywhere. Occasionally one blows away and bounces slowly round the estate, before being set upon by feral youths.

Every dwelling is buried under fairy lights and no self-respecting group of vaguely-related individuals would be without a troupe of penguins skiing down the roof.

Here at Dwayne's house, Santa has been adorned with a glowing icicle where I suspect one was not meant to be. Written on every window in spray foam is the greeting 'Mery Crismas!'

Traditionally, in these parts at least, Christmas is a non-stop, month-long orgy of theft, wanton vandalism, assault, burglary and violence, all fuelled by max-strength lager purchased from Mr Koshushko's Convenience Store. I am amazed that HM Customs do not take a greater interest in the foreign writing on so many of his products.

At St Jude's we also embrace the Christmas spirit early and wholeheartedly. The Art Department proudly began making Xmas cards on November 15th – a new record.

And with only three weeks left until we break up, it's War.

Today's lesson begins with a chorus of 'Why do we have to do work? It's Christmas!' (I check my diary; it's November 28th.) 'And we don't have to do work in any other lesson.'

This is true. Departments will do anything to get their hands on the TV and video. It is the only way to placate the kids. They associate Christmas with watching videos and nothing else will suffice. Not just any video either; only the non-stop violence of a good Hollywood action film can capture the spirit of Christmas properly.

Occasionally, teachers get presents bought for them by pupils and their parents at Christmas. At St John's, a decent bottle of red wine or a nice box of chocolates would be the done thing; here we get family packs of Dinosaur Crisps and stocking-shaped bumper packs of gaily-coloured chocolate bars. Still, it's the thought that counts.

Another Christmas tradition is the tabloid headline 'Blahville Council bans Christmas for fear of upsetting Muslims!'

This is an excellent idea, if you ask me.

Bah, humbug to you all!

THE SPRING TERM

Time-wasting meetings and training day

IT'S THE first day of the spring term, which means we're wasting time.

A fair proportion of each teacher's day is frittered away on pointless paperwork and bureaucracy, and today is a good example of that.

We're having a Training Day – by law we must have five of these each year – which begins with a staff meeting; the SMT will have dreamed up lots of pointless activities to follow.

In my long experience, meetings rarely achieve anything useful; they consist of hours of endless, tortuous waffle and no decisions about anything. As Supply I don't have to go to many, but I still avoid them like the plague as I did when I was a real teacher. It's a shame, really, because there's no reason why they shouldn't be informal, fun gatherings and potentially useful into the bargain.

Light relief can be provided by someone at the militant end of the spectrum clambering onto their soapbox, but otherwise they are invariably hogged by the dullest members of staff who will drone on and on about their pet subject while everyone else loses the will to live. Some poor sod has to record the minutes and run off dozens of copies in an effort to speed up the destruction of the rainforests.

Today, for the first time in a few years, I actually nodded off. I woke up with a yelp when I was nudged by Mr Blunt. When it dawned on me that everyone had stopped talking and was looking at me instead, I got slowly to my feet and hobbled around a bit, pretending I had suddenly got cramp. I think I got away with it.

The major difference between private companies and the public sector is that the former has to achieve things or go bust whereas the latter just has to go through the motions. In the modern British educational system, there is no suggestion so daft that it will not be taken seriously, noted down and discussed earnestly. If you should ever find yourself in one of these meetings – God forbid – try making a few, as long as you can keep a straight face. This is the best means of keeping your sanity.

There are other ways of getting through staff meetings, of course. Ask all the other teachers around you to join hands. If you can get them to do this, after a few moments ask 'Can you feel it?' in your most serious voice. Or pass numbered cards round at the start for no reason whatsoever. Or keep asking people to swap places with you. Or stand up and accuse the person next to you of having an affair with your partner. Or borrow a Geiger counter from a science lab and, wearing a set of earphones, slowly wander round waving the device here and there. Frown occasionally.

If you get really desperate just shout 'Oh my God!' and run out of the room.

Remember, if you get into trouble it is only temporary; meetings can scar you forever.

Unusually, I'm coming in to share today's delights, but only because they are paying me to be here. Training days are when real teachers (as opposed to useless, work-shy mercenaries like me) get to be bored senseless by a mix of patronising nonsense (*'Five New Ways to Encourage Positive Behaviour!'*) and seminars that explore the very depths of tedium (*'Driving Excellence In Curriculum Development!'*).

By the end of this day, I can guarantee that the Christmas break will seem like a very long time ago indeed. The only other certainty is that nothing concrete or useful will be produced. It never is.

Despite the school being closed for the last two weeks, you can also rest assured that there will be no ink in your printer, that the photocopier will be out of use and don't even think about trying to use a computer. The technician will start servicing them all tomorrow. This will take until May 18th. They will break down again the following day.

Today, we have a guest speaker and I can't wait.

She sweeps onto the stage in a blaze of multicoloured shoes with buckles, shapeless knitted jumper and huge, dangly earrings. It can only be the latest Advisor from The Council.

'Bloody hell, it's Coco the Clown!' whispers Mr Blunt, two rows back.

Mr Green is listening intently, simultaneously fascinated and horrified, as always.

Miss Simpson is noting down fashion tips.

'Good morning, my name is Janet and blah, blah blah… come to talk to you today about dyslexia… drone… .burble… but first of all I must just ask you, is there anybody here who is dyslexic?'

I want to stand up and tell my favourite bad joke, the one about my dad being a dyslexic devil-worshipper, who, one Christmas, sold his soul to Santa.

But to my shame, I haven't got the bottle.

I sit there and soak it up with everyone else.

Meet the parents

I HAVE always had a very strict policy towards parents.

I ignore them.

I ignore their phone calls, their letters and their visits to the school. I regard attendance in my lessons as a great privilege and have not the slightest interest in the opinions of those who simply had the misfortune to produce my customers.

Actually, let me start this again.

A small percentage of our parents are perfectly intelligent, decent people who are interested in and concerned about their children and their education.

Another, bigger percentage are well-meaning, pleasant people who make an effort to help their progeny but are sadly completely clueless.

I admire both of these classes of parents: people who try to bring their children up to be good citizens, especially in the trying circumstances in which many find themselves and their families. I believe we have a duty to teach the next generation good manners and good behaviour, a respect for law and order and for other people and their possessions. I am always happy to meet and talk to these parents.

It's the others I'm on about.

I would say that at least 50 per cent of our parents are dreadful people for whom I have nothing but contempt.

I do not make my dislike for them quite as obvious as Mr Blunt, who once headbutted a father after the man became abusive in the school car park. That's a tale for another day.

People who hide behind jobs with impressive titles (for example, 'Behavioural Psychologists' and 'Educational Advisors') dream up endless excuses for a pupil's bad attitude and worse behaviour. They may place the blame on poverty, deprivation, disillusionment, lack of opportunities or lack of 'relevant curriculum themes.' They might say that it is the fault of their teachers for having low expectations of them. (When teachers have low expectations of a pupil, they are usually proven right, I am afraid.) In fact, they blame these problems on everything except the obvious: the child and, mainly, its parents.

Kids misbehave simply because it is more fun than behaving and nowadays, in many cases, there is nothing stopping them. It is perfectly natural to explore the boundaries of what behaviour is possible. If no boundaries are enforced then the results are plain for all to see. Whether inside or outside school, they pretty much do as they like. Most of our problems come about through poor choices made when we were young – playing truant from school, experimenting with drugs and getting involved with petty crime, for instance. The chances of children making these disastrous choices, or failing to recover from them, are increased tenfold in the absence of suitable adult influences (or 'role models', as we must now call them).

We often hear in the papers about well-to-do parents who push their child relentlessly from an early age. This may be harmful, in some respects. But let me introduce the other end of the spectrum, here in Downtown.

Today, I am visiting a typical dwelling in order to give Leon an hour's home tuition. This is paid for by the local authority as he is unable to attend school for a while. He broke his arm falling off a bicycle. On further investigation, the bicycle turned out not to have belonged to him, so perhaps that's a kind of justice.

A note went up in the Staff Room, asking for (paid) volunteers, and I seized the opportunity, partly out of curiosity but mainly for the money.

We are sitting in Leon's house in the dining kitchen which, needless to say, contains a TV that blares away with nobody watching it. I ask if we could turn it off, so that we can concentrate on the work. They all look a bit puzzled by this concept and struggle to find the correct button. In the end, we compromise by turning the volume down low, so that mother can keep half an eye on some twaddle while she prepares tea. (I decline her polite invitation to join them with the white lie that Mrs Chalk will be slaving over the cooker even as we speak; I'd rather eat my own toes than share their meal of deep-fried burgers.)

The dining kitchen runs through to the living room, where I can see another TV. This one is an absolute monster and must have taken three men to steal.

Did I say 'steal'? I'm sorry, I meant 'deliver'.

I can hear the noise from two more sets drifting down from upstairs.

One wall of the living room is completely filled with shelving which groans under the weight of countless DVDs and video cassettes. There must be two or three hundred of them. I cannot see a single book anywhere until – all is not lost! – my eye alights on the autobiography of 'Jordan' (no, not the boy in Year 11) lying on the coffee table. This is common in homes of this type and it is a tragedy. A child's intelligence comes on in leaps and bounds if he or she is read to from an early age, but it hasn't happened for Leon or for many of his contemporaries. Poverty is always given as an excuse for this sort of thing, but ask yourself how much a library book costs? Ah, but getting to the library – even walking out to the mobile one that calls each week – and reading to your child… well, that takes effort, and making an effort is not a popular pastime amongst the parents round here.

Underneath the biggest of the tellies is a mountain of computer games, with an incredibly complex network of leads connecting various boxes and some sort of games console. Nobody is using the machine, but it, too, tinkles, squeaks and beeps away into the general cacophony.

Mother hears a baby screaming from upstairs and disappears. God, the constant background noise here would drive me insane. I wonder if they ever have any silence in the house.

We wade through some maths. Leon is quite glad of the change, at first, but after about fifteen minutes his concentration wanders. I have to keep encouraging him and try to resist his challenge to play him at *Blood Hound III: The Reckoning* instead.

I get mum to sign my form for the hour and leave some work for Leon to do for next time. Mum promises to make him do it, but I know full well that she won't. I mention that he could really do with some reading practice as well, and casually remark that the public library opens every day except Fridays. A look of confusion comes across her face.

I suspect I am wasting my breath so I say goodbye and wish Leon a speedy recovery.

Mum insists that next week I must stay for tea and I express my delight at the prospect.

Odd teachers

AT ST Jude's, as at all schools of my acquaintance, the teachers run the gamut from absolutely amazing to completely useless, with all points in between. (Note that this opinion is not accepted by most teachers or the teaching unions, who oppose any form of performance-related pay on the grounds that all teachers, without exception, are saints.)

We've met the brilliant (Mr Green and Mr Blunt), we've met the useless (Mr Jones and Miss Wade) and you're familiar, by now, with the merely mediocre (me).

So it's time to say hello to the eccentrics, weirdos and general odd-bods.

Mr Wilkinson teaches economics, which is mildly amusing as he is clearly penniless. He is about 50, wears thick-framed spectacles, lives with his elderly mother and rides a rickshaw to work. PC Pimblett once told me that, when he first met him, he wanted to arrest him for vagrancy.

Mr Griffin was a cheerful man in his late 40s, who taught music and always showed a great interest in the kids. Unfortunately, he had to leave us at the end of last year after a police investigation which found that all the rumours about him were true.

Mr Knutt teaches Design Technology, but his real love is wood-work. He spends every lunchtime and break churning out bookcases, bookends, boxes, coffee tables and CD racks, all of which end up in Knutts Furniture Shop in a neighbouring town. He must be a millionaire. He runs an after-school group where kids can help him make even more wooden things. He is round, balding and always wears a dirty overall. He smells of wax and varnish and woody things. He never visits the Staff Room as that would mean taking time out from the production line. He is always cheerful and I'm not surprised.

Mr Duncan is a short, skinny man of about 40 who is a good teacher of geography and a first-rate alcoholic. That is his defining characteristic. He does not openly admit it, but he joins many of the kids in getting the bus to and from school each day which no teacher in his right mind would do if he had a driving licence. The other giveaway is that he always smells of booze. The kids call him 'Mr Drunken' to his face, which is always blotchy and bright red. Oh, and there's the bottle of 'mineral water' from which he's constantly, surreptitiously, sipping.

Due to budget constraints, his dress is always the same: a huge woollen cardigan over a green v-neck jumper. He has an untidy mop of greasy, grey-black hair and is generally unshaven.

The kids quite like him, though, and look after him when he is having an off day. If he has fallen over in the classroom (he has difficulties with his balance sometimes) then a couple of kids will take him to matron for a lie down and generally get on with their work. It is not unusual to find him slumped over his desk, clearly the worse for wear, with the kids working reasonably well.

He is always full of good stories about all the different countries and capital cities, which the kids seem to find interesting. He has a battered, out-of-date map of the world on his wall.

Mr Rogers is definitely the oddest teacher in this place, and that really is saying something. He teaches English and is in his early 50s. He is slightly stocky, balding and would be picked out on any ID parade as a child molester. Nobody knows anything about his life outside school, which is probably just as well. He always wears a brown suit, a whitish shirt and a tie made out of some horrible man-made fabric, the sort of material used for old people's curtains.

The thing about Mr Rogers, though, is that he absolutely stinks.

I mean, he reeks, of BO, unwashed hair and stale clothes.

The kids aren't really sure how to take him, because of his short temper and rapid mood swings. He can be getting on fine with them and then, two minutes later, he is shouting like a madman. Some quite like him; others think he is some kind of nutcase. The staff are in no doubt that he is barking at the moon and cheerfully swap stories of his lunatic ways. He is also renowned for his writing, which is unbelievably bad. It is nothing but an indecipherable scrawl.

I hate covering for Mr Rogers, as his room also stinks. After years of his occupation, it has absorbed a permanent imprint of his aroma. As it happens, today I *am* covering for him and I have been expecting trouble from the moment I read his note to me on the Cover Board, which appeared to say 'W*nk on desk'.

After a few uneasy moments, I realised, to my relief, that it actually said 'Work on desk'.

I am standing in front of his Year 9 class trying desperately to decipher the illegible scribble that is the work that he has left for me.

Like him, his lessons are truly bizarre.

The instructions refer to some worksheets which do not appear to exist and a textbook of which there is no trace. It declares that the class should use the A4 paper which is entirely absent. If they finish this work, I am informed that they may use the coloured pens (not here) to draw the Tree of Life (none of the kids seem to have the faintest clue what this is and there is no clue in his notes). I hold my hands above my head in despair. Now the class is becoming restless and I have nothing to offer them. I am like that biblical chap in the lion's thingy.

Wondering if the whole thing is just the rantings of Mr Rogers' demented brain, I pick up Lorna's book. She is a good, hard-working kid, but as I look through her work none of it seems to follow on from anything. Instead, it's a random jumble of exercises and bizarre titles that do not correspond with the stuff underneath. I sigh deeply, for I cannot make any sense of any of this and I do not have the faintest clue what they are meant to do.

The lesson is balancing precariously on that delicate knife-edge, so familiar to the Supply Teacher, where the slightest pressure will tip it over the edge into freefall.

That push is thoughtfully provided by Shazney, who suddenly screams: 'You f*cking w*nker!'

Dwayne has decided to express his artistic abilities by drawing an erect penis on the cover of her exercise book.

Why are we wasting their time?

WHAT IS secondary school education *for*?

I ponder the question this morning, as I travel to St Jude's for another day of bedlam and chaos.

Well, on one level it's about opening up young minds to new ideas, teaching brains to reason, argue and compute and introducing kids to the world outside their immediate environment. It is also about laying the foundations for further and higher education, where appropriate.

But these lofty aims remain an elusive dream at St Jude's and at many hundreds, even thousands, of schools in Britain.

The best we can hope for, as things stand, is to turn out youngsters who understand how to behave, who can listen to and follow instructions, who are basically literate and numerate and who are punctual – in short, to ready them for the world of work, these being the entry-level requirements for 80% of the jobs on offer in this country, and the kinds of jobs our kids might get (we're not going to turn out many potential astro-physicists – even if the raw material was there, we're hopelessly ill-equipped to do that).

Even these simple goals are pretty elusive, too, I might add: after 12 years of full-time education, costing God knows what, the number of our pupils who leave school with even these basic skills is shameful.

Here's a radical suggestion: there is absolutely no point in trying to teach kids like Chelsey, Wayne and Coyne even simplified GCSE-level economics and French, for example.

If, redesigning our education system from scratch, it was suggested that we should attempt to teach Swahili to children but carry out those lessons in another foreign tongue, such as Swedish, this would rightly be derided as lunacy.

Yet this is not so very far from what we *are* attempting to do.

Take Coyne, for example. He is 14 now. His grasp of English is, at best, tenuous. Despite this, we are trying to teach him to speak French. Equally, his mathematical ability is next to nil; we are trying, in economics lessons, to explain concepts like inflation and money supply to a boy who can't add up properly.

Coyne has no aptitude whatsoever for learning French or economics.

Furthermore, he doesn't wish to learn them and he has been telling us, loudly, that he doesn't wish to learn them for the past three years. What he *does* want to do is to learn to be a plasterer, so he can follow in his step-dad's footsteps.

Would it not be a better idea to concentrate on improving his numeracy, reading and writing – the three Rs of old – while teaching him some basic personal life skills which will enable him to get along with a future employer and that employer's clients and fellow contractors?

Earlier, I said that we shouldn't allow children to make poor decisions for themselves. But, equally, we shouldn't prevent them from making good ones. What this means, in practice, is listening to Coyne when he says he wants to quit French and economics (because the empirical and objective evidence is that he is wasting his time, and that of everyone else, in those subjects) but *not* listening to him when he says he's not interested in learning maths or English, (because, as responsible adults, we know that it is important that he learns to read and add up and that, maybe, he will thank us for it later in life).

This would reduce the workload on Coyne to a more manageable level, both for him and for the school. It would also improve the prospects of those kids who *are* interested in French and economics.

Coyne has the potential to become an excellent plasterer, feeding and supporting his future family through honest hard work. He has no chance of becoming an economist. Some will say that this sounds snobbish and elitist, that I am 'pigeon-holing' him and closing down his horizons. I disagree – I think I am being realistic and that honesty will produce a better outcome for Coyne than garlanding him with false hopes and dreams.

The people whose horizons are *really* being closed down are the bright kids, with real potential, who can't learn anything in their economics and French lessons because of Coyne's antics.

There will always be kids like Coyne – it is a fact of nature – but currently far too many other, more capable children end up wasting their potential.

There is no reason, in theory, why bright youngsters from poor backgrounds should not learn French and economics, and calculus, algebra and geometry, and the major exports of the world's leading countries, and the rules of grammar, and what Shakespeare was on about, and how to bake a sponge cake, and even Latin. All of this and more was taught, and learned, in schools 50 years ago.

But practice is different from theory. In the current climate of generations of neglect, of parental indifference or even opposition, of the removal of discipline and of politically correct interference and meddling in teaching, it is impractical to expect even bright kids to tackle most of these subjects in any depth because the proper understanding of them requires discipline, application and years of study, starting at the age of five.

The intelligent need to be stretched from the start – then they will be able to tackle foreign languages and the like with confidence.

That's not to say we should forget Coyne and others like him. We should most certainly not. But neither should we coddle and indulge them. We should abandon the ridiculous 'one size fits all' attitude in our modern system and adjust the academic curriculum they face to better suit their needs and requirements. We should also teach them things that, just a generation or two ago, we took for granted that their parents would teach them.

Alongside basic maths and English, they should learn good manners and a pleasant demeanour. Employers only employ people they get on with. Most don't really care how many GCSEs their staff have. I know employers who use a simple tick box system during an interview to decide whether to take on a given applicant:

Punctuality?

Attitude in interview good/bad?

Likely to be able to concentrate on getting the job done?

Likely to be able to do a multi-stage task without asking unnecessary questions constantly?

The kids would be better served, too, by being given general information about their lives, and how and why they can go wrong. That would be more useful, surely, than not really knowing the French word for 'cat'?

Why not give them a grounding in:

How your house works – the basics of central heating, roof insulation, and the supply of gas, water and electricity.

How to clean yourself, your clothes and your house.

How to fix things when then they go wrong – I mean fundamental stuff, like changing a light bulb.

How tools work and how to use them safely to put up a shelf, or hang a door, or repair your fence.

How to save money on your bills, without resorting to the innovative methods of Shazney's stepfather, Gary.

How to manage a bank account and how to budget on a set amount: 75% of our kids, at least, come from homes where the adults in charge have absolutely no control over their finances. They fall victim to greed and endless offers of loans, borrowing money they can't afford to pay back to buy things they don't need. They rob Peter to pay Paul, sometimes literally, and have no sense of the importance of saving for the future, of living within your means, of at least trying to build up a pension.

Our kids don't know how interest works, whether on a mortgage, or a loan, or a savings account. Why not?

We could teach them face-to-face communication skills, because with all the time they spend wrapped up in their iPods, mobile phones, computer games and DVDs they don't have the first idea of how to talk to a stranger. (Mind you, I wonder if people said the same when books first became widely available.)

We should teach them how buy good food cheaply, how to store it safely and how to cook nutritious meals, rather than simply heating up ready-made ones which cost twice as much and turn your kid into a loony. A little understanding of basic medicine (colds, coughs, sprains, grazes) wouldn't be a bad thing either, to take some of the burden off GPs and A&E.

They should learn how advertising works, and how not to fall for it – what an item *really* is, as opposed to what the advertiser says it is. That way, maybe they wouldn't be quite so obsessed with branded designer stuff.

Why are kids not taught the basics of the law? Not the intricate details, just why we have it and roughly what the penalties are for infringing it. They should hear from and meet the victims of crime and be shown the nightmares that the Police have to go through to deal with it.

School should re-instil the now-alien idea that you can be happy by looking for things to celebrate rather than to complain about. While we're on happiness, we should teach kids that their lives will be vastly better if they don't compare themselves with TV celebrities, famous footballers and gangsta rappers, but work instead on improving themselves.

Most leave our school without the faintest concept of the pleasure and satisfaction, to say nothing of the pride, to be gained from doing a job well, rather than just doing the absolute minimum allowed.

We should teach them the importance of developing a hobby. We need to get them to find out what they are passionate about and hope that it is something like playing sport or helping orphans, rather than sniffing glue.

They need to learn about relationships: that children are best brought up in stable families, that sex is worth waiting for, that it is damaging to your life if you fall pregnant at 13.

They need to learn that material possessions are like salt water. There must have been a time when everyone was happy with a 12 inch television, before the first 14 inch screen came out. Now you can buy a TV 12 feet across and everyone wants one. For many people, what they currently own is merely the baseline. Every time they acquire something new they simply reset their happiness level to a new baseline. That way lies madness.

A little instruction on the realities of life wouldn't go amiss – the fact that life itself is not risk-free (it is, in fact, invariably fatal) and that accidents are not necessarily somebody else's fault, along with the importance of fortitude in the face of trivial problems, of not making a scene when things don't go your way but of behaving instead with dignity and quiet acceptance. Our pupils have no understanding of the forgotten values of perseverance, patience and dedication.

Every teenager should spend a few days in A&E seeing that the affects of guns, knives, drugs and alcohol, senseless violence and driving recklessly are not glamorous, as they are portrayed on the television or in Hollywood films, but gruesome and bloody.

Finally, we should teach them to try to live a good life, regardless of whether they are religious or not. As a basic rule, treat others as you'd like them to treat you in return is hard to beat.

Of course, we shouldn't really have to teach a lot of this stuff in school.

But if we don't, who will?

My pondering done, I arrive at St Jude's.

As I walk across the playground to the main doors, a small boy – I think it is Kyle from Year 9, but I can't be sure, shouts 'Chalk, you f*cking w*nker!' before dodging round a corner, cackling.

Yes, we should teach them about bad language, too.

Parents' evening

THE BEHAVIOUR today was disgraceful – the school was full of gum-chewing yobs wearing baseball caps and shouting abuse at us... yes, it's parents' evening again.

This one is for Year 9 and I have been asked to attend because I teach (well, I spend time with) a lot of the Year 9 kids. I have no intention of letting on to my full-time colleagues that I managed to negotiate being paid for being here. What I do intend is to give some of the parents some serious abuse. Assuming they bother to turn up.

Each of the parents/guardians/'Primary Care-Givers' or random 'adults' responsible for producing and/or looking after these kids has a five minute slot set aside for them. They have had every opportunity to book that slot over the last month. But only a few parents managed to do this; the rest just turn up when they can be bothered.

It's a good crowd tonight – we have been unable to schedule the event to coincide with a major football match, so we have a few more customers than usual – and mostly female, reflecting both the high proportion of single parents and the sheer lack of interest from the father/current partner. Many are blathering mindlessly into mobile phones while they await their appointment; in Declan's mother's case, she's gabbing away at the same time as Mr Green is trying to talk to her.

All the teachers have dressed up in their finest outfits. I have never seen so many jackets. Even Mrs Simpson is wearing something vaguely matching.

Mr Wilkinson certainly seems to have pulled out all the stops this evening. Gone is his threadbare jacket, replaced with a smart, well-fitting, dark affair. Unfortunately, he gives the game way by constantly glancing down and nervously checking it. Ah, I see it now! The price tag has been tucked carefully into the pocket and it will be back on the shelves tomorrow!

I wish I had a concealed camera because it's non-stop comedy. Shazney's mother informs me that her daughter wants to become a doctor. I can barely keep a straight face and have to pretend to be having a coughing fit.

'Maybe she should think about being a nurse, or perhaps the secretary in the surgery, or maybe a cleaner in the surgery, or…'

Maybe I ought to feel guilty: whatever happened to inspiring children, encouraging them, helping them to 'be the best they can be'? But I don't feel guilty; through a combination of genetics, upbringing and schooling, Shazney will have done really, really well if she makes it as a doctor's cleaner, and there's nothing wrong with that anyway. It is sad, but being sad doesn't mean it isn't true.

Mrs Scroggins accuses me of picking on Declan. I admit, regretfully, that I do. She was obviously expecting an argument so is unsure of what to say next and just settles for a sympathetic, 'OK, then.'

I have to admit that I *am* prejudiced against Declan, just as I am against all the really unpleasant kids. We all have prejudices (although you must never admit to them if you want to get anywhere in teaching). If Declan were a nicer boy I'm sure I would be less prejudiced against him.

Lorna's mother asks about our school's position in the league tables.

I tell her to turn to the final page and work backwards: it will be quicker to find us that way. I also tell her, for the third year running, that she should get Lorna out of this dump before it is too late. I fear my warnings are falling on deaf ears. Although their daughter is in the top set for everything, I cannot get through to her parents that, in most other schools, she would not be. Already, she has gained rough edges and is demonstrating the potential to go off the rails. It is genuinely depressing. Lorna's a good kid, with a lot of potential that we are not going to help her realise.

Dwayne's turned up with his mum. It's always a bit weird when parents bring their kid along: how can they possibly imagine that I have any desire whatsoever to see him or her during the evening, as well as during the day?

It's called PARENTS' evening.

Can't you read?

Actually, don't answer that.

As I tell Dwayne's mother that he is a pain in the neck because he cannot go five minutes in a lesson without interrupting, he proves my point by doing exactly that while I speak.

Over in the corner, I see Mr Duncan, clearly flustered as he hasn't had a drink for over an hour. His face is redder than ever and he is becoming increasingly animated. His arms whirl around as he describes some misdemeanour. I hope he doesn't fall off his chair like he did last year.

Next to him, Mr Jones is busy telling Sherry's mother what an excellent pupil she is and how if she works really hard, one day she might become a dentist's secretary. He is clearly mixing her up with Catherine who is a much better child and, in a better school, could certainly go to university and go on to do well in her life.

Look, there's Li-Anne's mother blowing a bubble with her gum while waiting to see Miss Wade.

Leon's mum has brought about half-a-dozen toddlers and babies with her. They scream constantly and she snaps and growls at them, aggressively, loudly and repeatedly. It all adds to the relaxing atmosphere.

Tracey's mother is storming off, slamming the door as she goes. Mr Blunt has just told her not to smoke. I can't help grinning: the parents are just bigger, fatter versions of the kids, really.

Mrs Simpson appears to be having a cosy chat with a parent. How strange. Then I twig it: the woman is also covered in dog hairs, so no prizes for guessing what it is that they are discussing. A queue has built up but they ignore it. Later, it transpires that in the whole evening Mrs Simpson saw only the dog-owning parent.

Bravo!

The children know what
they are doing

LIKE ALL Supply Teachers, I breathe an audible sigh of relief when I discover that the absent full-timer has actually left work for the class to get on with. I then scan it carefully to see how useful it is. I always look for traps, such as references to textbooks that are not in the room.

Phrases such as 'They can carry on with their projects!' are always worrying because all the naughty ones will claim to have left said project at home or finished it and handed it in last lesson.

One I particularly dread is 'The children know what they are doing, and can just get on with it.'

I know perfectly well that they will claim not to know what they are doing, and, even if they do know, that they will certainly not be able to 'just get on with it'.

Clear, precise instructions are like manna from Heaven.

The worst of all possible worlds, however, comes when there is no work at all.

There can be any number of reasons for this. Maybe some enterprising pupil has removed it from where it was Sellotaped neatly to the teacher's desk. Perhaps the teacher simply didn't leave any, or left it with someone else. However, none of this is of the slightest importance when the problem confronting me is quite simple: 'What the hell am I going to do?'

This is exactly what I am facing now as I stand in Mr Jones's empty classroom with the sound of his Year 8 group approaching. He is off on a Behaviour Management Course and, boy, does he need one of those. (I never seem to get to go on any of these courses; I fancied the sound of an Assertiveness Course they were touting around last week, but I wasn't brave enough to ask.)

I hunt around to try and find out what they were doing last lesson. A quick search of the desk and cupboards reveals nothing. Nor any textbooks. So I must try some subtle questioning of the group and, if that fails, I may have to do that horror of horrors – the 'off the cuff lesson', where I simply make up some random piece of work and hope to be able to persuade the kids that is what they should be doing. Surprisingly this is often harder than it sounds: the kids are very quick to refuse to do anything that they do not believe is the correct work set for them by their own teacher (as though they'd actually do the correct work).

The teacher next door assures me that she knows where the work is, and has sent someone to get it. I have heard this one a million times before and it no longer convinces me. I'll try the delaying tactic and hope somebody comes to my rescue.

Here goes.

We all line up outside the classroom. We are not going inside until we are in one straight line, absolutely silent, chewing gum put away, cigarettes extinguished. It is time for my stern talk about standards, behaviour, crime, society, bringing the correct equipment to lessons and anything else I can think of, with an emphasis on the fact that I am their only hope of avoiding a long slide into the abyss.

I add lots of glaring and menace; in a school like ours, they must be wary of you or they will take advantage.

A glance at my watch confirms ten minutes gone.

I let them into the room in small groups and tell them to put their coats on the pegs, sit down and take out their pens, pencils and rulers. I separate any grouping I do not like the look of and remind those that have forgotten to put their coats on the pegs to do so. I make sure that anyone who is on report places the card neatly on my desk.

This brings us up to the 20-minute point.

It is clear that they do not have the faintest clue what they are supposed to be doing this lesson so I continue. I have identified class snitch (as always, a smartly-dressed, well-behaved and normal child whose book is not covered in graffiti). I send her off to find the Head of Department or any other stray maths teacher. There is a slim chance that she will return.

While she is gone, I get everyone sitting properly, ties straightened, desks neatly lined up. Get all the litter off the floor and secure any posters that are falling off the wall and need to be stuck back properly. ('Put that drawing pin down this minute, Tyler, yes, I can see you.')

I give another talk about how if we look smart we will work smart and get good jobs. We must not accept anything less than a clean and tidy environment for our lesson.

This brings us past the 30-minute point and into the second half of the lesson. What shall we do next? Ah, I know; it's time to inspect their exercise books. I collect in all those that are covered in graffiti and announce that this is simply not good enough.

I ignore cries of 'But Mr Jones lets us write on the covers.'

This may be so, but he is also a waste of space who should have been sacked 24 years ago. (I don't bother saying this; they all know it anyway).

With great theatrical effect, I call out each name in turn and tear off the book cover. They are absolutely astounded, and we have reached the 40-minute point. Two-thirds of the lesson down.

Next we must make sure that everyone has a pen, pencil and ruler. How can great work be done without the correct equipment? Those that do not have a pen must borrow one from their friends, or use a pencil.

There is the inevitable cry of 'Can I lend a pen?'

I carefully explain (with examples) the difference between lending and borrowing and inform them that if they cannot get something to write with, then they may borrow equipment from my stock. They must give a deposit for anything borrowed in order that they appreciate the importance of returning goods in the state that they were lent out. I will accept money (minimum of 20p), a shoe or their mobile phone. Giving my own equipment out is always a last resort because it will usually be lost, chewed or wantonly destroyed. It also encourages the benefits culture in which so many of them exist: 'I can get anything I need provided for me, so why bother to bring my own?'

I collect £1.50, two shoes and three mobiles, write each of their owners a little receipt, and put them in a box in the cupboard.

For reasons that are beyond me, the pupils are allowed to bring mobile phones to school 'as long as they switch them off in lessons'. Needless to say, they do not do this and your lesson is punctuated with amusing ring tones. The Head is too frightened to get a grip and simply ban them, facing down the inevitable tirade of abuse from Wayne, Dwayne, and Shazney's mothers, who will claim that they are the only thing stopping their little angels from being kidnapped. (Any kidnapper would soon be begging you to take your child back, Mrs Scroggins, I can assure you.)

I always keep an old mobile phone in my jacket pocket (any mobile phone shop will give you a dozen old phones if you explain what you want them for). If I spot a pupil playing with his when he should be doing sums, I immediately grab it and walk back to my desk. Ignoring protests and using simple sleight of hand, I smash my own phone repeatedly on the desk before throwing it on the floor and stamping on it. The look of horror and outrage is priceless, as the precious phone disintegrates and bits fly everywhere. But this trick only works for the first thirty to forty times in our school before the pupils cotton on.

Dishing out the pens has taken another ten minutes, so 50 minutes gone.

I now have a problem. As I have ripped all the covers off their books I cannot tell whose book is whose; instead, we will have to use some A4 lined paper from the cupboard.

I go around the class, reverently placing a piece of paper on everybody's desk. I do not allow them to snatch it from my hand.

In these declining times, I regard it as my moral duty to teach good manners to all who pass through my classroom. This includes the correct use of 'please' and 'thank you', the prohibition of snatching and grabbing, and an absolute veto on raising one's voice unless one is drowning or on fire (the former is unlikely, I agree, but the latter quite possible, given the proliferation of smoking materials to be found in our children's pockets).

I instruct them to write their name, class, Registration Form, my name and the date and then to underline everything carefully. Almost 55 minutes gone.

Now we write the Title on the next line down, in big wobbly capital letters, and underline it.

'OK. Everybody look at the board and put your pens down.'

I make sure that the board is spotlessly clean and then glance at my watch. Oh dear, there are only three minutes left.

Because of their tardiness, this work will be carried on next lesson.

Anyway, never mind, I go round and collect in all the paper and place them carefully in the centre of the teacher's desk. Class snitch arrives with the Head of Department and a long story involving the difficulties she has overcome in finding him. The boss enquires how the class has been.

'Very good indeed!' I assure him, and get everyone to pack

everything away, checking all items borrowed against my list and returning deposits. (Head of Department seems to think this is a bit of an odd scheme and frowns in puzzlement at all the exercise book covers in the waste paper bin.)

Coats off the pegs, stand up straight behind desks; well done everybody, very good lesson and then off we go, row-by-row, just as the bell goes.

Not easily led to the study of physics

EVERY THURSDAY evening, I do an hour's private maths tutoring for James, a pleasant Year 10 kid from our school.

It's probably unethical, but I don't care. This lad is polite and keen and a pleasure to teach, and both parents are well-spoken and intelligent.

Needless to say they do not live on the Cherry Tree Estate. God knows why they send him to our school. From chatting to them, it seems to have begun with a well-meaning notion about supporting the local school. Well, we've all been there: I had plenty of well-meaning notions of my own, once. Lately, the scales have fallen from my eyes, as they have from those of many of my colleagues (though we don't like to talk about it too much). The problem, you see, is that a notion of this type is all very nice, in theory – if you're living in a village where the local primary is under threat, it's probably even admirable. But for a kid like James at a school like St Jude's, forget the theory: the reality is seriously bad. I can imagine his gratitude ten years' hence, after a school life in which he stuck out like a sore thumb, was bullied all the time, got into petty crime and had to spend an extra five years studying to get to university. Well, at least you did the politically correct thing, mum.

It will be worse, of course if he really falls in with a bad crowd (yes, I know it can happen at any school but, statistically, he is more likely to fall in with a bad crowd at our place because there aren't that many other crowds within which to fall; as far as I can see, they range from quite bad to terribly bad). His chances of avoiding that aren't great, to be honest, people being easily-led, and all that (though, in my experience, people are rarely easily-led to the study of physics, say, or chemistry).

Sometimes I try to give him one of my pearls of wisdom: 'James, what you do now will have a direct effect on how you live the rest of your life.'

Well, I never said I was Confucius.

'Yes, Mr Chalk,' says James.

And we return to his maths. He has Mr Jones, so he doesn't get to learn anything. In fact, I am astounded by how bad his maths is. He thinks that I am a human computer because I can do all his Year 9 stuff in my head but actually it's just because Year 9 maths is incredibly easy.

His mum gives me a resigned smile as I pull on my jacket a little later.

'You know, Mrs Smith,' I say, pausing at the door. 'It's not really any of my business – I'm sure you have very good reasons for keeping James at St Jude's. I know it's the closest school, and so on. But I really do think you should consider trying to move James to St John's.'

It's a conversation we've had several times before, to no effect.

'I think James would do better there – there's less messing around and more focus on…'

She holds up her hand to silence me. 'We're seeing the Head next Tuesday,' she says.

And I very nearly kiss her.

Not going to St John's

ANTHONY FROM Year 10 didn't come to school today.

Details are sketchy at the moment, but it seems as though he's been arrested for burglary with two other boys from Year 11. His mother phoned the school and spoke to the Head. She was in tears, according to the person who put her through. Anthony will be in tomorrow, as normal.

I'm quite sad when I hear the news because I actually like the kid. He's entertaining.

His brother, Paul, is at a decent university reading maths – I taught him a few years back, when I was full-time, and I think I can take at least some credit for his success. We got on well; he was a diligent lad and, while not naturally tremendously gifted, he always tried his best.

Anthony's the youngest in the family, a brighter kid than either Paul or their sister, Sarah (an estate agent now, apparently), and he's probably been mollycoddled at home a bit.

He's certainly been mollycoddled at school. Standards of behaviour seem to drop every year and our willingness, and ability, to stamp on it is dropping, too.

It's all about 'progress' and letting kids 'express themselves', you see.

Thirty years ago, the majority of kids in our school were obedient, respectful and hard-working (I'm not just saying that, we have teachers here who can remember). They may not have been rocket scientists, all of them, and a fair few probably misbehaved outside school hours. But there would have been no seriously 'bad crowd' for Anthony to fall in with and his intelligence would have been stretched and rewarded. If he'd failed to perform to his ability, he'd have been pulled up for it. If he'd misbehaved, he'd have been given lines or a detention. If he'd *really* misbehaved, he'd have been caned. It's not particularly pleasant, and it can be mildly humiliating. But that's the point: it works.

Result: 30 years ago, Anthony would have been expecting As and

Bs in eight O levels, planning his A levels and thinking about Uni. The world, for a lad with his brains, would have been at his feet.

Instead, he's in a police cell and my prediction for him from here on in involves drugs, crime and a sticky end.

Still, at least he has all the rights to self-expression he could ever wish for.

Progress, you say?

Sex, drugs and fighting: A day at the seaside

TRIPS OUT of school are not for the faint hearted.

It takes courage to go on one of these, let alone to organise one (even the gentle nature rambles I remember from primary school would be a logistical nightmare today). A book of procedures must be studied, endless pages of forms filled out, letters written home requesting parental consent and Health and Safety Risk Assessments made and signed-for. Then there is the ever-present risk of being complained-about or even sued. While we're on the subject, we have got to stop suing each other so enthusiastically. Take the case of the 16-year-old pupil from Suffolk who was left seriously disabled during a school skiing trip in Austria in 1996. Despite the fact that the boy had been behaving irresponsibly at the time of the accident – he was skiing too fast and out of control – and had already been reprimanded by his teachers for skiing off-piste, he sued. The judge ruled that the school was 50% liable for his injuries because the teacher in charge of the trip had failed to stop him skiing (though the Court of Appeal later said he was entitled to no compensation). I sympathise with the boy, but it seems to me that what happened was, essentially, his own fault (especially when physically restraining him is liable to end in a visit from the local constabulary).

Unless this lunacy stops, the end result – according to the Law of Unintended Consequences, which covers much of what we do and almost all of everything any do-gooder ever tried to achieve – will be that trips out will one day become a thing of the past, and the kids will miss out.

As it is, staffing is always a problem.

There is a small number of teachers, however, who are undaunted by all this. They are either suicidally brave or howling mad. They laugh in the face of danger and think nothing of organizing skiing trips for groups of 50 kids to the Alps. These are the descendants of men who peered over the tops of their trenches at the Somme and snorted in derision.

Hats off to them. Think back to your own schooldays and imagine what disasters could occur on such a trip. Losing a kid, injuries, the language problem. The habit that British children abroad have of shoplifting dangerous items.

Let's look at this from the pupil's perspective.

The most important things for the kids on any trip abroad are knives, alcohol and fireworks. Sex, drugs and fighting with the locals are also vital ingredients for the success of such a venture.

The potential for a mishap is huge and the rewards for the staff member... well, how does a week of your holidays away from your family and friends, in some grotty hotel that the tour company considers unfit for adult groups sound?

Our own more modest excursion today is going far better than anybody expected. We are visiting the seaside and even the two decrepit old vehicles that we have hired from Mr Koshushko's new coach company have managed the journey swimmingly.

The trip was originally supposed to be a reward for all the kids who had behaved well this year. However, we would only have needed Mr Jones' old tandem for that so we decided to broaden the net a little.

First, we changed the criteria to all those who had not been given a detention, but that would still only have required Mr Blunt's people carrier.

So then we decided that all those who had not been put on report could come; which bulked the numbers up to half a coach.

Finally, we agreed to broaden it to, 'All those who haven't actually been expelled.'

Before setting off, the kids are gathered in the school hall, frisked for weapons and given a stern talk by Mr Morris about representing the school and setting a good example. The rest of the staff can barely keep a straight face. The thought of this lot representing anything other than a challenge to your self-control is ridiculous.

Somebody must have requested the extra grumpy driver for our coach, as he has no end of complaints and rules before we even set off. I listen dutifully until his speech has ended before launching into a fine rendition of 'Oh, I do like to be beside the seaside!'

He is more prescient than I imagined, though; by the time we have arrived, half a dozen seat covers have been thrown out of the vent in the roof.

We will punish Ashley and Conner severely by making them sit with Mr Grumpy on the way back.

It's a beautiful spring day; blue sky and big round sun, pretty much as I've had the kids draw a thousand times in lessons. I am sitting outside a surprisingly pleasant-looking little pub on the seafront, sipping a pint of beer, watching the passers-by and talking nonsense with Mr Green. We've left the kids at the funfair, having finished our own tour of duty.

We both agree that it was highly amusing to hear that Dale and Chesney had been paddling in what turned out to be the overflow from a sewer and even funnier to see Wayne fall off the log flume. Mr Green tells me that he bought him a Lilo afterwards and sent him off sailing. As I knot my handkerchief and place it on my head, I scan the horizon and hope the tide's going out. I also reflect that sometimes teaching really can be the best job in the world.

That changes on our return in the evening.

We told all the parents that we would be back at 7pm and it is now 8pm. We have been sat on the school steps for almost an hour with three children uncollected.

There is no answer from any of their parents' phones and I am becoming increasingly fed up.

Everybody else was here to meet their offspring and take them away; where are these morons?

They all live in different areas of town so we have decided that the best option is simply to wait here. We drew straws and the losing pair, myself and Mr Duncan, are now cursing our bad luck. We have interrogated Darren, Hayley and Wayne but all they can say is that either mother or father promised to meet them.

We have decided to wait another 15 minutes and then drive them home. No doubt there are all sorts of rules prohibiting such things, not to mention union guidelines etc, but neither of us are interested in that.

Suddenly, a car appears. It's Mr Scroggins, arriving to pick up Hayley.

Sorry he's late but he got caught up watching the first half of the match.

Oh, that's all right then. Don't trouble yourself on our behalf.

Sarcasm goes straight over his head, just like my cricket bat will if he doesn't agree to give Wayne a lift home too.

We drive Darren home to find it in darkness. Unfortunately, he has a key (if he hadn't, I'd have taken great delight in smashing a window to gain entry). He just shrugs his shoulders and lets himself in

Good, caring parents, looking after their 12-year-old son.

I drop Mr Duncan off and he offers me a drink. I politely decline.

I drive home as dusk is falling, thinking how lucky I was to have parents who cared about me.

Geography, and getting off your face

I'VE GOT the cover sheet in one hand, my briefcase in the other and trepidation in my heart. This is because I am headed towards Mr Duncan's geography room to cover his Year 8 lesson.

He is probably off with a worse-than-usual hangover and will, no doubt, have been unable to come up with any sensible work through the haze in his head.

He does not disappoint me. I notice, too, that he has left his room unlocked, with the result that it is full of kids throwing his rock samples around.

Bloody hell, there are millions of them.

Class sizes are far too big for the nutters we have now: 30 kids of this type in a class is just overwhelming.

After a brief rant from me, we line up outside and mess around for a while. I harangue them a bit more and, finally, we go back in again to tidy up the room. I stretch this process out for as long as possible while I interrogate class snitch and discover that all their exercise books were handed in last lesson.

Attempts to find the Head of Geography prove fruitless, as he is out on a course.

I end up pestering the poor teacher next door, who hasn't really got a clue what they were supposed to be doing, but does have some text books with maps of Australia in them for us to copy out.

Geography isn't a bad cover, I suppose, because there is always plenty of opportunity for colouring maps and you can do a little test of capital cities (as long as they have their atlases to look up the answers).

Much relieved, now, I blather happily to the class for ten minutes or so about the many fascinating aspects of Australia: its unique flora and fauna, its vast and ancient desert interior, Ayers Rock (which I believe we must now identify by its Aboriginal name of 'Uluru'), the concentration of population along the coastlines, the Great Barrier Reef and so on.

After about ten minutes, I foolishly ask if anyone knows anything else about this wonderful and exotic country. There's silence, and then Ashley declares: 'I don't give a sh*t, I'm gettin' off me face tonight.'

This neatly rounds off the discussion, so it's time to get down to work.

No, we can't have the felt tips yet, Jenna, we need to draw the outline in pencil first. (Thinking about it, why don't I catch the first plane to Australia at the end of this lesson? I mean, seriously? I could do it.)

Most of them are having a go at the map, so the lesson appears to be on the right course. There are a few notes to summarise, too; I notice that, according to Nathan's book, Australia was once a penile colony.

Ashley has other ideas, however. He is demonstrating his remarkable ability to juggle with one object. Under my glare, he stops with a dramatic sigh, puts the rock back and returns to drawing pictures of bizarrely-dressed characters smoking giant cigarettes.

I feel that we are embarking on a journey down a well-worn path. I suggest that he draw the map of Australia. He says he doesn't want to. I go back to the front hoping he will get on with it if I leave him alone; he helps himself to another rock sample and promptly drops it.

Ashley is a standard naughty boy with a record of wrongdoing as long as your arm. The fact that he remains in our school is testament to our weak leadership.

Stupidly, I decide to attempt to reason with him.

'Ashley, maybe this isn't the most exciting lesson you have ever had but just draw the map, colour it in and then we're going in 30 minutes.'

Sounds reasonable to me.

He replies in a loud voice; 'Nah. This is sh*t.'

That's a fair point, but I don't want to hear it from him.

He starts to scratch his name onto his desk with the rock sample.

'Come on, Ashley, we're going to sit at the front,' I announce, removing his coat from the back of his chair. He grabs for it but I have had years of practice at this manoeuvre and, with a flourish, I keep it just outside his reach, putting it over the chair at the front of the class. He runs after me, shouting, 'I ain't movin', gimme me coat!'

He snatches the coat but I still have a tight hold of it.

As he furiously attempts to wrench it free, there is a loud tearing sound and, to the general amusement of the class, I am left holding one arm while Ashley tumbles back and falls to the ground holding the rest of it. A few bits of white, feathery filling float gently to the floor between us.

Ashley is now absolutely livid and I probably do not help matters by bursting out laughing.

'You f*cking tosser!' he yells, face puce with rage and embarrassment. 'I'm gonna get me Dad and he'll batter you!'

He storms out of the room.

I am still holding the arm as the door slams and Ashley's departing footsteps fade away. I pin it reverently on my noticeboard, bending it slightly at the elbow for comic effect.

Then I sit down on the front of my desk.

'Well,' I say, 'poor old Ashley.'

Billie-Jo looks sceptical. 'Aren't you going to do anything, Mr Chalk? He's always running off and nobody bothers!'

She's right: Ashley is a well known for storming out. He does it every time he doesn't get his own way, with me and with other teachers.

Mr Chalk (looking thoughtful, before casting the bait): 'Well Billie-Jo, it's not really his fault, he can't help it. We've just got to accept it and not make a big fuss over it. I mean, it must be difficult for him.'

Tyler and Davina (hooked instantly): 'Yerwot, sir?'

Mr Chalk: 'No, I'm sorry. I can't really discuss it… it's not fair on him.'

I now have the undivided attention of the Year 8 group.

Every pen is down, every ear strains.

Nathan (echoing Tyler and Davina in his standard question when puzzled): 'Yerwot, sir?'

Mr Chalk (reluctantly): 'Will you all promise to be mature about this?'

Billie-Jo, Nathan, Tyler, Davina et al: 'Yes, oh, yes sir, we will, yes, yes, definitely, cross my heart.'

Mr Chalk: 'Well, it's like this. You know how sometimes you really need to go to the toilet quickly, say if you've eaten something that doesn't agree with you?'

(Nods of understanding.)

'Well, some people have that problem a lot and they can't control themselves like we all can.'

(Eyes widening around the room.)

'So we just have to be sensible about it while Ashley goes to Matron and gets himself cleaned up and sorted out. Anyway, come on now, back to work.'

Groans of disgust fill the room and we return to our maps, sans

Ashley, his arm on the noticeboard reminding us of our sympathies for his plight.

Inclusion, or trying to get rid of Shane

IN COMMON with many schools, we have a policy of 'Inclusion'. This essentially means that not only will we take anyone, regardless of their impact on the rest of the kids, but also that we send a clear message to our persistent offenders: 'Do that again, and you won't be thrown out!'

Well, that certainly teaches them a lesson.

As most children on the planet would give their right arm for the lifestyle and privileges our kids turn their noses up at, I refuse to fall into the apologists' camp.

So many of our students (I find it so difficult to use that word without giggling) must be perplexed when, in later life, they are sacked from work for persistent lateness, petty theft, disobeying instructions and so on. After all, for the previous twelve years at school, this behaviour has been perfectly acceptable.

When Heads and SMT *finally* get round to chucking some brat out, usually after years of persistently appalling behaviour, culminating in something beyond the pale – they've murdered someone, say, or are using the maths classroom as the base for a drugs-and-prostitution racket – they have to get the support of the school governors.

The governors are a shadowy bunch, whose job seems to be to hinder our best efforts to teach by preventing the exclusion of such children.

Even if they do back us up, the pupil's parents can still appeal.

What a joke.

Let's consider the case of one of our ex-pupils, Shane, (whom we met earlier when he came to show us 'his' new motorbike).

For those of you who have no idea of what goes on in schools nowadays (maybe you have a position on a SMT), the exclusion procedure goes something like this.

Shane joins the school in Year 7 and is a pain in the neck from the word go. We expect this: we've heard that he was a nightmare at his Primary School. He is rude to teachers, disrupts lessons, gets endless reports, detentions and whatever. He does not turn up to most of his detentions, with the backing of his mother, who claims that the school picks on her Shane; she phones up endlessly and threatens school staff with violence or prosecution, or both. (She is familiar with court; that is where she met Shane's father.)

By Year 10, Shane is a serious problem child. He causes constant, low-level disruption, though the term 'low level disruption' is misleading: we use it to describe swearing and shouting out in lessons, fighting, refusing to carry out simple instructions and arguing with teachers. All of these would once have been considered serious incidents and dealt with accordingly. Occasionally, Shane is involved in what we still do call 'serious incidents' – he might have threatened someone with a knife, or been caught with drugs on the school premises. These result in a few one or two-day exclusions, but are more often simply brushed under the carpet by SMT.

By this stage of his school life, there is more effort, time and resources being spent on Shane than on 20 better-behaved children. The Behavioural Psychologist comes to see him once a week for a nice cosy chat; she refers to him as a 'Casualty of the System.' She doesn't seem to notice the real casualties: the other children in Shane's class, who have lost literally hundreds of hours of their education by now.

Halfway through Year 10, Shane assaults a teacher. The teacher demands his exclusion, but Shane claims that the teacher pushed him out of the door and two of his friends (both known liars) back up his story. The Head wavers and asks the teacher if he did anything to provoke the incident. The teacher backs down. The Head calls in mum and 'arranges a Package of Measures'. This is a teaching term which means 'backs down completely'. Effectively, this means Shane must attend only those lessons that he feels he can cope with. How nice!

A month later, he assaults another teacher. This one is made of sterner stuff and, despite Shane trying a similar argument with the backing of the same two friends, the entire department refuses to have Shane in their lessons (a rare example of teachers sticking together, caused by fear that they will be next and that it might hurt). The Head is faced with the option of having him taught on his own, at huge expense, or permanently excluding Shane. He reluctantly takes the latter course.

You may think it's all over for Shane at this point. No, no, gentle reader.

The School Governors decide not to support the Head's exclusion. They believe the little brat's claim that the teacher provoked him. This is no ordinary teacher, however; as we have seen, he has persuaded each of Shane's teachers to refuse to have him in their lessons. The Governors are eventually talked around and Shane is thrown out.

However, he now has the right to appeal to an independent panel and mum intends to exercise this right.

She has persuaded a GP to diagnose Shane as suffering from ADHD or ODD and is claiming that the school is discriminating against him because of his disability.

While this appeal is going through, the school must accommodate Shane on the premises and provide work for him to do. As none of the Staff will teach him, he has to have his own Supply Teacher, which costs the school a couple of hundred pounds per day.

If he wins his appeal, we're back to square one. If he loses, he just moves to another school and he's no longer our problem (though Wayne, Darren, Coyne and two dozen others still are).

Madness, isn't it?

Headhunted by Elmwood

I HAVE been headhunted today by the man who organises Supply at Elmwood.

He called me on my mobile – goodness knows how he got hold of it – as I relaxed in the Staff Room. What an executive world I live in!

Elmwood is only a couple of miles from us and has a similar intake of pupils.

It is our arch-rival and we are neck and neck in the race for mediocrity. After all, as John Prescott has rightly pointed out, if either of us were to become a good school, parents would want to send their children to us and that would never do.

This chap asks me if I would like to cover maths for a few weeks for a teacher who is off with stress. I can't help but think that he shouldn't apply for any jobs in sales or advertising.

As I'm free before lunch, I head over to see him. The whole school was rebuilt a couple of years ago and, in contrast to ours, the buildings are modern, light, and airy.

Like ours, though, they are vandalised, covered in graffiti, and absolutely filthy.

I think to myself what an excellent demonstration this is of spending a large amount of public money to make no real improvement whatsoever (in an astute aside, one of the staff later says that it wasn't the buildings that needed changing, it was the pupils).

As I make my way to the Staff Room, I notice that they have a similar amount of litter to us (ie beyond belief) and that there are enough computers in the school to control a space launch.

Once ensconced on a spongy, orange chair below the pigeonholes, I am regaled by relaxing staff with familiar-sounding horror stories about the kids and their parents. I reflect that it's nice to see another group of staff with exactly the same problems as those at St Jude's.

Unfortunately, I have to decline the cover as I'm already booked up at our place for the dates required.

But I can't help feeling it would have been nice. Sometimes, a change is as good as a rest.

Techers shuld stick to lerning them

I KNOW I said I don't talk to the worst of our parents, but that wasn't entirely true. I'll do it on my own terms.

However, it's usually a complete waste of time.

I'm in the Staff Room, just after lunch, on my mobile.

'Hello Mr Scragger, it's Frank Chalk here from St Jude's. I'm just phoning up about a few problems we've been having with Kyle.'

'Uh? Wahyouonabout?'

'Kyle – your son?' Bloody hell, man, are you drunk? It's only 2pm.

'Uh? Right.'

'Yes, he won't ever keep quiet in class. He keeps shouting out and being a nuisance. He's disturbing my lessons and I wondered if you could do anything to help?'

'Nah. We can't do nothing with him these days. I know what the little bastard's like, mate.'

'Well, perhaps if you sat down with him and had a talk – you know, father to son…'

'Have you ever tried to 'ave a conversation with our Kyle? He can't sit still for two minutes before he's up and out.'

Through gritted teeth: 'Yes, I have tried to talk to him as well, but… HE IS YOUR SODDING KID!' (This last bit is only screamed in my head.) 'But I just thought you might be able to connect with him a bit better than we can.'

'Oh… right. Yeh. I'll gi' it a go. OK? Bye.'

Clunk. The phone goes dead in my ear.

He's obviously anxious to get off. Something must be starting on the telly.

Thank you, Mr Scragger, for the interest you have shown in the latest set of behavioural problems exhibited by the apple of your eye. I'm reassured tremendously; you clearly intend to deal with him harshly, and to ensure that we don't have any further problems with him.

If phoning the parents makes you feel that you are wasting your breath, writing to them is even worse. The letters are almost always ignored. If there is a reply it will be illegible, unintelligible gibberish, along the lines of: 'We will se whot we can do with are Shazney now the soshal worker is helping us all together Thank You'.

Sometimes there is an attempt to argue the case.

'We never have no problems with Dwayne at home schol shuld stick to whots going on in school and techers shuld stick to lerning them and mind there one biussness.'

Ah, that makes it all so much clearer, Mrs Grott.

An avenging angel

MR BERESFORD stands in front me, his hands on my desk. I can smell a faint mixture of beer and cigarettes on his breath. He is in a furious rage; gesticulating and threatening all kinds of unpleasantness should I ever chuck his little angel, Tyrone, out of my class 'for no reason' again.

We are alone in a classroom right at the end of a lonely corridor, in a part of the school building where many of the rooms are locked up and disused.

It is remote and he knows it (he is an ex-pupil of ours, so has had little difficulty entering the school unnoticed).

School has just finished and Tyrone has summoned him by mobile phone. I have thrown his son out of the previous three lessons for messing about and disrupting the class. As dad has nothing else to do, he races over to school like an avenging angel.

He has the bully's confident swagger; he is used to getting his own way and knows that he can threaten me with impunity. His confidence increases as he rants at me. He is bigger and stronger than I am and that fact is not lost on him. He senses an easy victory and is taking great pleasure in humiliating a teacher. His son is hanging around in the corridor outside, mightily impressed by all of this.

Mr Beresford informs me that I am not going anywhere until I have apologised to his son. I sit behind my desk, saying little, looking frightened (actually, I am frightened) and absorbing the tirade of threats and abuse.

When he finally falls silent, I speak. 'Mr Beresford, I have the greatest admiration for you,' I begin, in a calm and quiet voice. He is a bit taken aback. 'You have had the courage to admit that Tyrone is your offspring. I would rather stick pins in my eyes if I were you.'

He is now less impressed.

'Here's my plan,' I continue. 'In a moment, I am going to bang my nose on my desk. Not too hard, but hard enough to start a nosebleed. I will then leap over the table and jump on top of you, shouting 'Help, help... he's attacking me!' at the top of my voice. When help does arrive, I shall demand that the police are called to arrest you for your unprovoked attack on me, a defenceless teacher.'

He is standing up now, slightly more defensive: I press on.

'Now, who do you think the police will believe? You? Well, you've got into the school through a back door, uninvited. I bet you're known to them already?' This is a cheap shot, but it's probably true. 'Or do you think they'll believe me, a helpless teacher? I must be three stones lighter than you. I've never been in trouble with the law, have I? I've been attacked while marking my books, haven't I?'

The anger is fading from his face now; he's not the brightest of men, by any means, but he can see the sense of what I'm saying.

Out in the corridor, Tyrone is hopping from foot to foot. 'Tw*t him, dad!' he shouts.

'Shut up, you little bastard!' replies Mr Beresford.

I continue: 'I will insist on a prosecution and the judge will no doubt believe my story over yours. You will go to prison for six months, while I will take six months off with stress caused by your attack. Summer is on its way and I am looking forward to sitting on a deckchair in my garden, on full pay, sipping from a bottle of beer and toasting the image of you fending off amorous advances in the showers.'

He clenches his fists and then unclenches them.

Then, to my immense relief, he storms out, pausing in the doorway to grab Tyrone by the scruff of the neck and make a couple of additional threats towards me; but he leaves nonetheless.

I sit back and sigh, my hands trembling slightly with adrenalin. I've just come very close to being beaten up.

Unlike many of my colleagues, I have never been assaulted in school.

In fact, unusually, I've only even been jostled once (verbal abuse doesn't count, that's water off a duck's back). It happened years ago, when I was just starting out. I'd had words with a group of pupils in class and, as I walked past them after school on my way to post a letter, they deliberately blocked my path. I ignored them and went to walk through the group. As I did this, one of them elbowed me quite deliberately into the wall. It wasn't particularly painful, and I wasn't hurt, but I was quite surprised.

I couldn't belt him – apart from anything, there were lots of them and I'd have been filled in – but on returning home I did phone the police to report an assault.

Two officers came round and interviewed me for around half an hour, taking copious notes. At the end of this, they announced that there was nothing that they could do as I had no witnesses or marks upon my body. I gave them the name and address of the boy concerned and asked if they could visit just to give him a caution. They replied that they would not. It would be construed as 'harassment', apparently.

I tried the Head. He was sympathetic, but was able to wash his hands of the incident as it was not on school premises, though he agreed when I said I wouldn't teach the kid again (I probably should have taken some paid time off with some sort of psychological trauma, but I didn't).

Finally, I phoned the boy's father. He turned out to be quite supportive, and declared that he would 'give the lad a slap'. This obviously worked as I never had any trouble from his kid again.

The question in my mind then, and now, is why should I have to put up with this sort of thing? Would a teacher have had to suffer it fifty years ago? If not, what has changed?

As I say, I'm something of a rarity. Several teachers *have* been assaulted at St Jude's, as they have at many schools. Often these cases go unreported. Sometimes, it's because the victim has lost faith in the ability of the system to do anything about it. Other times, it's because the teacher fears he or she will become embroiled in some sort of Kafka-esque nightmare in which the victim becomes the accused. A woman teacher I know was pushed hard into a corridor wall recently but let it go because she had first grabbed the offending girl's wrist to prevent her from hitting another pupil. In the mad world of British schools, this made her an offender too.

Many do report assaults, of course. In 2004, 272 teachers in England were attacked badly enough to take three or more days off school.

In January 2006, a new milestone was passed when the first teacher was 'happy slapped' in a school – at St Chad's in Runcorn, since you ask. One pupil carried out the attack while another filmed it on his mobile phone.

If you think my school's bad, perhaps you should apply for a job at New College, Leicester, where they logged twelve assaults on teachers in four months. One boy, who injured a woman by barging her into a door and then threatened to kill her, was suspended for 15 days and then let back in.

Or perhaps move up to Glasgow where, according to a recent report, the kids manage to beat up a teacher every day. I hope it's not the same one.

Wondering where Miss Wade left her spine

I AM sitting in our Staff Room with my feet up on one of the crummy Formica tables, trying to make sense of what I have just been told.

Apparently, Miss Wade has put in a formal complaint to the Head claiming that she is being bullied.

Without exception, in my experience, this is always a precursor to a period off with 'stress'. She certainly looks as though she could do with a nice holiday, poor love.

Visions of the Head of Science demanding her dinner money wander in to my mind (actually that wouldn't be such a bad idea: she could do with missing a deep-fried dinosaur or two).

I had always assumed that bullying was something the kids did to each other but nowadays adults feel free to get involved as well. I really struggle to get my head round this concept and can't help but think that any adult who feels they are being bullied by another adult probably ought to be.

I mean, 'psychological bullying': it's hard to keep a straight face.

Frankly, if someone hasn't got the spine to stand up to a weedy, middle-aged man like the Head of Science, what use are they going to be in front of a class of unruly yobs?

Lots of people need a kick up the backside now and again (especially me) and a good boss (sorry, 'line manager') has traditionally been the one to provide it.

Unfortunately, this is now called 'bullying'.

Downtown college

DOWNTOWN COLLEGE is the local further education establishment where quite a few of the kids go after St Jude's.

From what I can gather, most appear to be studying Daytime TV.

There do not seem to be any entry requirements to get into the college, which makes it very difficult for us. For example, a teacher might say: 'Come on, Dwayne, make a start or you won't pass your GCSEs to get into Downtown,' but both he and the pupil will know that this is a farce (unless the child wants to study A Levels, or something daft like that.)

Downtown will honestly take anyone at all.

Even some of the Ghosts end up there eventually.

Sixth forms – that is, when kids stay on to further education at their school – are so much better for the pupils than colleges. They provide continuity for them and have a calming effect on the rest of the school. Best of all, they recognise that the sixth formers, as 16- and 17-year-olds, are not adults and that they still need plenty of pushing and encouragement. The colleges often treat their kids like university students but few are ready for that yet.

Guns, breasts and cannabis leaves

AS PREDICTED, Miss Wade is off with 'stress'.

But, joy of joys, I am not covering for her today.

Wandering down the corridor, reflecting idly on why our school never appears to be cleaned, I pass her science lab.

I wonder which poor unfortunate is covering this lesson and the sound of a manic cackle from within answers that question straight away. Such a sound could only have come from a madman and, sure enough, I can see the back of Mr Rogers through the door. I quietly go into the prep room next door and peep through the glass.

Inside the Lab, I can see a child standing with one hand on a large metal ball. Her hair is standing on end. She reaches out her other hand and there is a huge spark. She lets go quickly, shrieks and dances about, waving her hand and trying to flatten her hair. The next in line steps forward and Mr Rogers cranks a handle furiously.

For reasons best known to himself, Mr Rogers has decided to demonstrate the Van der Graaf machine. This device generates a huge static electrical discharge and there are quite strict guidelines for its use. I suspect Mr Rogers has not learned any of them during his career as a teacher of English.

He is wide eyed and looks slightly crazy.

God, it is virtually *impossible* to get sacked from teaching as long as you keep your hands off the children.

I want no part in this, so I start to slink away. I am free this lesson and have plans to catch up on a couple of miscreants who have been avoiding me. To my horror, however, Mr Rogers has spotted me. He comes into the prep room and asks that question that every supply teacher dreads: 'I don't suppose you could look after this lot for ten minutes could you? I've just got to nip out for something?'

I can hardly say no. After all, I'm paid by the hour and it's not really the done thing to refuse. Actually, the truth is that I can't come up with an excuse quickly enough because he has surprised me.

'Yes, no problem,' I reply, and saunter into the Lab.

'There's the work,' he says, pointing at the teacher's desk, which is covered with Sellotaped A4. And before I can ask where the Van der Graaf fits into all this he has disappeared.

'Bugger. I've been stitched up here,' is my first thought, as I search desperately through the work for today's lesson.

Bloody hell, this group seem to have been copying out of the textbook for the last two weeks solid! A glance through a pupil's book confirms this. They are slowly but surely replicating the textbook, like those Byzantine monks who painstakingly illustrated documents by hand in the Middle Ages. No wonder Rogers got bored.

To be honest, Dwayne's book doesn't look that much like one of those Byzantine things at all, with its crude representations of guns, breasts and cannabis leaves. Though there is some evidence of syllabus-related work: my eye alights on some pictures of various invertebrates, one of which has about 12 legs. Above it, a caption reads: 'The octopus has stinging testicles.'

This absolutely kills me and I have to look away from the group to recover.

Sometimes, things that the kids do make me laugh. (Usually, these are things that they don't mean to be funny, which means you are laughing *at* them. You're not supposed to do this, but it never causes me any problem; after all, they get to laugh at my expense often enough.)

I start to write the work on the board.

'Guess what we're doing today, Dwayne?' I say brightly.

'Copying out again?'

'Absolutely right!'

'This textbook's gay!'

'Is that because we lie all the textbooks that are the same on top of each other every night and put them in the cupboard and turn all the lights out, Dwayne?' I ask.

'No. It's just gay!'

On further questioning, it turns out that the felt tips are also gay, as is Assembly and French lessons. Some teachers would probably make a big fuss about homophobia or something but I'd say don't waste your time. You can't fight every battle so never pick the unwinnable ones, because you end up sounding like a prat.

A brief history of education in Great Britain

RIGHT! PAY attention! I'll be asking questions at the end.

In 1880, the Elementary Education Act made education up to the age of 10 free and compulsory.

In 1918, the Fisher Act raised the school leaving age to 14.

In 1944, the Butler Act split schooling into Primary (before 11) and Secondary (after 11). The same act introduced the tripartite system which split Secondary schools into three types: Grammar Schools, Secondary Modern Schools and Technical Schools (very few Technical Schools were ever built, so only about 2% of the population went to one of those and the tripartite system was abolished in 1976).

At that time, all children sat an exam – the 11-plus.

It was divided into three parts: arithmetic, problem-solving and an essay (it is still used today in some English counties and in Northern Ireland, but for most of us this is a past tense description). If you passed the 11-plus, you were eligible to attend grammar school; if you failed, you were not.

There were drawbacks with this; how serious they were depends on your ideology.

Firstly, it decided a child's future based on a single performance. I don't have too much of a problem with this – in a pass/fail test, the vast majority of results will be accurate, with only the most borderline child being affected by a 'bad day'. Once you accept the principle of selection, some errors are inevitable; it's just a question of whether there are more errors under that system or our prevailing one.

Secondly, there was some perceived unfairness in the fact that the pass rate varied in different parts of the country.

This could have been due to marking differences, but it could have been down to the quality of local primary schools. Again, it is not an insurmountable problem in my view.

There were two types of grammar schools: direct grant and State-funded.

Direct grant grammar schools took 25% to 50% of their pupils through the 11-plus and the rest had to pay to attend.

State-funded grammar schools took all their pupils free. Nowadays, virtually all of the old direct grant grammar schools are private, fee-paying schools. Fewer than 200 state-funded grammar schools remain.

Between the late-1960's and the mid-1970's, most of the grammar schools and secondary modern schools became Comprehensive Schools, open to all pupils, regardless of ability, who lived within a catchment area surrounding the school.

Nowadays 90% of children attend these state comprehensives.

Around 2,000 comprehensives in England (about two-thirds of the total) have become Specialist Schools, which means that they claim to specialise in the arts, business, engineering, humanities, languages, maths and computing, music, science, sports or technology.

They receive extra funding from the government for this (£100,000, plus £126 per pupil for four years) and they are allowed to select up to 10% of their intake (though most choose not to do so). They must raise £50,000 of private sponsorship and must still follow the National Curriculum. At the time of writing, the current plan is for all comprehensives to become Specialist Schools.

There are also around 30 City Academies, which are schools that are publicly-funded but independent of the Local Education Authority. Each has a private sponsor who pays 10% of the start-up costs, in return for a say in the curriculum and ethos (but NOT a seat in the House of Lords).

So, which system was better – the old or the new?

Well, the 11-plus had its flaws, as I have said, but I believe it is, fundamentally, the best way to go (and remember, I went to a comprehensive school). If you list children in order of academic ability at age 10, and then compare them at 60, the order is pretty similar.

The change to comprehensive education was introduced in an attempt to improve the chances of children from poorer backgrounds. More of them ended up going to secondary modern schools, the theory went, and the results at these schools were not as good as those at grammar schools. Lumping them all in together would even things out.

Ironically, the effect of this experiment with our children's future has been the exact opposite; social mobility is now much reduced in comparison to the situation thirty or forty years ago, as is the education our children receive. And the experimentation, and tinkering at the margins, continues: at the time of writing, the new Education Bill looks as if it is going to end up so watered-down that it will achieve little, if anything. Vague ideas about making schools into 'Trusts' are not going to help anyone.

The child for whom I have the most sympathy is the bright kid from a poor background. Grammar school offered him a way out, a lifeline for him and his family. It wasn't perfect, because life isn't, but it was there.

That lifeline has now been cut away and he is adrift in a vast, choppy sea.

Dog mess and a howling wind: Another day in paradise

WHAT IS the matter with these teachers? They are *always* off sick. Don't give me any of that nonsense about staying off so that you don't give whatever you've got to everybody else; that's just a handy excuse. Have you ever known anybody who is self-employed be ill? Of course not.

Anyway, don't expect any sympathy from me; I'm the poor sod drafted in to cover. It's not good enough.

You will have gathered by now that I am not one of teaching's high fliers. Not for me the office with a title such as Head of This or Assistant Deputy Head of That, or even an office without a title, for that matter. I am perfectly happy on the ground floor and I have never had a single day off. This is very rare in teaching and I am proud of it. I do not allow myself to become run down; I take plenty of exercise so that if I feel a bit unwell I can cope. This, and the fact that I don't get paid if I don't turn up, enable me to struggle on.

However, on seeing the rabble before me today, I begin to wish that I had broken the habit of a lifetime. The powers of my trusty glare have deserted me. Sometimes, as I stand framed in the doorway, a silent look can get them sat down and silent. Most times it doesn't work, though, and I am left watery-eyed and wondering what to do next.

Today is one of those days.

I am doing nothing more than crowd control. I am covering for Mr Jones again.

And there is another factor working against me today – the weather. For some unknown reason, the kids are always more of a pain when it's windy.

I'm trying to get them to shut up so we can start work, but this is always a nightmare when I am covering for Mr Jones, because he is a clown who 'lets us talk as long as we're working'. I hold up my watch up and write down the minutes wasted on the board. By halfway through the lesson, I am facing the daunting prospect of having to sit with the little idiots for an extra 16 minutes after the lesson ends. What have I done?

I have a flash of genius and announce that we will cross one minute off for every minute that they are good.

'Collect in the homework' is the first instruction on the bit of paper Mr Jones has left me.

Two minutes later I have discovered that 18 out of 28 have not done their homework. It doesn't surprise me, really. Many of the kids do not have a stable home life. Nobody makes them do their homework, or get out of bed for school, or study for exams. In fact, nobody takes the slightest interest in them beyond swearing at them for talking while the telly's on.

The kids are supposed to be getting on with their GCSE Coursework projects. Coursework is perhaps the biggest of the many jokes in our world: essentially, it is a way to fiddle exam results. For readers who were unlucky enough to miss the coursework revolution, here's how it works. A large percentage of the marks for your GCSE result will come from work not done under exam conditions, but in school or at home. When you hand it in to be marked, teachers can hand it back with suggestions on how you (or, more likely, your parents, or me, if I'm your maths tutor) can improve it. Then you resubmit it and get anywhere up to top marks. No wonder GCSE results go up every year. Of course, the downside of this is that the mark you get depends mainly on how affluent and concerned your parents are and the diligence and competence of your teachers. That's where many of our kids are out of luck.

Mr Jones instructs that if anybody finishes, or more likely does not have their project work with them, then they must get all the teachers' comments on their 'Records of Achievement' up to date this lesson. This is a new load of paperwork ostensibly designed to provide future employers with an idea of what pupils are like. Like many of these ideas, it's great in principle but shocking in practice. For a start, only positive comments may be written down and a child can always decide to 'lose' their record and claim that they never received it if they aren't happy with the finished result. As I say, I'm not against it *per se*: it just needs tweaking. First of all, every child should leave school with a comprehensive record of what he or she has spent the last 12 years doing, even if the resultant record is a blank sheet of paper. It should list all serious infringements of the rules, their exam results and their attendance record (which is very important to any employer), together with notable achievements outside and inside school. And let's enter, blinking in the white light of technology, the 21st century. The record should be stored, encrypted and secure, on the internet and kept by the school, and emailed to prospective employers as necessary.

Of course, these improvements will never happen because we must avoid honesty and transparency at all costs; what matters is that we *appear* to be assessing our kids. *Actually* assessing them would be a nightmare. Who knows *what* we might uncover?

The lesson is only going fairly badly for the first forty minutes, but then it really falls apart. A particular friend of mine, Wayne, walks in (ridiculously late) with dog mess on his shoe. Because he is such a fool, he proceeds to wipe the shoe on another boy's trousers. It's a revolting thing to do, but the reaction is bizarre: the other boy immediately starts screaming (he is, after all, only 15) and running around like the proverbial headless chicken. Now the offending material is on his bag, on the stool he was sitting on, on his neighbour's bag, on her chair, the work bench and so on. Half the class are now screaming and the lesson, as a means to impart knowledge, insofar as it was ever such, is over.

'Wayne, Wayne, you have no brain,' I murmur to myself.

It's childish, but it amuses me.

Getting away from it all

SOMETIMES, YOU just have to get away from it all. Today is one of those days.

There are twelve of us sitting on the floor in two rows facing backwards, like rowers. We're squashed so close together that it is impossible to move and relieve the ache in my legs. There's not so much banter now and I'm mentally rehearsing the exercise I am going to attempt in the next few minutes, occasionally glancing at the gauge on my left wrist: 12,000 feet, not long now.

There is a shout from the back and the side door opens, revealing a rectangular patch of blue sky. Cool, fresh air washes over us. With another shout, the engine tone deepens as the pilot throttles back, reducing forward speed to around 80 mph and raising his thumb to signal that all is well.

Now we are on our knees, shuffling forward in slow motion, legs protesting.

Those in front of me disappear, alone, or in pairs; then I move to the open doorway and kneel on my right knee. Ridiculous thoughts, like *Am I still wearing my parachute?* force themselves, unwelcomed, into my mind. My right hand is held high so that my chest will hit the wind as we exit; my left grips the front of Jimmy's suit. He is perched outside, legs bent, feet in the doorway, right hand on the thin rail running above the door, the other holding the tube running down the right arm of my suit. Firm grips.

His helmet completely covers his face and has a dark visor so I watch his head bob in countdown and match it with my own, grinning like a loon. He's a Red Devil, with 1,000 jumps to his name; I'm a buffoon with 30.

'3, 2, 1… out!'

I push forward, like a 100 metre runner as Jimmy throws himself backwards.

My stomach lurches as we plummet.

The wind starts to roar and we are doing over 60 mph only three seconds after leaving the plane; we're facing each other as we fall, horizontal and stable (more thanks to him than me).

Jimmy lets go of me and bends his legs, retreating until we are 10 metres apart. I snap my legs straight and adjust my hands, funnelling the air to push me towards him. As I approach close, I dip my left elbow and right knee, forcing the air to spin me on the spot like a propeller. He catches my feet as they come round. I continue the turn through 360 degrees so we are facing each other again. He is giving a big thumbs-up; I am elated and grinning like a nutter.

I glance at my altimeter: 8,000 feet, as he moves backwards again. This time I come in fast, turning to the right. Alas I have messed up and I am 12 feet below him. I stretch out arms and legs to make myself bigger, as if I was on top of a giant beach ball, and slowly rise up to him.

Glance at the alti again: 5,000 feet.

Less than a mile above ground, and we are doing 120 mph towards it.

Playtime is over. Jimmy waves his fingers across his throat and I turn away 180 degrees from him, dropping my hands to my sides like Superman. I count to three, bring my hands forward to stop, cross and uncross them quickly to signal what I am about to do, arch my back and reach round with my right hand to where my back pocket would be, grab the toggle, rip it out and throw it sideways in one quick, fluid movement.

I feel as if someone has just lifted me up with their hands under my shoulders; then, after three seconds, I look up and see what always strikes me as a minor miracle (especially if I have been involved in the packing). Less than 60 seconds after I left the plane, there is a big, multicoloured rectangular thing above my head that is holding me up in the air.

Two toggles await my commands. I reach up and take them after a quick look round the sky and at my alti (2,700 feet), still cross from my failure – my third in a row – to master the freefall manoeuvre. I drop the right toggle to my side. The chute seems to stand on one edge and I feel like I am being whirled round like a pebble on a string. Enough of that; it terrifies me. I head towards the landing area and below me I can see my friend Tim, who exited before me, coming into land less than 50 metres from the buildings. The DZ (drop zone) controller is already shouting at him – he's way too close – before his feet have even touched the ground. (They're followed rapidly by his knees, his elbows and the side of his helmet; he's about as good as me). I hang around above the rubbish dump for a few minutes, contemplating my jump and watching the gauge lazily approach 1,000 feet before I start my run in. An easy out-and-back run sees me land as lightly as if I had stepped off a kerb. I gather up my chute and walk the 400 metres or so back towards the hanger; no telling off for me today.

There is more to life than teaching. No matter how bad your school might be, no matter how useless your Head of Department may be... when you're floating around serenely under a big canopy, half a mile above the countryside, none of that stuff matters one jot.

And it's such a transcendental experience that it occurs to me that giving kids the chance to do this sort of thing – if Health and Safety would allow – might stop some of them hanging around on street corners, taking drugs and shagging in the bushes.

We could try it without parachutes on one or two of them.

Reflections from the prep room

I AM engaged in my favourite pastime, of sitting around doing nothing in the prep room next to Mr Green's science lab.

If I have a free lesson, I always try to hide up here.

The reason I am free at the moment is because I was scheduled to cover English for Mr Rogers, but he has returned early from his Team Building Course. Apparently he did not get on with the others. He can therefore take his own lesson.

The lab technicians are good company and rarely throw me out, as long as I help them with various trivial tasks. Mrs Tomkins is a jovial woman in her forties who is always laughing and joking. Her sidekick, Mrs Devonshire, is older but equally good fun. They have not a care in the world and are always happy to poke fun at kids and staff alike. Their job is to look after the equipment for practical lessons, to clean and repair things and to make sure that what has been asked for ends up in the right lab for the right lesson. They often get it completely wrong.

Today, they have got me going through a huge pile of text books, removing graffiti with the aid of a white eraser pen and a 1,000 metre roll of sticky white labels which can be used to cover up rude comments and drawings.

Unfortunately, it is difficult to do this without obliterating most of the book itself. They cost fifteen quid apiece and are completely destroyed after a year or, at most, two. I can remember being given text books that were thirty years old when I was a kid.

Graffiti comes in three varieties: Comments, Drawings and Modifications.

'Comments' are often puzzling, due to the low standard of spelling and grammar in our school.

'Mr Chalk is a Gig!' screams out at me from the inside cover of one textbook. The two lab technicians and I ponder this and suggest various explanations, none of which is entirely satisfactory. It seems unlikely that the child is suggesting that I am a pop concert or a 19th century horse-drawn carriage. But you never know.

'Mr Green is a Penus!' is a bit easier to work out.

'Drawings' by girls consist largely of heart shapes and declarations of undying love for a burglar two years above them. It's always easy to identify drawings by boys: it is a well-known rule in teaching that if you give a class of thirty young male lowlifes a piece of blank A4 and tell them to draw whatever they want you will get a mixture of cannabis leaves, pneumatic naked women and bizarre-looking characters wearing baseball caps and outlandish jewellery smoking giant cigarettes.

As for 'Modifications', well, modern textbooks are chock-full of photographs and pictures. They are, therefore, open invitations to the witty modifier. A chapter on the effects of alcohol on the body, with a picture of a drunken tramp collapsed in the street, is inevitably linked with poor Mr Duncan, while Mme Dupont will no doubt be delighted to hear that she plays a starring role in the chapter on human reproduction.

A note to textbook manufacturers: in order to make my job easier, could you please stop printing photographs of people bending over? Images of women or animals should avoided, full stop. In fact, don't put any photos in at all and use the space for long lists of facts and questions, instead.

Nowadays, the textbook stays in school for fear of it not returning and thus doubling the number of books in some of the kids' homes. I was once laughed down for suggesting that the Head should charge a deposit for each textbook. Maybe it was a bit naïve of me.

Of course, it's difficult to get the kids to take their lessons seriously when each page of every textbook is adorned with pictures of drug paraphernalia and/or erect penises. It's the same with their exercise books. In my day, you backed your book and if it got scribbled upon you had the back ripped off by Sir and you rebacked it. End of story.

Not any more.

Every exercise book is covered with graffiti. How have we *possibly* got to the stage where we allow the kids to deface everything to do with the subjects we are teaching? Can you imagine what would happen to a child in a remote African village school, where they value education, if he scrawled on text books?

Sensible ideas, such as each child having their own textbook, with their name on it (rather than that of some gangsta rapper), for which they will be expected to take some responsibility, are laughed out of court.

Most schools have a chronic shortage of textbooks, although there is money aplenty for interactive whiteboards, computers and any other hi tech stuff you can think of.

I look up. Shouldn't Mr Green be teaching his class, rather than standing in the prep room watching them through the glass in the connecting door? When I mention this, he beckons me over and steps aside for me to have a look. I can see his Year 9 group inside. Although Kerryann, Ashley-Jade and Colleen have their traditional bored expressions, Dwayne, Leon and Lewis seem to have discovered a sudden interest in the scientific world that I had certainly never noticed before.

One possible explanation is the new student teacher taking the lesson. She is very attractive, which is unusual in our school. There is a law, discovered many years ago, which states that the attractiveness of the teachers in a given school is proportional to the quality of that school. I have conducted much research into this phenomenon and found it to be inviolable. Student teachers obey the same law too, but only half the time because they do two placements. One is meant to be in a school that roughly matches their background; the other is meant to be quite different.

Unfortunately, her outfit is not suitable for school. Her top is pleasantly low-cut, a fact which is not lost on the boys. She is falling for the age old trick of being called over to look at somebody's work so he can look down her top and goggle at her cleavage as she bends down, while the boys nearby make rather rude gestures at her posterior. I grin ruefully; if I'm honest, I remember attempting the same stunt 25 years ago as a pupil.

Damnation! Dwayne has seen me gawping through the glass and is already nudging Lewis frantically and pointing at me. Act now. I push the door open and walk in. Mr Green nearly falls in after me: 'Good morning Miss…' I babble. Oh, bloody hell! I can't remember her surname.

'Can I er… just borrow the Year 9 textbooks for a minute? They're in a pile over here…' as I walk over to the book cupboard.

'This is a nice top. They shouldn't need much help with their work.'

God, did I really just say 'nice top?' I meant 'a nice group'.

I can feel my face reddening as I beat a hasty exit to the prep room, where I must endure the hushed sniggers of Green and the lab techs.

The power of positive drinking

I SUPPOSE I should have picked up on it sooner.

Perhaps I ought to have realised something was amiss when Leon fell off his chair and lay sprawling on the floor for a few seconds before getting up in slow motion and staggering around for a couple of seconds, to the delight of the class.

Or maybe when I actually spotted Declan drinking from the bottle of 'mineral water' and noticed that everyone else was watching him too.

Yes, I think, looking back, that these were important clues but, actually, I only realised that they were both completely drunk when they burst spontaneously into song, half an hour into the lesson.

Mr Phillips had the bright idea of allowing the kids to drink water in lessons because he had read that some academic said it improves learning.

I predicted that we would have endless water fights, and I have naturally been proven right, but I must confess it never occurred even to me that some bright sparks in Year 9 would decide that Mr Chalk's lesson would be far more interesting if the bottle were filled with vodka rather than Evian.

There is no chance of any work being done now; all I can really do is shove them both, none-too gently, out of the classroom, phone the duty member of SMT and wait while they don't turn up for twenty minutes.

After which the lesson is over and, like Leon and Declan, absolutely wasted.

It occurs to me that no doubt the Ed. Psych. will love this: she will be able to declare that Leon has 'turned to alcohol in a vain attempt to counter his feelings of low esteem'.

In fact, this sort of stuff trips off my tongue so easily nowadays that it frightens me. What also frightens me is that the kids think nothing of drinking huge amounts from an ever earlier age. A favourite trick is to nick a bottle of wine from home, the supermarket, or the local off licence and drink it at lunchtime. It makes the afternoon lessons so much more fun. It's worse in the evenings and at weekends, of course. Kids of 12 and 13 are regularly to be seen getting plastered in the park. Their parents either don't care – most of them can't wait to get shut of their kids – or are too far gone themselves to realise.

Schools are also awash with drugs. I was only saying recently how well Callum and Tyler were behaving in my lessons lately. They seemed, somehow, calmer... more mellow. This was before I discovered that they had been getting stoned before class.

Drugs – primarily cannabis, but occasionally harder things like ecstasy and amphetamines – are widely available in our school, as in society, because the penalties for dealing in or taking them are insufficient to deter people and the risk of being caught is extremely low. We should stop buggering about and face up to the fact that drugs are really dangerous and that there is no safe way of taking them, despite what some fashionable group of drug experts said when they came to give a talk in school last year. That pretty much confirmed my low opinion of academics. I have always believed that most of them simply make up their results (all the ones I knew at university certainly did), especially when they are looking for a new grant. It's a mystery to me that we must always embrace their ideas so enthusiastically when our own common sense is a much more reliable guide.

Of course, it's no use teachers telling the kids not to touch drugs; they have no regard whatever for what we think or say.

No, we need some decent weapons to fight the drug culture which is so pervasive in schools nowadays. For a start, a few celebrities or footballers, bullied into coming round schools and denouncing drugs, drink and cigarettes would be a good idea. At least they might get the kids' attention.

Drug testing should be compulsory in all schools and professions and done on a regular and random basis.

And miscreants should be dealt with harshly.

The 15th circle of hell, and poor little Liberty

THE SIGNS of late spring are all around us – there is a noticeable warming of the air, leaves are sprouting on the trees and, praise-be, the grass is starting to grow, which means it will soon cover the cigarette packets, sweet wrappers and vast numbers of doggy do-doos which litter the area.

I am feeling pleasantly relaxed: I went out to a nearby pub at lunchtime, as it is one of the lab techs' birthdays today, and I felt that I could do with a little light anaesthetic before reluctantly returning to face the afternoon lesson.

Well, if it works for the kids.

I know from bitter experience that they will be totally hyper after their chemical-soaked lunches and fizzy drinks. In fact, Dante didn't invent enough circles of hell to describe this horror: we'll be down around the 15th or 16th if the nutters have forgotten their Ritalin.

There are more than a few nutters in the Year 9 class I am covering for Mr Phillips, the Deputy Head, this afternoon.

There's supposed to be a support assistant, to watch my back, pass the ammo, that sort of thing, but she doesn't seem to have returned from the pub. She has to deal with these fruitcakes all day, so I can't say I blame her.

And they are on fine form, roaring outside the room, running up and down the corridor and generally being a nightmare. It takes me ten minutes to get them in a straight line. I try to calm them down and then let them into the room, standing in the doorway, as always, so that they have to pass through in single file. I am a control freak and proud of it. In fact, I'm smug about it.

I separate one or two known problem kids. They refuse to move, at first, but I throw Carl out of the room and the other three move places, albeit reluctantly.

I have placed some economics worksheets on each desk and written the work on the board.

It's not the easiest of lessons. Carl is being a pain outside and the others are being a pain inside. Dwayne is performing a traditional trick: he calls me over for help and then wafts his hand around as if I have bad breath. And, no, it's not because I've been to the pub, it's a common diversion. It amuses his simple-minded friends no end but I always stamp down hard on any minor rudeness, so I chuck him out as well.

Five minutes in the classroom and I've got two outside already.

Bloody hell.

Carl and Dwayne are making a racket, banging on the walls and throwing things in the corridor. I go outside. I know that one of them has a stepfather who is not allowed near his house so I casually mention that I might have a word with this freak if they don't behave.

Back inside, all hell is breaking loose. I go to the front and, as calmly as I can manage, tell them all to put everything down, fold their arms and listen carefully. Treating them like primary school children is surprisingly effective sometimes.

I am rhythmically moving my bunch of keys back and forth in front of me, hoping to hypnotise them. I try this all the time and am convinced that it works.

I explain how we have to keep quiet from now on or we will be staying behind at the end to make up the wasted time.

'No, no, no, put your hand down Shazney. Don't worry; I know I'm only allowed to keep you ten minutes. Stay calm.'

Eventually, they settle down and start not doing the economics questions.

My eye falls on Liberty. She's a slight little girl, who looks under-nourished to me. Her hair is lank and she always seems rather sad, with a faraway look in her eyes. It's a shame: she's a nice kid, and bright too, and she deserves a better home life.

Some of our children are seriously neglected.

They come to school without having had breakfast made for them, for instance. This is not because mum is 'deprived'. It's either because she's too stupid to understand the importance of a good meal first thing or because she is simply too lazy, and doesn't give a toss.

In the case of little Liberty, I suspect it's the latter.

Poor thing.

Write 100 lines: no modern idea in teaching ever works

I AM covering the second half of double science today. Science covers aren't as bad as you might think. You're not supposed to do experiments these days, which is a shame, since these are the only interesting bits of science, but the textbook usually has at least a few questions in it and the kids can design (ie draw) some experiments.

I am in the prep room, wasting my time as usual by trying to combat textbook graffiti. It has become a pet project of mine recently and I am worried that I might be becoming obsessive.

Outside in the corridor, I can hear Wesley, a Year 11 pupil, arguing with Mr Jones about his coursework. He has missed the deadline for handing it in and, for no obvious reason that I can discern, was given another week to complete it. Needless to say, he has still not finished the work and Mr Jones is telling him that tomorrow is absolutely his final chance.

There's an indignant screech from Wesley.

'Well, OK, then,' says Mr Jones. 'Wednesday, since you've got football after school today.'

This charade simply reinforces the idea that they can ignore all deadlines while we bend over backwards to accommodate them. As preparation for the world of work, it is absurd.

I glance at my watch and realise that it is nearly time. I put down the eraser pen that I was about to use to remove a textbook comment which suggests that Mr Chalk's parents were unmarried when he was born. It's strange how this term of abuse has survived when in an era when more than 50 per cent of our kids literally are bastards.

Moving over to the door between the prep room and the science lab, I carefully put my eye to the small hole in the poster that covers the glass panel in the door.

I know what I am looking for and it does not take me long. There's Dale, sitting in the back row, happily chewing his gum and staring into space with an air of bovine contentment. And what have we here? Next to him, Brett is rather furtively listening to his mp3 player. A few moments later, I see Chesney tearing out a page from his exercise book and scrunching it up, ready to throw at someone.

I leave the prep room and then knock loudly on the science lab next door. I enter and pause, looking all around the class, before walking casually over to Mr Jones, who has been covering the first period, to a satisfying chorus of groans and protestations. A couple of pencils are thrown down and arms are folded.

Excellent.

If I wanted to be popular with children I would have become a circus clown.

Mr Jones glances at his watch and gives me a grateful look. It's about five minutes before the interval, and he clearly cannot wait to be out of here. He shows me what they are doing and I pretend to take interest. He assures me that they are no problem at all. (He obviously doesn't realise that I've been listening to the near riot for the last half hour.)

I need to make a clean break between the two halves of the lesson, otherwise they will carry on being a nightmare. I adopt my favourite 'talking to the class' position, standing in front of my desk but leaning slightly back on it with my arms folded. One time I did this, the desk slid backwards and I nearly broke my neck, which wasn't great.

I tell them to put everything down and look at me. I have no idea why they should want to look at me, but it gives them something to do and stops them casting around for mischief.

I then tell Dale to put his gum in the bin. He is absolutely astounded – am I psychic, or what? – and obeys without the usual protestations of innocence. I then tell Chesney to put the piece of paper which he is concealing in his right hand in the bin too.

I stare hard at them and try to conceal my own amazement when two others get up and empty their mouths into the wastepaper bin. (I hadn't spotted them at all). I save the best till last, by cocking one ear slightly and then sternly announcing that whoever has an mp3 player (they get all stroppy nowadays if you refer to them as Walkmans, and I'm trying to avoid any unnecessary arguments) had better put it away. Two kids do, neither of them Brett. A further glare, and he complies also, slightly disconcerted. Maybe my mum *was* a gypsy.

I tell them to start the questions on page 51, having further established my reputation as an all-seeing, all-hearing psychopath.

However, my joy is short-lived as one half of the class groans 'It's too easy, this work!' and the other half frowns with concentration, desperately trying to work out what the strange squiggles on the page could mean. Their traditional cry of 'I don't geddit!' soon fills the air.

I realise that I am facing that nightmare of nightmares, the mixed ability group.

Rather than 'set' the kids, the Head has decided that the Year 7 and Year 8 classes should be Mixed Ability. He believes that the children should not be 'labelled' (whatever this means). The Head is a numb-skull.

So while Alex, Becky and Jonathan race through the work and finish it in five minutes flat and then get bored, Dale, Chesney and Damon cannot even read the instructions.

Honest teachers will admit that we can all teach a lesson for a narrow band of abilities but that, as the range of abilities in the class grows, the lesson becomes less and less effective.

As I wander around trying to help, I reflect that, like most great ideas, this came from academics who would not dream of setting foot inside a school like ours.

And why would it? Imagine if you decided to go skiing for the first time this winter and discovered that the ski school had adopted a policy of mixed-ability teaching? I can just hear Pierre the Instructor now: 'Mais oui, le mixed ability teaching c'est bon!' as he leads the beginners and advanced skiers alike in one group over an icy cliff.

Well, at least you can't say that you have been labelled as less capable than the other skiers and I'm sure your self-esteem will not have been damaged (even if we can't say the same for your limbs).

This reminds me of a few other 'Great Ideas from Academics'. Teaching seems to attract them – I don't know why.

Firstly, 'Group Work'.

Because I am a dull traditionalist, I always sit the children in neat rows facing the board. They can all see you and the board and you can see them scratching rude words into the surface of their desks. However, more progressive teachers delight in 'group work', where the kids sit in little groups and 'work on problem-solving together'. You can imagine exactly what happens and it certainly isn't problem *solving*.

Second, the death of rote-learning.

We knew how to teach children a thousand years ago. Show them how to do something, repeat it lots of times, get them to call out their answers and see who's not got it yet. It isn't particularly difficult, and it works. I'm the proof – I rote-learned *everything* in mathematics up to A level and I did very well, thank you, as did lots of other kids.

No group work, no posters, no fancy methods.

OK, I haven't a clue how calculus works but, at my level, that doesn't matter, I don't need to. I can do it, that's the important thing. I don't know how my car works either but I manage to drive it without too many problems.

If I could have the traditional three wishes, the first would be for teachers, *en masse* across the country, to forget all the nonsense they were taught on PGCE and use their common sense: for God's sake, let's get back to traditional methods before it's too late. I'm not telling you what the other two wishes would be.

With a sudden bump I am returned to earth and the reality of this Year 8 science group. Mary has done all the questions on the page and is writing a letter. Perhaps it is to the Head, demanding immediate setting. Sam is playing with his mobile phone and Ashley is banging his head repeatedly against his desk to the amusement of Billie-Jo.

Write down 100 times: *No modern idea in teaching has ever worked.*

A bee, and the descent into gibberish

THERE IS a lot of debate at the moment about the pros and cons of supply work being done by unqualified teachers. I rarely manage to teach anything at all in the subject that I am qualified to teach (maths). In fact, I often cover lessons for subjects that I haven't even got an O Level in because of the way the cover timetable has to be organised. I may be an extreme case, but the general picture is repeated across the country. In 2004, 40% of physics lessons in our schools were taught by someone without a degree in the subject, which is rather shocking.

Having said that, 90% of my job could be done equally well (that is to say, not particularly well at all) by someone with no qualifications whatsoever and in all my time in our school I cannot recall ever being asked a question that I could not answer. It's different at a school like St John's: the pupils there really need their teacher to have a deep knowledge of the subject, not just a vague familiarity with it.

Anyway, enough pointless daydreaming. Let's get back to the nightmare in hand.

I'm covering for Miss Keebles, the new English Teacher. She is in her first year of teaching – she only looks about 14 – and is massively enthusiastic about every aspect of teaching. I think she might be completely mad. She was given the job by virtue of being the only applicant. Miss Simpson interviewed her, as it was felt that only a good actor would be able to hide the fact that we were in dire straits and would have taken Jack the Ripper if push came to shove. When Miss Keebles was offered the job – about 30 seconds after the interview had finished – she asked for a couple of days to make up her mind. You could almost hear the entire English Department shouting 'For God's sake, woman! Can't you see we're desperate?'

The classroom is so quiet and peaceful before the kids arrive. I am sitting in the room trying to make sense of the note she left in my pigeonhole about the lesson.

I can understand bits of it, but struggle with 'Hiya' which I mistake, at first, for 'hymn'. 'Cul8er' had me flummoxed for a while, as did 'afaik' and 'bfn' (for the terminally elderly, these translate as 'see you later', 'as far as I know' and 'bye for now'). Still, at least she's made the effort; there are even a few smiling faces dotted around for good measure.

As I crumple the note and lob it into the bin, I reflect that it's sad that we have become so desperate that we can employ teachers, in any subject, who can't even be bothered to write letters in proper English. People say that grammar isn't important, and that you don't need it to pass your degree. That's true, but only because it is marked by someone who doesn't have a clue about grammar either. I know that all languages evolve, but if you just throw away all the rules overnight then they descend rapidly into gibberish. Even I understand that and I'm just a maths teacher.

Tyler hands me a note as he comes in.

'Shouldn't you have given this to your form teacher, Tyler?' I enquire.

'Yes, but he's away and nobody came to register us.'

I look at the note. It offers an explanation for his recent absences, mentioning 'are Tylers bad stumock'. I will not repeat the mistake I made several years ago when I phoned up Mrs Boggs to tell her that her son had been truanting again and forging sick notes into the bargain. I explained that I knew it was a fake because his poor writing and spelling gave the game away, and read out a couple of examples for her amusement. That was when she suddenly remembered that she had written the note herself, a few days previously.

Miss Keebles wants us to do a 'mind map'. The only reason I have the faintest idea what that means is because the support assistant who is helping some of the drongos has told me that it is the new word for 'brainstorm'.

'So why don't we just say brainstorm, then?'

'Because it is offensive to epileptics.'

'Do we have any epileptics to offend?'

'Well, er... no.'

I can't help but think that if half the time and effort spent thinking up new words was actually spent teaching kids how to spell and punctuate using the words we've already got (after all, the English language is not exactly short of them) we might not be in the mess we're in now.

Anyway, we soon settle down to the easy task of drawing a few lines and writing the odd word between them. At least, we do this until a bee flies through the open window and reduces the class to screaming madness.

Have kids always been this scared of bees? I mean, 14-year-old boys shrieking in terror, girls hiding under their desks? Do they think it's a miniature alien or something?

The support assistant frantically checks her list, to see if anybody suffers deadly allergies to bee stings. Meanwhile, I simply open the door and it flies out harmlessly into the corridor. A few minutes later, I am rewarded with the sounds of screaming from next door.

I sack the mind map stuff after half an hour and write down a few essay titles on the board. Ignoring the groans at the word 'essay', I get them to suggest a few ideas for each one and note them down on the back page of their books. Next lesson we will write a story and then draw a picture illustrating it. Proper English, in my opinion.

And this lot certainly need to be teached proper English!

Standards, both written and spoken, are unbelievably poor. Years ago, people left school at the age of twelve able to read and write to a standard that would be about average in a 16-year-old today (and they were taught in classes of up to 100 pupils). That is the progress we have made in the last 80 years.

To be honest, it's not just the spelling and punctuation that is missing. There's never any logical structure or argument. Points are made that are simply not relevant to what has just been said or refer to something that I do not know about.

Maybe I'm just losing my marbles and can't understand them.

A mental note on stab-proof vests

I LOOK through my pigeonhole to see what nonsense has landed in it this week.

What have we here? The new school policy on Positive Assessment.

This is an absolute joke. It means you can only say nice things about a kid.

For example, you write, 'Wayne does his best work under close supervision', when what you really mean is, 'Wayne is a lazy, bone-idle lump who will not do a stroke of work unless you beat him'.

Here is a note from SMT. It says that they are very worried about the continuing rise in staff absences. Then it goes on to say that they are not going to do anything about it. I actually laugh out loud, and stifle it quickly as a few staff members look up in surprise. Like most schools, we are very sensitive about this topic; we refuse to pin up details of who is always off or reward those who are always in.

There is a yellow note concerning the recent problems on the school buses.

Apparently, there have been complaints from people because the kids are spitting out of the windows at them as the bus drives past. Lovely! Actually, spare a thought for the driver of the school bus. Day after day, he endures a barrage of abuse and foul language from the kids. Can you imagine a more thankless job? Hang on a minute, I think I can... teaching!

It's Your Time You're Wasting

Another note, this one on nice pink paper, reminds us that this Friday is 'NON UNIFORM DAY.' We have one of these every so often. It's an excuse for the kids to dress up like rappers or prostitutes and generally cause mayhem. They are supposed to donate 50p for the privilege, but most won't and nothing will be done about that either. A few well-meaning but foolish staff will wear some sort of fancy dress. I remember this was parodied very successfully in an episode of the amusing TV comedy *The Office*.

Next are the conclusions of the 'Working Group' set up to improve the school's image. They have come to the conclusion that we need to have a school motto. It will be displayed above the Main Entrance and on all school notepaper. Most schools have some sort of motto – good schools tend to have theirs written in Latin, the rest have some sort of sickly, PC collection of random words such as 'Striving for Excellence' or 'Moving Forward Together'. As I crumple yet another sheet of wasted paper and chuck it in the bin, I can't help but think that we should be a bit more realistic: how does 'Striving for 50% Attendance' sound? Or maybe 'Chew Gum and Swear'?

There is also a letter announcing that someone is coming from Downtown University to talk to the kids about further education. In my opinion, far too many kids go to university nowadays. It's only worthwhile if you are bright, say in the top 10 to 20%, and you are intending to study a genuine, academic subject (that is, not media studies, leisure centre management or advanced knitting). What on earth is the point in encouraging kids to load themselves down with debts of twenty grand while doing a degree whose title makes employers double up with laughter? The current government wants 50% of students to go to university and is marching, relentlessly and unthinkingly towards that target. Already, the consequences are becoming clear; almost all degree courses are objectively easier now than they were a decade ago, as the universities drop their pass mark to cope with the influx of unsuitable students (many of whom drop out before graduating anyway). This will only devalue the degree further.

Am I alone in suspecting that the real purpose of all this is to keep our young adults off the unemployment register?

I sit down with my cup of tea and open a newspaper.

But my ears prick up; apparently a child has been quite badly beaten up in the school. Could it be that one of my colleagues has finally snapped? Ah, no. It sounds as though one of the fifth-formers is to blame. The level of violence in our schools is frightening, both in its frequency and its severity, and is getting worse on both counts. You may think that I am exaggerating, for dramatic effect. If so, take a moment to consider the following three cases (all of which happened during October and November, 2005, as I was tackling this mammoth undertaking).

Shanni Naylor was slashed across the face by another 12-year-old girl, who used the blade from a pencil sharpener in the attack in Sheffield. Shanni will probably be scarred for life.

Natasha Jackman, aged 15, was attacked with a pair of scissors at her school in Surrey.

Jade Headleand, another 12-year-old, was attacked by another girl with a cigarette lighter. Her face was badly burned in the incident.

As I sip my tea and listen to the chatter, I wonder at the factors which combine to generate the circumstances where these sorts of crimes can take place in a school? I know that generalisation is foolish, and that it's wrong to use these individual cases as an excuse to get on my soapbox, but saying one thing and doing another is one of the quickest ways to make SMT, so here goes. In cases such as these (I make clear I am not talking about the specific cases themselves because the details available to me are incomplete):

1) The parents of the perpetrator are almost certainly separated from each other (if they were ever together).
2) They have made no effort to teach their child discipline, respect or even how to interact with their peers.
3) Teachers in the school concerned are not being firm on discipline.

   Many have been brainwashed by PGCE; the newer among them probably lack the confidence to take firm action and will keep quiet about behavioural problems which they may feel are their fault. This might well be partly true, but there should be no shame in asking for advice or help.
4) The SMT will be weak and will not back up the teachers who are firm.

It will not take a strong line on incidents reported by teachers, it will be reluctant to exclude, reluctant to stand up to parents and reluctant to insist on police involvement and prosecution.

5) The local LEA will be more concerned with employing advisors whose job it is to irritate the teachers on training days, than with supporting schools who try to get rid of badly-behaved pupils. It will not have learned the lesson that it is no use making schools jump through 20 hoops when they want to exclude a drug dealer or violent kid.

6) The local police force will be swamped with paperwork. Many officers do not want anything to do with crime; it takes too long to fill out all the various forms and the outcome simply doesn't justify the effort. Additionally, arresting kids is a sure fire way of getting complaints made about you, which will be thoroughly and painstakingly investigated and which will hinder your promotion chances.

7) Everyone involved knows that the government and its legal system simply refuses to punish criminals.

I finish my tea and slope off to a drama cover, making a mental note to look at the prices of stab-proof vests.

We are not used to seeing young girls with scarred faces, the victims of violent assaults inside their schools.

We find it shocking and perplexing.

Perhaps we will find it less so, the more often it happens.

I can never resist a challenge

FOR THE 500th time, the classroom door has been left unlocked so the Year 9 group are running around inside.

They have broken a chair and are as high as kites, so it takes a good ten minutes to get everyone outside and vaguely calmed down. Darren then destroys all my efforts by treating us to his party piece –

dancing around, like some half-witted rap star, jabbing his finger in the air to the amusement of the group. I resist the strong temptation to club him over the head with a chair leg that is lying alone on the carpet and instead start again the process of quietening them down. I don't care how long it takes; there's no way I'm letting them in to someone else's room when they're like this. Although we're close to Easter, it's turned cold and it's been snowing for a couple of hours, which means the kids are absolutely hyper (don't ask me why).

Ages after the lesson should have begun, we finally go in and sit down.

I get them started on the work and then notice that Declan is reading a magazine under his desk. I couldn't really care less, but several others have seen him and it is not the sort of magazine I would show my mother. I manoeuvre myself into position, edging closer but facing away from him, pretending to be helping Janet with her work. Then, like a trapdoor spider, I pounce; the magazine – *Big Ones* – is in my hand and I'm away from Declan before he has time to notice. He shrieks and flails around. I quickly reassure him before he gets too agitated: 'Sorry Declan, I'll give it back to you at the end of the lesson.'

No I won't, I'll burn it or shred it. I'm a classroom kleptomaniac. I take everything I can get my hands on. And I never *ask* anyone to hand anything over, as I don't like to put myself into a position where they can refuse; I simply take it, while apologising profusely. If they freak out, I just chuck whatever I've got into the corridor and them with it.

As the lesson drags inexorably on, Shazney suddenly asks me 'Sir, How much do you earn?'

'£100,000 per year,' I reply, in a matter-of-fact way and wearing my most serious expression.

There are cries of disbelief.

'No way! Mr Wilkinson said he gets £30,000!'

I explain how Mr Wilkinson is simply being modest and that we all get paid around £100,000 because nobody else will work in schools like this.

They look suitably impressed, and treat me with a new respect for a moment or two, before they forget what they've just been told.

It all corresponds with my theory that there are only two things that modern kids respect: money and appearance. The simple fact of being an authority figure doesn't wash these days, a general problem shared with teachers by the police, doctors, nurses, firemen and pretty much anyone else who we once looked up to.

Lewis is showing the magazine-less Declan his new trainers. This is a current bugbear of mine. Like the Government, our SMT comes up with endless new ideas to combat problems but has no real plan on how to actually carry them out and deal with the consequences. Any fool can come up with lots of ideas, it's working out the answers to all the 'what ifs' and 'how do we' questions that is difficult (and therefore not attempted). Recently they have decided to clamp down on kids wearing trainers in school. I'm all for clamping down on anything and in principle this is fine. But in practice it's a nightmare, because there is no coherent plan laying down what will happen if a pupil refuses to change his shoes, or – quite likely – simply doesn't have any others.

The kids know this and more and more of them have actually started flouting the prohibition. I overhear Lewis boast that he is 'not taking them off for no one'.

Well, I can never resist a challenge.

I look over.

'Gosh, they're smart trainers, Lewis; I wish I had some like that myself.'

The bait is cast, and he shows them off in all their garish splendour. They are absolutely foul – white with some sort of gold braid. They even seem to have lights of some description on them. I ask him for a closer look at the lighting facility and he passes me one to examine. One fluid movement of my arm and – whoops! – there it goes, out of the window and into the snow covering the playground below.

With a roar of fury, and various promises of what dad is going to do, off he hops to find it.

The rest of the class think it is hilarious and I even feel a bit guilty for ten seconds or so. It's worked, though; I can see several kids furtively changing their footwear underneath their desks.

There's only a few minutes left and I close all the windows, as we don't want to hear Lewis's foul language as he searches for his white shoe in the drifts outside.

When the lesson ends, I tell Declan that he can have his magazine at lunchtime. When he returns at the start of lunchtime to collect it, I regretfully tell him that I thought he had forgotten it, so I have posted it home to his mother. The look on his face is priceless.

Lewis's funny-looking father arrives just as I am leaving.

No doubt Mr Morris will be writing me a note tomorrow.

Benefits culture, and why this makes a teacher's life a misery

AS A teacher, my job – obviously – is to try to assist in the education of those youngsters who are unfortunate enough to spend time in front of a worthy plodder like me.

Some readers might be forgiven, then, for believing that my interest in these children ought to begin and end in the classroom.

If we lived in a vacuum, that would be the case. But we don't; the lives our pupils lead away from school directly affect their academic performance, which is why I (along with many other teachers) bother myself with matters like the family lives of my kids, the areas they live in and their homes (where they are supposed to complete their homework and coursework, after all).

Of course, you'll be aware that the home lives of many of the pupils at St Jude's are shambolic, unstructured affairs, full of verbal and physical violence and the unthinking neglect of uncaring parents.

Once upon a time, as a naïve and well-meaning innocent, I was full of explanations and even excuses for this. But after having observed many of these families at close quarters for many years, I now believe I have at least a partial explanation: it's down to our benefits culture.

It seems to me that, a few toffs apart, and allowing for exceptions, there are two broad classes in Britain now: middle class, which is everyone who works, and underclass, which is everyone who doesn't.

The underclass survives on benefits and the proceeds of crime.

Many badly-behaved pupils come from families on benefits; these are poorer than the average UK family. That much is undisputed.

Poverty is entirely relative, however.

These families all have shelter, clean water and sufficient food (years ago, the poorest people in Britain died of malnutrition; now many of them are morbidly obese). This puts them well into the top half of the world, wealth-wise, straight away.

In fact, their housing is all warm and dry. They have a variety of food and drink extending far beyond the mere essentials. They have television and radio and spare money with which to buy treats for themselves. Importantly, they have unlimited access to opportunities to learn, and thereby improve themselves and their lot. There is free education until the age of 18. There is a public library two miles away in central Downtown which has 50,000 books, none of which costs a penny to borrow, and free internet access. By the way, two miles takes the average adult of average fitness 35 minutes to walk. All of this brings them into the top 20% of the world's population.

Beyond that, in many cases, these families possess genuine luxury items. Satellite TV, with its diet of 1,000 channels of drivel, is commonplace. Often both parents smoke and they are regular bingo players at the Cherry Tree Social Club. They have a fridge-freezer groaning with unhealthy things from Mr Koshushko's Convenience Shop. They consume vast quantities of illegally-imported lager. They wear ostentatious jewellery and their houses are filled with flashy electronic consumables.

In terms of their material position, then, they are in the top one or two per cent of the world's population.

To call this 'poverty' is grossly to insult those who live in mean shelters, thirsty and hungry, all over the world.

The modern British underclass has a far higher standard of living than I did as a student, when I often had no heating, could scarcely afford to drink at weekends and struggled by with just the BBC and ITV on the box. I don't remember stealing, vandalising property or spraying graffiti on everything in sight, while hiding behind excuses.

Let's get one thing straight: when gangs of youths throw stones at passing cars, shout abuse at innocent people going about their daily business or beat up random passers-by, they are not doing it because 'there is nothing for young people to do'; they are doing it because it is fun and, in modern day, punishment-free Britain, there is no reason for them not to.

So, despite the regular suggestion that they are deprived, the families of my pupils want for very little.

One thing most of them do lack is 'get up and go.' Because they are relatively comfortable, they have no drive to better themselves through learning and see no value in work for its own sake. They certainly see no value in education.

The unemployment figures are down, the government regularly tells us.

Hmmm. In 1983, unemployment stood at three million, with a further 400,000 on sickness benefit. At the beginning of 2006, we have around a million unemployed and 2.7 million on sickness benefit.

Technically, then, the government is not lying. The punters are happy, too: it suits them to receive sickness benefit rather than unemployment benefit because you get more money and you don't have to get up early and sign on once a fortnight. Many GPs of my acquaintance tell tales of patients demanding to be signed off 'sick'. Even when there is nothing obviously wrong with these people few doctors will argue, as *The Times* discovered recently, when it sent an undercover reporter round some GPs in Birmingham; the medics simply sign them off to avoid a confrontation.

So: same meat, different gravy.

This is the benefits culture – 40 years of people, families, and whole housing estates, increasingly unwilling, even unable, to work.

It is a vicious circle, of course. Once you have been unemployed or signed off sick for a long period of time, no employer will touch you. Once a family gets used to the benefits lifestyle, they find it too difficult to break out. The culture of laziness is endemic.

The relevance of this to me, as a teacher, is obvious.

Many of the children I teach are growing up to follow the same path as their parents. They see no value in education, because they either do not want to improve their lives or are too lazy to do so. Instead, they spend their lives ruining other peoples' opportunities.

Dealing with the worst 10% of pupils takes up most of my school's resources.

In later life, these same people will go on to take up most of society's resources.

I could write their names on a piece of paper now, together with predictions as to their outcomes; if we looked at it in 10 years' time, I would be hailed as a new Nostradamus. But in truth I simply see what we all see; it's just that so many look the other way.

The chemical was unfortunately harmless

WHILE WALKING along the second floor corridor, on my way to the peace and tranquillity of the prep room, I hear the sudden rush of footsteps behind me, followed by the Ashley's shriek as he slaps me on the back. Turning round just in front of me he shouts 'How are yer Mr Chalk – my mate!'

This kid is a complete nutcase. I threw him out of my lesson yesterday, but it's quite clear that he has completely forgotten the episode. At 13 years of age, he is capable of very little but playing around. It terrifies me to think that he will legally be able to drive in just four years' time. Mind you, I don't suppose the legality of the situation has much bearing on it. He probably does already. Visions of him cheerfully running me over in a stolen motor flash through my head. The last thing I'd hear would be the whump-whump-whump of some awful rap rubbish; how bad would that be?

We have so many kids like him in this place that I actually run out of words to describe them over the course of a day. I long ago gave up assigning any value to what they come out with. Mostly, they just open their mouths and words fall out. There is no thought involved whatsoever.

I go in, sit down in my usual place between the two ladies and start to listen to the tale of the mother who is claiming against the school for injuries supposedly sustained by her child in Mr Green's lesson.

Apparently, while doing an experiment, one of the kids had asked him what to do next. He enquired whether the child had measured out 10 grammes of a chemical and the child said, 'Yes. What do I do now?'

Mr Green told him to heat it up and then watched in utter amazement as the child popped the sample into his mouth and swallowed it.

It turns out the simpleton thought Mr Green had said, 'Eat it up.'

Mr Green called an ambulance and the child was taken to hospital, from where he was released a few hours later. (The chemical was unfortunately harmless.)

Rather than the note of thanks he had been naïvely expecting, Mr Green then received a solicitor's letter.

Now the LEA has sent him further correspondence indicating that it is going to settle out of court, even though it is virtually certain that there was no real negligence involved. This is a common policy. We get 30 to 40 claims every year against the school, nearly all of them nonsense. Parents are keen to try to sue the school because it costs nothing and they might get something in return. It's another simple cost vs benefit calculation and I'm amazed we don't get more of them trying it on.

No sooner have we mentioned the man than he arrives, telling me cheerfully to clear off because the desk I'm sitting at is reserved for 'real teachers.' I point out that at least I haven't poisoned any of my pupils and move to another one so that he can do his marking while eating his lunch.

Marking isn't something I do a great deal of any more because I'm not paid to do it and, anyway, there's not a lot to mark. However, it is a task proper teachers still face from time to time and they are constantly being told new ways of doing it. Long ago, when it was part of my life, I just used to write 'Excellent', 'Very good' and so on, down to 'Absolute rubbish, do again.' (On one occasion I wrote

'CRAP!' in big letters without thinking, across one pupil's work. I received no complaint whatsoever. Which says as much about our pupils and their parents as it does about me.)

These days, however, marking has to 'emphasize the positive aspects', another bit of educationalist-speak, so there is a whole plethora of acceptable comments and 'CRAP!' is not one of them.

It would appear, though, that Mr Green is as blissfully unaware of this as he is with most modern aspects of teaching. He has just ripped out the page from Declan's book and declared that he could train his dog to produce better work.

My mobile rings and I answer it, only to discover that it is an attempt by a rival phone company to sell me a new tariff. I put on a slightly agitated voice and reply: 'Hang on! I can't hear you properly up here, I'll just climb down' and then let out a blood-curdling scream, followed by a couple of low moans. Then I press the red button. I quite like it when people cold call. I always show great interest in whatever they are selling, asking for details of the various options, and then ask them what their home address is, because we've got on so well and I'd like to come round sometime for a chat and a cup of tea because I don't have many friends. They usually hang up at that point, occasionally with an abusive comment or two. I have always loved the simple pleasures in life: eating a nice meal, sitting in the sunshine, ignoring the alarm clock on a dark winter's morning. Best of all, I love it when two or more items of junk mail arrive through my letterbox. The kick I get out of opening them, finding the prepaid return envelopes and stuffing each full of the other's promotions before sending them back… it's almost second to none.

Mr Green lets slip that he is thinking of applying for a job at a local private school. Some state-employed teachers are quite vocal in their opposition to private education. Personally, I'd say that if you can afford to send your kids to one – and it's a good one, not all of them are – then it's money well-spent, unless you are very lucky in where you live. People called Oliver, Josh and Anabella go to private schools and it sounds jolly nice.

Teachers only work in schools like ours for one of two reasons:

1) They can't get a job anywhere else.

2) They believe that they can improve the chances of the kids.

I always think the latter kind of teachers are very noble. After a bit, though, they usually go mad, or quit with stress, or become deeply cynical about everything.

Over-bearing, over-authoritative and rigid in my approach

THE GREAT day arrives. We have spent weeks preparing our attempt to pull the wool over the eyes of the Ofsted Inspection Team.

All sorts of policies and action-plans are in place, whether or not they work or even have any meaning. I have passed on my suggestion of a Behaviour Improvement Policy whose targets should be: Clear, Realistic, Achievable and Permanent. If it's adopted I'm hoping the Head will shorten it to an acronym.

A couple of miniature bay trees have appeared outside the school entrance. The whole school has been half-cleaned. The caretaker has been woken up and all the bits of wood fixing the Temporary Classrooms have been given a new coat of paint.

In short, we have done everything except address any of our real problems.

I predict we will fail miserably, unless the Inspectors are completely stupid.

If we do badly, we may well become a 'Failing school' (and if we're not failing our pupils things must really be bad) and have to be inspected more frequently or even closed and reopened under a different name. All the teachers would then have to reapply for their jobs (don't worry on their account, they'll be fine: I can't really see anyone else wanting them).

Reopening under a new name would be great. I wonder if they let the teachers decide what it should be. I can certainly think of a few ideas. We would get a new Head, who would be given all sorts of emergency powers to chuck out all the bad kids and send them to other schools in the area. That would make us popular locally. You'll often hear on the news how a heroic new super-Head has managed to turn a failing school around. What is rarely mentioned is that he or she will usually have negotiated *carte blanche* to exclude any troublesome pupils; otherwise there's not a damn thing they or anyone else will be able to do.

Obviously, we need school inspections. Firstly, we need to know how schools are doing. Secondly, we need to provide employment for thousands of ex-teachers, who would much rather check up on how other teachers are doing than risk doing any teaching themselves.

But let's be serious about them: make them unannounced, so that these busybodies can see what really happens, how the kids really behave and how (in)competent everyone really is. Under the current system, a school gets lots of notice of an inspection which gives the staff time to put on a great show. Or to commit fraud, as you might term it. What a nonsensical idea this is.

While I was covering French today, one of the inspectors came into my lesson. He was a mild, slightly nervous-looking man in his mid-fifties, with thin, grey hair and a nice, dark suit. I'm not sure if he was supposed to be there, given that I'm on supply, but I didn't have a problem with it. They might as well see the full horror of what goes on here.

I thought it all went quite well, actually; the kids didn't play up to him as much as I'd expected. They seemed to like him a lot, especially when he put on a tape of soothing music for them to listen to. I quite enjoyed this too.

Afterwards he gave me a debrief (see, I know all the terms already).

He started by telling me that I was over-bearing, over-authoritative and too rigid in my approach to seating and behaviour.

I thanked him; it's nice to get a bit of praise now and again.

He noted that I had spent five minutes lining the kids up outside (though he called them 'students'), five minutes sitting them down and a further five minutes getting them to write down the title and the date and then underline them.

I thanked him again, and was about to enquire as to whether I might apply for some sort of pay rise when he continued by saying that he was very disappointed in the lesson content, which apparently did not stretch the pupils sufficiently.

They had been drawing pictures of various objects and writing the word next to them. This was in English, admittedly, but if they had worked a bit quicker and got on to the next bit they would have started looking the word up in their dictionaries and writing it down in French. If that isn't stretching them, then I don't know what is. They really struggle with the dictionaries and constantly announce that the word is not listed, as they cannot spell and have no perseverance.

He was also concerned about my knowledge of the language. I had to admit that my degree was in another subject, but I said I had been to France quite a few times on holiday and loved the food, especially the pasta and the pizzas cooked in those proper wood-burning ovens. He seemed a bit puzzled, but eventually praised me for my efforts in what must be a difficult subject for me. He finished by urging me to raise my expectations of the children. He then went to leave, remembered his cassette recorder and discovered that one of the kids had nicked it.

After lunch, he went into Mme Dupont's lesson and was much happier, apparently. He told her that she had an excellent grasp of the language and that her accent was first rate. He never seemed to notice that she only spoke about six words of English.

Meanwhile, I meet up with Mr Green in the prep room. I am loafing about, finishing off a cup of coffee that the lab techs have made for me in return for labelling a few test tubes.

All over the school there is still a frantic hum of activity, with teachers rushing around looking for equipment for their next lesson or just generally panicking, hoping they won't be singled out by the Ofsted lot. For the thousandth time, I thank my lucky stars that I have given up regular teaching. I'm able to relax, safe in the knowledge that none of it matters in the slightest.

Mr Green exhales loudly and informs me that the inspector has told him that his lesson had 'great contextual relevancy'. He had to admit, however, that he didn't know whether this was good or bad. He was disappointed to hear of shortcomings in his 'Related Learning Objectives' and I wished him a speedy recovery. Mind you, he was delighted to be praised for involving all the children in his lesson. He wondered if the inspector had thought he might just teach half the group.

I tell him my latest plan: I've been surfing the internet and have found a place where I can purchase a gown and mortar board. I have had the sudden desire to be a Victorian Teacher and, as far as I know, nothing in the school rules precludes me from dressing in this way. Discipline problems will be a thing of the past when my supply of canes arrives.

He is suitably impressed and nods sagely. I can see he's on the verge of asking me to send off for two sets.

None of this is to say that I don't want to embrace modern trendy teaching methods. Just because telling kids how to do something and then getting them to do it was good enough for the likes of Galileo, Newton and Einstein, that doesn't mean it will do for Bradley, Coyne and Dwayne. In fact, I outline to Mr Green and the Techs a new scheme all of my own. In order to Facilitate Memory Retention Skills, Give Experience of Public Speaking and Build Self Esteem, first thing each day each child will come out to the front and be quizzed on his or her multiplication tables. The one who gets the most sums wrong will be allowed to stand in the corner on a small box wearing white conical hat with the capital letter 'D' written on it.

We all agree that this ought to impress the Ofsted people and the Techs make more coffee.

Wishing I had a cattle prod handy

THE WORST of all possible worlds. I am covering for Mr Jones and we have been moved, into Mr Blunt's room. The reason for this is that we have just had a wet break (it's tipping down, so no-one's allowed outside in case they die of rain) and a group of kids somehow got into Jones' classroom and completely wrecked it. There is not time to clear up the mess so we have moved. I am becoming more and more convinced that someone has copied a key somehow. I will have to ask class snitch later.

We tramp across the school, the kids causing havoc and hysterical mayhem as we go, me wishing I had a cattle prod handy. As I approach Mr Blunt's room with my motley band of Year 8s, however, I notice the calming effect that proximity to the great man has on them. Even though his room is clearly empty, they are standing in a reasonably straight line, most have got rid of their chewing gum and some have even stopped talking (except for Davina, who is enthusiastically telling her friend that Mr Blunt is a 'right bastard'). This is a proud moment for any decent teacher: to be acknowledged as a 'Right Bastard' is to be praised indeed. Right Bastards do not court popularity; they demand, and receive, respect.

I try the key that I have been given, but to no avail. I examine it closely, while trying to ignore the whoops from my crowd. The bloody key is quite clearly labelled 'B1', but it doesn't work.

I get Nathan to run to the school office for another one.

While we await his return – me fretting and hoping, them screaming and bouncing around – Mr Rogers emerges from the storeroom next door. He mutters darkly to the group and they quieten down a little. He brandishes a huge bunch of keys, selects one and, to my surprise, opens the door. He acknowledges my thanks with more incomprehensible mumbling.

The room is immaculate, spotlessly clean, and every desk is laid out with military precision. Along one side of the room are various old maps, and some work done by his classes. There is no writing on any desk; I expected nothing else. I know that he makes the naughty children clean them after school each day. This is a great trick that I've employed myself occasionally; to be honest, almost all the useful things I have ever learned about teaching (or, more accurately, crowd control) I have learned from Mr Blunt and a similar character, Mrs Peters, at another school.

Nothing has been vandalised at all. His own desk at the front is bare and his store room is double-locked to safeguard it from children and supply teachers.

He has an amazing collection of contraband that he has confiscated over the years hidden in a locked box at the back of his cupboard.

First of all I just let them look in through the open doorway in small groups to admire a room like no other. Then, after several more warnings, I let the brats in one by one, settle them down and remind them to treat Mr Blunt's room as if it was their own. Aaaargggh! Scrub that! Don't treat it as if it was your own, treat it like you'll be summarily executed if you make a mess of it.

Mr Jones is off with stress today; he was assaulted by a pupil yesterday. Apparently, Sean from his bottom set in Year 11 punched him after he tried to chuck him out. I think back to when I took that group last week and managed to bore them into submission. Sean is quite a lively character but he is more nuts than malevolent. Like 90% of the kids, on a one-to-one basis, or in a group of three or four, he is OK. He just isn't suitable for a standard school. Apparently, the police have not been involved. I cannot believe this. If the little tyke threw a single punch at me I would go straight to the police and camp there until they prosecuted him.

Actually, I have discreetly spread a little story around the school over the years and it has passed into folklore. I occasionally refer to a man called 'Jason'. I have even made up a card from him and stuck it on my classroom wall. He punched me while he was a pupil here, the story goes, and I had him sent to jail because I knew the judge. He is still there, seven years on, but is now a reformed character. Why, he even sent me this card asking for forgiveness, revealing how awful it is in his prison and confessing that he now wishes he had behaved better at school.

The kids have fallen for it, hook, line and sinker and it has helped me on a number of occasions. In one lesson, we even wrote cards back to Jason, assuring him that we were all behaving ourselves and would not be following in his footsteps.

Anyway, the lesson drags on and the kids get on with drawing some simple graphs reasonably quietly.

Ashley asks me what I would do if I won the National Lottery.

I inform him that I don't do the Lottery on principle because they give money to various nutty groups, such as the Communities Empowerment Network which helps parents appeal against their kids being excluded from school.

'Kids who are bad should just be chucked out,' says Billie-Jo with no apparent sense of irony. If I ruled the world, Billie-Jo would be sailing, head-first, out of the door right now.

These graphs are actually extremely simple; they have to be because, for some reason, our kids cannot do graphs. They always end up as a straight line; they don't seem able to understand the concept of scale, and simply copy down all the numbers.

While I am trying to persuade Charlotte to at least attempt to use a ruler, Nathan returns; apparently they didn't have a spare key at the office.

Soon, there's only five minutes left and I stand them all up and inspect every desk. I am completely paranoid but they have behaved extremely well, by their standards. Only Rachel had to be sent outside and her cries of 'Can I come in now?' soon subsided. The bell goes and off they troop, row-by-row. A successful lesson, in my book.

As I walk past the school office the secretary calls out to me, 'Can I have the key back that I gave Nathan for Mr Blunt's room please?' and my blood runs cold.

The bruised egos of a few pompous asses

I HAD a run-in with Ashley this morning.

Nothing out of the ordinary, but it led me to ponder the nature of rules.

Out there in the real world, society is confused; as a nation we want to have our cake, stuff it into our mouths and then go on a seven-day detox plan. We want judges to lock away burglars, but we fiddle our expenses. A train crash kills five and we demand jail terms for the company bosses, but we don't have a problem chatting on our mobile phones as we roar past speed cameras. This schizophrenic attitude is understandable; no-one wants to live in a police state and, in a free society, we're always going to seek to bend the rules occasionally.

The balance has tipped, of course, because while we have rules aplenty we lack sufficient numbers of people able, or willing, to enforce them. When they do, they are enforcing the wrong ones.

At the same time, society's attitude to those who transgress has altered; where once it was shameful to be falling-down drunk and foul-mouthed in the street, now it is celebrated as evidence of our freedom of expression. This combination, of apathy on the part of the police and courts and increasingly bold and belligerent wrong-doing by some members of society, sees more and more serious rules ignored and society sliding closer to anarchy, day by day.

You will not be surprised to learn that it's not much different in schools, which are nothing if not society in sweaty microcosm.

Schools ought to be different, of course, and they once were, in the time when schools were not a free society, or a democracy. Once, the teacher was a miniature god whose writ extended to every area of a pupil's life. Clear rules existed, with clear punishments for those who broke them.

That has all gone, replaced by a haphazard approach to discipline, across the state school sector at least, which is genuinely astounding. The teaching profession has brought some of this upon itself by abandoning the strict disciplinarian approach for which it was once renowned in favour of attempts to make school 'fun' and 'entertaining' for the kids, as if we were children's entertainers. Another name for a children's entertainer is a clown.

It isn't as though children, even today, are incapable of behaving themselves: the behaviour of kids varies hugely from school to school. Even within St Jude's their attitude and conduct changes according to a number of variables, including which subject they are doing, which teacher they have and what they had for lunch.

Some teachers genuinely seem to believe the politically correct nonsense that children should not be punished. Others are simple-minded and have allowed themselves to be brainwashed until they think they believe this. Most, I suspect, are simply worn down by years of watching standards slide while being told there was nothing they could, or should, do about it.

We all reach the point where we wonder why we bother. And shortly afterwards, we stop bothering.

The situation is so dire, and the grip of the 'experts' so firm, that this cannot be reversed on a case-by-case basis.

The last but one education secretary, Ruth Kelly – recently replaced by Alan Johnson – demanded a 'zero tolerance' policy to all forms of disruption in class. Hear, hear! I'll bet my house nothing happens.

I am broadly against too much state interference in our lives. But I have reluctantly come to the view that discipline in schools should be legislated for. We need a standard set of School Rules which apply across Britain, with a corresponding set of punishments for breaking them.

These rules, and the punishments for breaking them, should be displayed in a standard diagram in every classroom in the land. They should be arranged so that multiple infringements earn steadily greater punishments. Every time a pupil breaks the rules, it should be noted on their record. The police must be involved, without exception, whenever a violent or criminal incident occurs.

Every teacher would be required to implement the rules, whether or not they agreed with them. This would have the important benefit that pupils could not argue with an individual teacher over the breach of any rule or the resultant punishment, since neither would be a matter of choice or whim.

Eventually, the kids would get to know the rules, the punishments and the boundaries of acceptable behaviour.

No doubt some Heads will see this as undermining their authority, and they may be right. But since they have failed as a group, signally, to demonstrate that authority for many years now, who cares? Anyway, consistency (a vital cog in the machinery of a young life) is far more important than the bruised egos of a few pompous asses.

Crucially, we would need someone permanently based on the school premises to ensure this policy was faithfully carried out. It would be no use the Duty SMT staffer turning up and getting the same load of abuse from poor misguided Ashley. The person I have in mind would need to be able to arrest and search if necessary (kids and parents): I'm thinking along the lines of a School Bouncer, with the necessary legal backing.

Let's have a look at how this would work in practice.

Mr Chalk asks Ashley to sit in a desk at the front.

Ashley shouts: 'No, I'm not moving. F*ck off!'

Mr Chalk points at the Rules Board, which states that any pupil swearing at a teacher earns one week in the Dull Room. Mr Chalk then phones the School Bouncer who comes along, ignores Ashley's protests and frog-marches him off to spend five days copying out Latin verse and learning French vocabulary, on his own.

No benefits to be paid to parents during this time and the whole family has to do an hour's work picking up litter at the school.

OK, it's pie in the sky I know, but we all have to have a dream.

One day, perhaps, those at the top will admit that there is a behaviour crisis in our schools; until then, the pleasure of using nunchucks to bring Wayne and Darren into line will be denied me, I'm afraid.

Incidentally, when I visited a friend in the local hospital last week, I couldn't help noticing the plethora of CCTV cameras and the proliferation of bright yellow notices proclaiming that anyone abusing the staff, verbally or physically, would be dealt with by the police and could also be refused treatment.

Why don't we have any of this in schools? Perhaps it's a fear of 'sending the wrong message'?

Don't stand so close to me

I NOTICE with some concern that Stacey is wearing her miniature scarf again.

I remember it well, because I found it lying in the mud as I walked across the school field at the end of a Wednesday afternoon several weeks ago. I brought it to the School Office, still dripping mud, earning me a snarl from Mrs Borrowdale. It turned out that Stacey was being bullied by some yobs from her year group who had taken her scarf and jumped up and down on it on the field. A lovely bunch of kids; their parents must be really proud.

In an unusually kind gesture for me, because she is a decent kid, I picked it back up, took it home and washed it for her as I knew that her own parents were probably too idle to bother.

Alas, due to my own incompetence, I put the machine on too hot and the damn thing shrunk. She was still delighted to receive it the next day (although her ungrateful parents wanted me to pay for a new one).

Things then became far worse when Stacey decided to become the male teacher's worst nightmare: The Pupil Who Has A Crush On You.

They are a far, far bigger issue than other problem children such as The Maker of Animal Noises or The Projectile Thrower. The only way to deal with the smitten pupil is to be absolutely horrible to them and to their whole class for a while, until their feelings disappear and group pressure finally convinces them that you are, in fact, a complete bastard.

If they try to stay behind at the end of the last lesson when everyone else is leaving, just run away screaming. You only have to read the tabloids to see how these things can go horribly wrong. The slightest accusation or suggestion of impropriety and you will be suspended pending an investigation quicker than you can say, "Yes, I'd love to see your new tattoo Chelsey."

I was so worried I nearly informed the SMT (I can just imagine Mr Morris, our elderly headmaster, dealing with this situation.)

I'd always thought that this sort of thing was exclusively a male-teacher-with-female-pupil-type thing, usually followed by a spell in jail.

Nowadays, however, with equality and all that, female teachers have been getting themselves into all sorts of bother with male pupils. I don't remember any of this happening when I was a lad (despite my best efforts) but it seems commonplace now.

Samantha Grixti, 30, was given a three month suspended sentence for having an affair with a sixteen-year-old that she taught. She had even booked a hotel room for them both to celebrate the end of his GCSEs! I can't imagine the judge suspending that sentence if it had been a male teacher, somehow.

Obviously keen not to be outdone, Shelley White, 24, was found guilty of an affair with a fifteen-year-old boy at her school. On one occasion, they retired to the stationery cupboard to get to know each other better. Imagine the romance. Oh, a suspended sentence for her too.

And guess what punishment was dished out to Nicola Prentice, a dance teacher who admitted an affair with a fifteen-year-old boy?

Hannah Grice didn't get away with it so lightly. She received five months for her affair with a 14-year-old which ended when her husband caught them in his wardrobe. I'd love to have seen that. Imagine her explanation: 'Er, he's doing a project on shirts and I'm helping him with his coursework.'

Susan Hogan was jailed too, for seducing a 14-year-old with Special Needs, as was Beverley Miles, who received six months for having sex with her sixteen-year-old Special Needs pupil.

Come on now, ladies: there must be one or two decent-looking male teachers at your schools, surely? I can send our PE teacher, Mr Pullen, round if that will help? He's got an eye for the ladies, as we'll discover later.

The right to an education

I'VE MANAGED to avoid taking this lot for French for some weeks now (the last time was before Christmas, when the lesson almost degenerated into mass hysteria after Darren's sit-down protest), but I couldn't dodge them forever.

I'm worried that I may have my work cut out today, but they line up, nice and quiet. I explain how we don't want to have to bother Mr Phillips again. Some of them look puzzled, so I move on quickly and get them sitting down in the classroom.

This time, the work that has been left instructs the children to get on with 'ze posters'.

Where are we going to put them up? I wonder. Posters already cover virtually every square inch of wall space. I decide to stick them on the ceiling if we finish any.

'Oh, not posters again!' is the opening gambit from Sherry. I'm amazed at this; it takes a lot to get them fed up with drawing.

Most of the work they do with Mme DuPont seems to involve drawing scenes and labelling them with the odd French word. Their exercise books are in a cupboard and the last bit of written work was a list of words three-and-a-half weeks previously.

This is disgraceful, by any standard.

I decide to test them on a few words that I can see on the walls.

'What's the French for dog, then?'

'Dunno.'

'Come on, you've all done a picture of Fido and labelled it 'chien.'

'Chien, then.'

'Good. What's the French for cat?'

'Dunno, we just draw things and put them on the wall.'

The lesson soon starts to degenerate and, before long, Leon starts to be a pain, kicking Dwayne's chair and stealing Shazney's pencil. I move him to the front and he starts to hurl a tirade of abuse at me, so I throw his bag out into the corridor and encourage him to follow it.

'I'm goin' to phone my mum and she'll come up here and sort you out!' he informs me as he picks his bag up. 'I've got the right to an education!' He's getting out his phone.

'Well, you can lead a horse to water, Leon,' I say, remembering Mrs Chalk's wise words of a month or two back.

'Eh?' he replies. 'Worrayeronabout? What horse?'

'Nothing,' I say. 'Where did you hear that phrase, Leon? 'That you have a right to an education?'

'On the telly, when I was off last week!' he enlightens me. By 'off', he means playing truant. Ha, ha, ha.

He's got a point, though. Nowadays the rights of one scumbag are considered far more important than the collective right of the 29 others to be taught without being distracted. I leave him in the corridor, whining to mother on his phone, and go back inside the classroom.

Five minutes later, Mr Phillips knocks on the door and informs me that when Leon went to see the educational psychologist last week she decided that he suffers from low self esteem, so the teachers need to try harder to boost his 'feelings of self-worth.' I patiently explain that it's not Leon who has problems with his self esteem; it's me who is having problems with mine. And that's hardly surprising: not ten minutes ago, he informed his classmates that I was a 'f*cking bastard.' Mr Phillips reluctantly takes Leon away, no doubt for a reassuring chat.

Shortly after this, a crowd of girls turn up demanding that Kerryann be allowed out because they need to practise their dance for assembly and Miss Simpson has said it's OK. As you might imagine, I tell them where to go. Kerryann starts moaning about how it is not fair and, two minutes, later the whole damn crowd returns, this time with a note from Miss Simpson asking if it would be OK for Kerryann to miss French 'just this once' so she can practise with the others.

Furious, I scribble on the note that she can bloody well practise at lunch time.

The group then hangs around in the corridor, knocking on the door every few minutes and driving me up the wall.

Then, just to keep my blood pressure rising, the mysterious projectile thrower leaps into action. This is a classic teaching problem: as soon as you turn your back or look the other way something is thrown. Unpunished, it escalates and it can rapidly reduce your lesson to chaos. But catching the offender is hard: often, he (it's always a boy) is highly skilled at escaping detection.

He plays on the fact that monitoring the whole class, all the time, is very difficult. That's not to say it is impossible. An expert can keep his eye on the class over one shoulder while simultaneously writing on the board; it needs practice, but it's worth the effort because it really freaks them out. After many years' experience, I am proficient at this: the main thing is consciously to raise your writing to stop it sloping down to the right.

If you do miss an incident, there are a number of ways of tempting the miscreant into breaking cover. Practise subtle feints with your eyes and body. Move unpredictably and see who reacts. If you pretend not to have noticed the first throw, he will always get over-confident and you will be ready to spot the second one.

This time, however, I am too fed up to use any clever tricks and simply announce that if it happens again I will keep them all in for twenty minutes after the bell. They know I will do this because they know that I don't care about their parents moaning that they lost their place in the dinner queue and missed all the chicken dinosaurs in the canteen.

I half-hear Dwayne making a casual remark to Coyne about a television that has been stolen and is being sold on the estate. Many of our children have an easy familiarity with crime that is disturbing. As someone tried to burgle my house recently, causing hundreds of pounds worth of damage, it is a topic close to my heart at the moment. I should concentrate on the lesson but I can't help myself.

'What about the person that owned that telly, Dwayne? What if someone stole yours?'

'I'd batter 'em!'

'Yes, Dwayne, but let's assume that you don't know who has taken it (though they're likely to be acquainted). Can't you imagine how fed up you'd be? The cost of replacing it, the damage caused to your house.'

'Insurance pays for all that!' declares Dwayne, with the certainty of one who has never experienced the aggro that goes with making an insurance claim.

I give up on the lesson and spend the last ten minutes trying to convince them that house burglary is an awful thing, and that home contents insurance is not a magic fairy that makes everything better.

I can't help the nagging feeling at the back of my mind that important ideas like this shouldn't be taught, off-the-cuff, by a supply teacher at the end of a failing French lesson.

Ah well. The Easter holiday starts tomorrow.

THE SUMMER TERM

Free crisps and chicken nuggets

THE SUMMER term is in full swing: the sun is shining, the birds are twittering and the inhabitants of Cherry Tree Estate are proudly displaying their new tattoos.

The traditional sounds of early May in England can be heard all around: police sirens, rap music blaring from stolen car stereos, the thwack of willow on somebody's head.

Listen carefully now and you can hear the faint tinkle of the jukebox flying through the Cherry Tree Social Club window. Is that Mrs Jones' voice I can hear in the distance, shouting accusations that Declan has been putting dog dirt through her letterbox again? Surely not.

It really is a lovely day, the type that reminds you of how lucky we are to live in Ingerland.

To make things even better, I am not teaching. Instead, I am visiting some of our pupils on their Work Experience placements.

In the fourth year (Year 10), all state-educated pupils do three weeks of work experience. It's a tremendous opportunity for them to experience the world of work (for many of our pupils, unfortunately, it's for the first and last time). They can organise a placement themselves or we can sort one out for them. As you might imagine, we usually have to sort one out for them.

This is harder than you might think. We are blacklisted by quite a few companies due to various unfortunate incidents which have occurred on past placements. When you phone a company, they often become a little reluctant, to say the least, when they discover the identity of the school which is trying to palm a pupil off on them. Phoning round begging work experience placements is a depressing task indeed.

After a few (say 50) rejections, it is very tempting to exaggerate a pupil's devotion to duty, his attendance record and his willingness to learn.

I sit in when Mr Green telephones a local employer, let's call them Grillfords Machinery, in an attempt to get Shane a slot.

A man called Dave answers the phone.

'Hi Dave, my name's Mike Green. I'm just phoning to offer you a pupil for work experience this year.'

He's having a good stab at making it sound like we're doing them a favour and Dave is clearly quite receptive. But, awkwardly, he wants to know where Mike is calling from.

'Well, Dave, I'm calling from St Jude's…'

Long pause.

'Right… I see… yes, I see. Well, this lad's called Shane Boggis, he's a hard worker, good attender, nice lad…'

I can almost see his nose growing.

Another pause. Mr Green is wincing slightly.

'Yes, I did hear about the unfortunate incident last year… no, this lad's nothing like Liam.'

How can he say this and keep a straight face?

More chat from Dave.

'Yes, we're all very sorry about what happened… No, I didn't realise that it went to court, did it really? No, no, he's an honest fellow is Shane, Dave… no, no, no, entirely different family, just same surname… No, I don't think you're off your rocker at all… Oh, OK. Well, thanks for your time anyway.'

Phone down, another one crossed off the list.

I have witnessed dozens of similar exchanges and I have to say that, in general, firms bend over backwards to help. If you phoned me up and asked if I would like to entertain a 15-year-old pupil from St Jude's for three weeks I would fall off my chair laughing. Unless a kid shows exceptional aptitude and unusual willingness, it boils down to a hell of a lot of trouble for the firm for which they receive nothing in return. They can't just use the kids as tea-makers: they have to show them several areas of operations, appoint someone to look after them and come up with useful work for them to do. This last part alone is a major challenge.

Needless to say, we struggle to find placements for our kids.

Of course, parents and children rarely appreciate your efforts anyway. Only today, Mrs Scroggins has phoned in to complain that Hayley is used as cheap labour and has not yet been allowed to cut any of the customers' hair in her placement at the local salon. She has spent the last week sweeping up clippings and arranging the wigs, apparently.

'She's not a cleaner, our Hayley. Blah, blah, blah…'

I'm tempted to ask whether she would let an untrained simpleton loose on her own head, but then a vision of Mrs Scroggins comes to my mind's eye. To be blunt, she's no stunner; I'm forced to conclude that it would probably improve her.

Wayne's mother is not happy either; he has been called 'a f*ckwit' by the garage proprietor who has been good enough to accommodate him. I mentally note that the man is obviously a good judge of character.

'Wayne knows all about cars,' she rants.

'Well, he certainly knows how to bypass the locks and start them without the ignition key,' I almost say, but don't.

'He never meant to drop that spanner and they blamed him for all them other tools that went missing. He'd never nick nuffink.' This last statement is grammatically accurate, but accidentally so. She drones on – 'blah, blah, blah…' – while I let the receiver dangle in my hand and look out of the window.

Occasionally, however, a child really shines, really takes to their work, does far more than they have been asked to and gets a glowing report. Some even get the promise of a job when they leave school. Gillian, for example, has been offered a job at the chicken nuggets factory. Alas, she has turned it down for, apparently, it is 'Right scuzzy' there. I sympathise (though I can't help wondering whether she thought the nuggets arrived in nice little cubes from the farm where they were grown and the operators reclined on velvet sofas while packing them?) but I'm disappointed; she won't get too many shots at gainful employment.

More often than not, however, I have to face an earful from some irate supervisor because a given pupil is not the credit to the firm we suggested he might be.

'Yes, I know you requested a hard diligent worker, Steve.' (Don't they know who we are?) 'Maybe Bradley was tired from all the long hours and that's why he fell asleep and was slumped over the desk when the company owner arrived. Yes, it is meant to be full time... What! He told you his placement was only two days a week? The little swine!'

Sometimes employers do not wait for our visit, but phone up the school to give us a piece of their mind.

'What? She called you a f*cking bitch? Yes well, Collette does have a bit of a mouth on her, but she's got a heart of gold and I'm sure once she's calmed down... what, she's stormed out? Oh dear...'

Today, I am visiting Connor, our champion truant, who is working for Smeggins the Builders. When I turn up I discover that he is happily mixing cement and has nothing but praise for the firm of Smeggins. This is most unusual and my antennae immediately begin to twitch. Ah. Mr Smeggins turns out to be his dad, though he has a different surname of course.

Back at school, the scrapings from the bottom of the barrel (the kids who we couldn't find anyone to take) are in the woodwork room making bookcases for the enterprising Mr Knutt, woodwork teacher and entrepreneur extraordinaire, so he can flog them later in his furniture shop.

Lauren is a nice girl who has managed to get a placement in a solicitor's office. They are a bit miffed because she has just told them that she would have preferred to work in the crisp factory with Kelly and Courtney. They got free crisps, you see.

Fun and games with Mr Pullen

MR PULLEN teaches PE and sleeps with the female teachers.

I honestly think it is part of his job description. He is not the brightest of men, but his success rate is astounding, perhaps because he is good-looking and drives a Golf GTi. He has branched out into the neighbouring schools and is even chancing his arm at those further afield which he visits with the football teams. It took me ages to work out why we had so many more away fixtures than home ones.

Every day he wears a different designer tracksuit and he always sports brand new trainers. He has a deep tan. I suspect this is not simply the result of days spent outside in the weedy sun that overlooks our field.

Today he has to shoot off to the other side of town immediately after the start of the lesson. Now I come to think about it, the winsome Miss Johnson, our new student teacher, lives on the other side of town and she called in sick today. I'm sure it's all just a coincidence.

PE can be an awful cover. Some schools insist you are PE-trained, whatever that means, and if you're not (I'm not) they insist that you do some really bad worksheets that the staff have cobbled together, usually word searches. When you give them out, be prepared for the inevitable cries of 'We've done these before', which they will have. If any of them ask what this has to do with PE, feel free to confess that you don't have a clue. The kids will never settle as they feel that they have been robbed of something.

However, Mr Pullen is a cowboy and is quite happy for me to do whatever I want. If you can get outside, and it's a nice day, it's a great cover.

Today, I'm taking a Year 9 group out for a game of rounders.

Mr Pullen tells the kids to shut up and sit down and they all immediately flop, cross-legged, on the floor. PE teachers are usually very good with the kids because they don't muck about. He explains how I have generously agreed to take them outside blah, blah, blah and we expect them to be on their best behaviour etc.

About half of the kids have their PE kit. Those that don't are divided into two groups: those with no notes and those with forged notes.

Those with forged notes are told to sit on the field in a line and keep score. Those with no notes are given ancient Stanley Matthews shorts to wear. When they refuse they are told to get them on, or else. I like the PE Department.

There is too much nonsense babbled about the importance of children 'choosing' to do this or that. Mr Pullen ignores this, which is one of his redeeming features. We fret too much about giving choices to people who don't yet know what is good or bad for them (and maybe never will). Treating 14-year-olds as adults, with multiple options, is all very well on a one-to-one basis, when you're having a cosy chat, but it has serious flaws as a general policy. In my experience, below the age of 16 kids usually make decisions based solely upon what their friends are doing or what they think is 'cool'. Nine times out of ten, these are bad decisions. Decide for them, and save them from themselves – that's my motto. It doesn't matter whether they agree with you. You know better than they do; you're an intelligent adult, for God's sake.

Mr Pullen departs, combing his hair and sniffing his armpits, and we make our way over to the field. I am carrying the bat and ball for reasons too obvious to bother explaining. Leon and Sherry (another child named after mother's favourite tipple) are carrying the bases.

It may surprise you to learn that our kids are not just academically poor; they are also hopelessly badly-coordinated. Many of them cannot catch even an easily-thrown ball. Take Lewis; I chuck a tennis ball to him, just above head height. He raises both hands to catch it and it sails right between them as he flails hopelessly.

I line them up, number them 1 or 2, and that gives us two teams. (This is the modern, PC way to pick teams, rather than have two captains who pick their players in turn, which gives you teams of balanced ability, but upsets the fat and weedy kids left until last.)

The game progresses with much cheering and shouting of abuse from the non-doers behind the line. I am umpire and conduct the match with great seriousness. The kids get really into the game and love running about. It's a gorgeous day and the early summer sun is beating down. I've rolled up my sleeves and jettisoned my tie. No doubt we should be worried about the kids getting sunburned, or dehydrated, or suffering grass allergy, or being killed by a sparrow, or swallowing a tennis ball, but instead we all just play happily.

At times like these, my job truly is actually enjoyable.

Exercise is a major key to solving behavioural problems, I think, as I watch them hare around the field having fun. Nowadays, they do far less physical activity than the children of the past. Labour-saving devices are everywhere to enable more time to be spent in front of the television. Kids are driven to school because parents have got it into their heads that child molesters lurk behind every hedge. But our bodies have not evolved to be sedentary and need regular exercise; kids have loads of energy and they can either use it up through running around or they can use it up in your lesson, causing mayhem. Young men, especially, need an outlet for their natural physical aggression to prevent it bubbling over at an inappropriate time. Ask any teacher who has taken kids on a walking holiday, or has been on a school ski trip abroad: they are no trouble after the first three days. They burn it all off during the day and are pleasantly tired in the evening. I've seen kids with the most awful records and every fashionable acronym-complaint under the sun sit still and listen for the first time in years, simply because they are doing what their bodies have evolved to do, often for the first time in their lives. When they return home they immediately revert to their former behaviour.

If I was in charge, daily exercise would be a compulsory part of education as it is in many private schools. We should increase dramatically the range of sports that the kids are introduced to, as well as the time spent on them. This would increase the chances of them finding one they like and keeping it up in later life. People with a hobby or interest tend not to want to hang around vandalising bus shelters and getting into petty crime. Of course, most schools have abandoned traditional sports days and forbid any playground game that is deemed in the slightest bit 'rough'. And as we build over more and more fields, both Local Authority-owned ones and school playing fields (we had 78,000 in 1994, now we have 44,000), the kids have fewer and fewer places where they can get out and about in the fresh air (the Cherry Tree is littered with 'No Ball Games' signs). Many roads have become too dangerous for them to ride their bikes on.

We are encouraging an ever-increasing number of overweight people, with no idea how to look after their bodies; the country is in the grip of an obesity epidemic. In 20 years, the average person will be wider than they are tall and soaring rates of heart disease, cancer and diabetes will follow, as surely as night follows day. I often think that fat teachers need to get their act together and give an example by losing weight. Or at least dying off early to show the kids the dangers of too much eating and too little exercise.

Towards the end of the lesson, Tyrone starts to make fun of Lewis because of his complete inability to catch the ball. Lewis takes offence at this and they start fighting. Tyrone is a little swine, just like his father. In the interests of justice, I let Lewis whack him a couple of times before stepping in to separate them both by the simple method of pushing into the middle with both arms outstretched and shoving the two of them backwards. They both fall over and everyone else laughs. I send them to opposite ends of the pitch so they can sulk for a bit.

I have done this sort of thing a hundred times, without ever worrying about the consequences. Others are not so lucky. Here are a few unfortunate cases from 2005.

Willem van Trotsenburg, a maths teacher at Hobart High School in Norfolk, ended up in front of the magistrates for chucking a 14-year-old girl out of his lesson. He was found not guilty of using excessive force, but no doubt the accusation will linger on some record forever.

Ian Mackay, a headmaster in Cumbria, was suspended for months while his school governors dithered over what to do with him. His offence? He had forced two 10-year-old boys to free a girl whom they had locked in a store cupboard.

Carron Downer, a PE teacher, who had worked at the same school since 1982, was found guilty of assault by North Avon magistrates after he pushed two boys who had deliberately barged into him. (I believe he's appealing, and good luck to him).

Finally, Olive Rack from Kettering. Olive isn't a teacher, but I'm sure she would make an excellent one. We learn that she was to be prosecuted after stopping a toddler from hitting another child with a plastic brick (despite the fact that none of the parents of the kids complained).

I wonder what the various Crown Prosecution Service lawyers, police officers, magistrates and social workers involved in these and a hundred other cases think they are doing?

Can the CPS and our JPs and judges *really* be so stupid as to believe that it is right for Carron Downer, for instance, to have a criminal record for what he did?

I fear they are.

All of these cases send a clear message to pupils: do whatever you like and if a teacher tries to stop you, accuse them of anything you want. They'll get into a lot of trouble and you might get compensation.

The message to teachers is pretty clear too.

Don't try to stop anybody causing trouble in your classroom.

A lifetime away

IDLY GAZING out of the classroom window at a grey sky, my mind drifts back to a carefree day over a decade ago now when I did a ski season in the Alps.

The scene around me is achingly beautiful. We're at the top of the mountain with a stunning view of the huge red sun setting behind us. The sky is almost completely clear, a deepening blue with a few thin, horizontal wisps of cloud near the horizon, changing colour before our eyes – gorgeous shades of yellow, oranges, reds and purples reflect the sun's dying light.

We watch as a group of school kids and their teachers trudge, as quickly as they can in the snow, into the gondola which will ferry them back down to their hotel in the village, a vertical mile below us.

They're on a skiing trip from their school in Sussex and both staff and kids seem a good bunch. We wave and they throw the odd snowball at us. Most nights we'd be on there, too, but every Tuesday we attempt to race the cable car using a route that is more direct than the piste and a hell of a lot more hair-raising. It's been a ritual around here for years, they say. Usually, the locals from the ski school just about manage it. My friend Dave and I have so far failed miserably every time.

It's getting a bit colder now and I glance nervously at my watch, much to the amusement of the others. It's much harder to ski once the sun starts going down – you can't see the dips and bumps properly in the flat light of dusk – and I don't want to leave this too late as I need all the help I can get.

Finally, the whole group, teachers and kids, are crammed into the one cable car, and the doors close. We wave to them and the driver prepares to take them home. He gives us a grin and a wave and Hannes shouts something in his dialect that I can't understand. The kids are looking puzzled through the glass doors, unable to work out what we are up to. They know that this is the last gondola of the day and the slopes are now deserted.

In time-honoured tradition, we wait until the horn sounds and the cable starts to turn, and then push off across the slope, poling furiously, with Gabriella leading the way, the rest of us following in single file, gradually picking up speed, heading towards a gap in the low wooden fence that marks the edge of the piste. The kids and teachers watch us curiously as the gondola starts to move off slowly downhill on its thick steel wire.

Faster and faster now, through the gap and onto the wide open meadow that slopes away in front of us. Fanning out, we all make our way down, throwing in tight, 'S'-shaped turns (not so tight in my case) in the smooth powder and whooping with exhilaration. From what I can gather, the rules of this 'race' appear to involve showing off at every opportunity whilst demonstrating as casual an attitude as possible, only taking it seriously, and going hell for leather, in the lower stages.

Suddenly, Dave cuts right across the front of my skis, glancing back over his shoulder, with a rude gesture and a huge grin. I narrowly avoid falling and all hell breaks loose as everyone starts doing it, until Gabriella shouts at us to grow up. She is the Head of the English-speaking part of the local Ski School, and has a firm manner.

The terrain becomes a nightmare, now, constantly changing from ice, to crust-topped snow, to fresh powder, and back again. Well, it's a nightmare for me; they're all locals, apart from me and Dave, and they handle it like it was a beginners' green run.

I see a blur to my left and Mattheus goes full tilt at a gap in the trees. Bloody hell, he really is nuts. It's a mini cliff, a good fifteen feet high, and the rest of us just cruise, watching open-mouthed as he flies off the drop that we all know is there. He is an awesome skier and judges it beautifully. The rest of us follow, lower, where it's not as vertical, with a lot less speed; I still nearly have to change my trousers.

We hurtle downwards in a frenzy, suddenly ripping across the piste, then off the other side, down a bowl full of powder after the recent heavy snowfalls. I can ski confidently on any terrain, but I lack the natural ability of the locals who have grown up on snow. Unbelievably, Hannes is using a pair of skis that I lent him from the shop where I work. They are absolute rubbish and the previous school group rejected them. I suspect that he hasn't bothered to wax them and I'm sure their edges are about as sharp as chewing gum. I should know – it's my job to look after the equipment. None of this seems to bother him, however, and he is flying. Dave and I are desperately trying to keep up.

I hear whistling below to my left. It is Gabriella and at first I can't work out what's happening. She's sitting down but still moving at speed. Then it dawns on me; a tennis court-sized area of the hill is moving and she's going with it. Everyone's eyes are on her. There's nothing we can do, except watch carefully in case she goes under the snow slide. After just a few seconds, however, the snow stops and she scrambles upright and launches herself diagonally away from where she was. She brushes herself down when she gets back to us and with nothing more than a laugh and 'Keep well away from that bit!' she is off again.

We head at breakneck speed through a wooded section, which is terrifying in the low light and then fly down another short length of piste as the gondola glides overhead, kids banging on the windows, shouting and waving in astonishment. The race is definitely on now and it's no holds barred (unfortunately for me): 200 metres of piste and then we are off again down a narrow valley with ever-tightening, icy walls that terrify me. It is impossible to slow down at all as we are close together and there is simply no room to turn. It spits us out onto the last stretch of meadow. Everybody is skiing absolutely straight towards the final corner of piste that we can just about make out in the distance. There is a stream to cross, which is usually frozen over but once gave me a good soaking (my clothes all froze solid on the long walk back to the village afterwards and I arrived looking like I was wearing a suit of armour). This time, we're OK. Hannes picks a good spot and we all follow in his tracks. On to the piste now and one last bend where everyone pulls ahead of me again. I can hear the whine of the gondola following us overhead as we straight-line down towards a crest which provides a stomach churning launch and short flight. Ten seconds later, I arrive at the gondola station as the kids are spilling out. Once again alas, two of us failed to beat it. Hannes brandishes the remains of his right ski at me and I gape. One metal edge has completely broken off; how can he beat me on that?

Tradition dictates that as long as everyone got down in one piece, the fastest and slowest skiers must now split a round of drinks. I get out my wallet with comical reluctance and we all traipse off towards the village, laughing.

And then I blink, and I'm back in the greyness of St Jude's, and it all seems a lifetime away.

Educational welfare officers are often completely mad

IT'S LUNCHTIME and I am eating the gourmet delight that is my carefully-prepared packed lunch: ham and tomato sandwiches, an apple, some of Mrs Chalk's flapjack and a bottle of mineral water. I look forward to it all morning. Thoughts of it help me through the darkest moments.

The teachers next to me are discussing the Educational Welfare Officer (EWO). These people are often completely mad, and ours is no exception. She has apparently decided that there's nothing wrong with 12-year-old Josie living with her 19-year-old sister, who is a known drug-user. I've often found that social services tend to think the very best of everyone (cynics might say they are a bit gullible). Unless you happen to be white, middle-class and vaguely normal, in which case they regard you with the utmost suspicion.

The group on the other side of the room are whining to each other about something or other. Teachers, even my friends, are the worst whingers I know, bar none (what's this book, after all, if not an extended whinge?). Thirteen weeks' holiday a year, incredible job security, short hours, a pension the private sector would die for and a salary that's not bad either: what the hell do they have to moan about (apart from the kids, who they can just ignore)? Teach some stuff as best you can, let all the rest of the nonsense wash over you and you won't go far wrong. But that's not good enough for some. I have lost count of the number of times I've heard someone say 'If I worked in the private sector, I could earn three times as much.' Well, go on then.

I finish my lunch and sit back, feet up and both eyes closed, half-listening to the continuing babble all around me. Mr Burton reminds the table of the time when I ruined his electronic whiteboard by writing on it with the marker pen. I start paying attention when I realise that he has referred to me as 'Mr Chalk'. We are in the Staff Room – no children are present and he knows my first name. This is the mark of The Strange Teacher. If you are talking to other adults while kids are present you use Mr, Mrs or Miss and you change seamlessly to first names as soon as the kids are gone. The strange teacher – every school has one, but we have loads as you know – does not. He insists on calling you 'Mr Chalk', or even 'sir', even when you have told him your first name three times. I always keep a watchful eye on such people; they could be capable of anything.

The group opposite are now discussing 'Citizenship'. They don't seem that impressed, though I can't help thinking that this much-criticised subject is actually a very good idea. What's wrong with teaching our kids to be kind and respectful, to obey rules and respect other people's possessions?

The discussion moves on again, to the rumour going around that St. Jude's might be knocked down and a brand new school built in its place.

This sounds like a good idea, but it isn't. Our Victorian forefathers were marvellous builders. Their modern equivalents, I'm afraid, don't seem to have quite the same pride in their job. New schools lack the imposing and classical character which the old ones possess and which, if they were properly maintained and cleaned, would delight even the most jaded eye. They are built using cheap and flimsy materials, often under a Private Finance Agreement (that is, the naïve Head gets taken for a ride by some sharp suits). Additionally, every new school I've ever seen has been far too small, with some pretty fundamental design faults: narrow corridors, too few classrooms or laboratories and a hall and canteen only big enough for half the school. They look super, for a while, but once the vandals take hold the new buildings decline very rapidly. Classrooms are always painted in bizarre colour schemes which some psychologist has lately decided is ideal for the 'learning environment'. I'd sooner spend the cash on padlocks.

I am not an expert, or a role model

I AM eating my breakfast toast and listening to the *Today* programme on Radio Four.

There is a discussion about the violent and evil lives many of our young people are leading these days (tell me about it) and an expert, some do-gooder or other, says it's all down to a lack of 'role models'.

I think it is at least possible that it's all down to a collapse in discipline, good manners, morality, respect and decency, but I don't expect that I qualify as an expert, or that the BBC would invite me onto their programme if I did.

But it does give me pause for a moment.

What 'role models' do kids have nowadays? Some ridiculously overpaid footballer prone to childish tantrums? The morons in the *Big Brother* house, perhaps? Or maybe the various gun-toting rappers who regularly delight us with their expletive-laden vocabulary and eccentric attitude to women?

It could be that their 'role models' are closer to home: their work shy, immoral and amoral 'parents', obviously. The local drug dealer, who tours the Cherry Tree in his souped-up BMW, resplendent with extra-powerful speakers and those tasteful blue strip lights cheering up the underside, also springs to mind.

If I had to hazard a guess (and bear in mind that, as I say, I'm not an expert, employed by the government to draw up strategies in return for a fat salary), I'd say it was a combination of all of those people.

One thing's for sure: they rarely see their teachers as people to follow. Their impression of us is at an all-time low. Shabby, poor and boring is the general consensus, and they are hardly going to look up to that when there's bling in the air.

Teachers who do something interesting in their spare time – play rugby or cricket for the town, teach karate or travel widely (the Costas and Balearics don't count) should break my cardinal rule about revealing details of their life outside school and let the kids know about it. But do so with subtlety: put a photo up discreetly and wait for them to ask you about it. Don't bore them, whatever you do. By the way, if you are a keen birdwatcher, or you collect stamps, keep that to yourself.

A moment's pause

I'M WALKING idly across the yard back to the main school entrance to collect my bike, which is chained up, very thoroughly, even though it is in the Staff Cloakroom. Bikes that are not chained down around here have a habit of riding off on their own.

It's a lovely late spring afternoon and, although I can hear the mayhem in the distance as several hundred lunatic children spill out of the school gates to descend on the town, my ears are full of the sounds of blackbirds and starlings twittering in the nearby trees.

It's Friday and we have just broken up for half term so I'm in fine spirits.

Then I hear a heavy tread behind me. Hmmm. Fake Nike Air, by the sounds of it.

I quicken my pace as I don't want to be engaged in conversation.

But the legs rising from those lurid, multicoloured trainers are longer than mine and I'm caught within a few strides.

'Alright, Chalky?'

I look to the side, but continue walking. It's Liam, teacher-beating thug, petty thief and all-round Year 11 waster. Oh, joy.

'Hello, Liam,' I say.

'Alright, sir?' he repeats, a little more politely.

What do you *want*, boy? 'I'm fine thank you. Yourself?'

'Not too bad thanks, sir,' he replies.

We walk in silence for a moment or two; the entrance is closer, now, and soon I'll be away.

'Sir?' says Liam, as we reach the door.

'Yes?'

'I'm leaving school this summer, right?'

'Yes.' (About time, I don't add).

'Well, it's just… I know I ain't been that good at school and that.'

'Yes.'

'I could have learned more, like.'

This strikes me as the understatement of the century but I refrain from saying so and pause by the door, committing myself only to a nod and an 'hmm-hmm'.

Liam looks away, into the distance. Red brick houses stretch almost as far as the eye can see, away to the factories and industrial estates on the other side of town. He appears almost wistful.

'When I first come to St Jude's you told me I was wasting everybody's time,' he says. 'You said I weren't thick, and I ought to knuckle down and do some work. But I never.'

'That's true, Liam,' I reply.

'I suppose you was right, really,' he says, looking back at me, quite sadly. I actually feel sorry for him. What's going on?

'Well,' I say. 'Er…'

'It's too late for me now, here,' he says, quite the philosopher. 'The exams is in a couple of weeks.'

He laughs, hollowly.

'I ain't bothered. I'm gonna fail them anyway. But I tell you what, I ain't spending the rest of my life over there.' He looks over in the direction of the Cherry Tree Estate.

'No,' I say. 'I don't blame you.'

There's an awkward silence.

'So what are you going to do?' I ask.

'I'm gonna join the Army,' he says. 'Me and Jordan and Sean went down the recruiting place in town and there's all sorts of things you can do, be an electrician, be a mechanic, learn stuff, travel places. And it looks a right good laugh, and all.'

'Oh, so you're all joining up?' I ask, as my brain struggles to deal with the terrifying idea of this trio armed with automatic rifles.

'Nah,' says Liam, looking at the ground and scuffing away at the loose pea gravel. 'Jordan and Sean didn't fancy it in the end. The guy was all, like, you've gotta get up early in the mornin' and that, yeah? You've gotta do as you're told.'

'That's too bad,' I say. He looks up, half embarrassed, half confused.

'I just wanted to say that some teachers, like Mr Blunt, and Mr Green, they was alright really and I wish sometimes I hadn't f*cked about so much… you were alright sometimes too, a bit. Sort of.'

I reach over and grab his shoulder. 'Liam,' I say. 'Get yourself into the Army, treat it as a new start. Remember, they won't know what a pain you've been here. I won't tell if you won't! But you will have to try hard, and not just give up. It won't be like school, where we just let you do what you want. Do you know what I mean? If you don't do as you're told they'll chuck you out.' I'm not sure about that, these days, but I gloss over my uncertainty. 'We haven't prepared you for that and it will be a big shock.'

He nods and I glance over at the Cherry Tree. 'When it gets difficult, just think of it as your ticket out of there.'

And I push open the door, unchain my bike and push off, feeling happier than I have in quite some time.

Exam practice

TODAY I am covering science for Miss Wade again.

She made a brief re-appearance after her bullying-induced stress but the problem has recurred, this time as a result of an unfortunate incident with Darren. She locked her keys in the car one morning and unwisely accepted his offer to help her get them out 'because me brother works in a garage.'

Anyway, he caused quite a bit of damage to the area around the door lock so when he later demanded payment, she refused. That afternoon, he demonstrated an alternative method of gaining entry by throwing a brick through one of her car's windows.

I think that was pretty much the final straw for her.

The kids do a modular science course, which means that Miss Wade's Year 10 science group must do a multiple choice paper. I say 'multiple choice', but we all know it's really a matter of multiple guess. Anyway, it involves the kids putting a line through one of four boxes on a special piece of paper to indicate their choice of answer.

The first exam is coming up soon, and in order to get used to this format we have decided to practise doing a past paper and answering it using copies of the grid sheet.

Great, in theory. In practice, it goes something like this.

First of all, I make the fatal mistake of only spending ten minutes explaining the concept of 'Exam Conditions' (for example, not copying off the person next to you, remaining in your place rather than running around the room and not shouting out 'I don't geddit!' every two minutes). These are difficult, even alien concepts to many in the class; it really needs a whole lesson.

Yes, you do have to use a pencil to put your line through the box because it is read by a machine that recognises pencil marks. No, not a Sony PlayStation, Lee; a different kind of machine.

Out of interest, I time the ensuing fiasco on my stopwatch.

Twelve seconds to the first shout of 'We haven't done this!', from a child whose attendance is considerably less than 50%. He then throws his pencil on the floor and folds his arms in protest. I ignore him and continue timing.

Thirty-six seconds to the first hand up.

'Yes, Kelly, what is it?'

'How do you do this?'

'I can't tell you, Kelly, because, as I said earlier (six times, in fact), this is an exam.'

'No it's not!'

I feel like I have somehow been transported into Monty Python's 'argument' sketch.

Firmly: 'Yes, it is. You must work the answers out for yourself.'

'But what if I can't do it?'

Then you will have failed, you dimwit. 'For goodness' sake, Kelly, if you can't do it just go onto the next question.'

Kelly reacts in the traditional manner, slamming her pencil down on her desk, folding her arms and sulking.

I look around and notice half a dozen hands are now reaching skyward.

'What is it?' with a vague nod to Wayne.

'I don't get this…'

Through gritted teeth: 'If you can't do a question, just go onto the next one.'

Pencil down, arms folded.

Lee has his hand up too. Exasperated: 'What is it Lee?'

'I don't get this, either.'

Are they, just possibly, taking the mick?

No, they really are this stupid.

'OK, everybody! Put your pencils down, look at me.'

I explain – again, painfully – every last detail of how to conduct yourself in an exam: what to bring, what to leave at home, how the questions test our knowledge of the work we have done in the lessons and how the idea is that, if we pay attention in class and learn something, we can prove this by actually answering some of the questions, rather than just missing them out. How they can further improve their chances of doing well by revising at home. (Startled looks from one or two, those who understand the meaning of the word 'revising' mainly.)

227

Wayne counters with a comment every supply teacher must have heard: 'How do you know? You're not a real teacher!'

Whenever a pupil suggests this, I wholeheartedly agree that I am no longer allowed to be a real teacher 'due to an unfortunate incident.' If I'm feeling mischievous, I like to add something vague along the lines of, 'I have paid my debt to society and that it's all in the past and come along now Wayne, let's see that drawing finished by the end of the lesson.' On this occasion, I don't bother gilding the lily.

Taking advantage of a sudden silence, I launch us back into the exam again. This time we manage nearly two minutes before the first hand rises.

The faint sound of running footsteps

MISS KEEBLES' tyres were slashed while her car was left in the school car park overnight and she will not be coming in until after break. Once again, the police do not seem to have been involved; I can never understand this.

Anyway, I will have the pleasure of her group today. I am greeted by screaming mayhem in the corridor outside her room, and soon discover why.

Her classroom is on the ground floor and overlooks the school field. Several windows have been smashed and the classroom is full of broken glass. She has clearly upset somebody, although I cannot imagine how as she seems pleasant enough and appears to go out of her way to avoid confrontation.

CCTV would be a major bonus here. Again, I can't understand why we don't have it.

We must, therefore, find another room. This is always easier said than done, as the only time rooms ever seem to be locked is when you desperately need to get into them.

We traipse around the school, heading for a room that the Head of English has promised is empty. Transporting a class anywhere is always an absolute nightmare, as they inevitably do everything they can to cause mayhem.

Unfortunately, the new classroom is occupied. However, the teacher in there knows that one of the temporary classrooms is available. Off we go, only to be intercepted by an eager child with a message from SMT saying that room H11 is free. I scribble on the note that we have just left that room, and it clearly isn't.

We continue on our way. I pause to pick up something I need from the Staff Room as we pass it.

The behaviour of the group continues to be an embarrassment and the feeling of helplessness begins to annoy me. I stop them, line them up against a wall and roar at them. I don't usually bother shouting as it doesn't impress them, so when I do it is, at least, unusual. Halfway through my rant, however, I am rather distracted by the sight of a large brown dog walking unaccompanied towards us along the corridor. We carry on and it follows, quite happily.

This lesson is rapidly developing a surreal quality.

One or two seem to know something about what happened to Miss Keebles' car and windows. I casually mention that the police told me who did it, to see if I can tease out any information.

We cross the playground with our faithful hound in tow, in order to get to the temporary classroom that is our final refuge. I shoo the children up the steps and inside. There's a trainer lying discarded in the mud (I have no idea why it's been left there, but these things are not unusual) and Fido obediently lollops after it.

Two of the Waifs spot us from their hiding place and hurl obscene abuse at me. They are wearing hooded tops and baseball caps, which provide a simple but effective disguise. I pretend not to hear them; I never get into confrontations that I cannot win.

Once settled in our truly awful classroom, we get down to our work. This consists of looking up words in the dictionary and writing them down, together with their meaning. It used to amaze me that many of the kids could not manage this. It's a classic example of the problem of their short concentration spans: they flick through the pages wildly and complain that a given word isn't there.

I write down the first word on the board. It's 'illiterate'; whoever wrote this worksheet obviously had a sense of humour.

There is a frantic turning and creasing of dictionary pages, arguments between those who have to share them and the odd tearing noise.

Wayne is outraged. 'This one's got pages missing, see!' He brandishes the book. 'How can I do this work? It's crap!'

The dictionary is flung down in protest.

I pick it up and examine it. 'Hmmm,' I say, after a moment or two. 'I concede that there are a couple of pages missing, Wayne, but they are under 'W', and illiterate starts with an 'I'. So let's not worry about it yet.' I hand it back, trying to straighten out a few of the pages he has crumpled.

Jade shouts out her answer with an air of confident finality: '*Not recognised as lawful offspring!*' She starts to write it down, copied by the rest.

'No, that's not the definition of 'illiterate',' I protest.

'Yes it is, I've got it here!' pipes up Dannii.

'So have I!'

'No it *isn't*! You're finding '*illegitimate*'.'

'What's that mean, then?'

'Er…'

'What's he know about English, anyway?'

'He's not even an English teacher!'

They're in full flow, now.

'Yeah, he took us for maths last week!'

'We had him for French!'

'Sir, *are* you a maths teacher?'

I sigh. 'Yes, I am. I also teach French, as you know. And English, as you also know. I'm like… er… superteacher. Let's just concentrate on looking up this word, eh? Here's a clue: it starts 'I-L-L-I' not 'I-L-L-E'.'

'What's he on about, 'I-L-L-E'?'

'That's how you spell it, dur-brain!'

'Spell what?'

'This word… "*illuminate*"…'

And my head sinks into my hands in despair amid a fresh burst of protests that there is something wrong with the dictionaries.

Before long, a familiar character appears.

Like 'The Projectile Thrower' we encountered earlier, 'The Maker of Animal Noises' appears in different guises with monotonous regularity. I ignore him (again, it's always a boy) for now and hope that he will get bored, as I can't be bothered to try anything clever.

I have announced that they owe me 15 minutes at the end for being a nuisance, but they can win one minute back every time they find the word that I've just asked for. The words are getting easier, as I can't bear to spend much of lunch time with them. Especially not in this hell hole, which I know will become surrounded by a crowd of irritating kids as soon as the bell goes, banging on the walls constantly and shouting abuse.

The temporary classrooms are awful places. For a start, there's nothing much temporary about them. This one has been up for decades and is in an advanced state of decay. To make matters worse, because they are isolated from the main building, if it all goes wrong (let's face it, this is a strong possibility) you're on your own.

My quick dip into the Staff Room was to collect a bucket. I always take one out to these ghastly Portakabins, not, as you might think, to protect me against the rain but to combat an altogether more sinister menace: Ghosts and Waifs. They tend to gravitate to the temporary classrooms, drawn by the combination of isolation and cover that they offer. I fill my bucket three-quarters full from the sink in the corner of the room.

Since the lesson began, twenty minutes ago, I have been regularly snatching furtive glimpses out of the window to see if the forces of darkness are afoot. Suddenly, a stone hits the window – a sure sign that the Undead are nearby. It's best to keep the windows open, as it gets very hot and stuffy in here during the summer, but, ignoring the protests of the class, I lay my bait by closing all but that nearest to me. I know exactly what will happen next.

Suddenly, some toe-rag jumps up outside the window, knocking the handle so that the window slams shut with a loud crash. With a shriek of delight, he disappears. I casually re-open the window a touch wider and, less than a minute later, the same thing happens again. I re-open the window again but this time I pick up my bucket.

He's mine.

I am positioned carefully to one side of the window, just out of sight. The class are looking at me, but I motion them to keep quiet.

I hear the faint sound of running footsteps and seize the moment. With perfect timing, the bucket of water soaks the Ghost. I give him a cheerful wave and close the window, to protect our delicate ears from his obscene tirade.

Exam practice, only easier

MY MIND drifts back to the previous day, where I sank without trace shortly before lunch in this very room.

Exams are looming, now. I am covering for Miss Wade once again and, to my utter shame, I confess that we are again attempting to practise filling in that answer grid; but first, and even I cringe before I admit this, we're going to try it *without the questions to distract us*.

I get all the desks moved apart, with only a pencil on the top, just like in the real exam (glossing over the missing question sheets), and off we go.

Frowns of concentration as we decide between the four squares, each with a letter in it. Then, decision made, we carefully draw a horizontal line through the relevant box.

On to the next question. My stopwatch is running again and we almost make the three-minute point before the first hand rises.

'Yes?'

'What do we do when we've finished?'

'Don't worry about that, Wayne. You're only on question five and there are 50 to answer.'

God, I can barely keep a straight face when I say 'answer'.

After ten minutes, I can bear it no longer.

'Right, that's enough of that. Put your hand up if you cannot put a line through just one square?'

No hands up, good.

'Right, now that we've had a bit of practice, let's try it with the question paper!'

I quickly give everyone a question sheet and a new answer grid, trying to make the most of the sudden improvement.

'OK. We'll do 30 minutes, so you should be able to answer about 10 questions, but don't rush! Shut up, Lee. There is a clock on the wall and we will stop at ten-to.'

Wayne starts being a nuisance. This new idea of having actually to think about the answers doesn't go down well with everybody. He has taken Kelly's pencil case and is now kicking the chair in front of him. I move him to the front but he continues to be a pain. I eventually get sick of him.

'Come on Wayne, let's have a look at how much work you've done… Oh dear. Absolutely nothing.'

'But anyone can put lines through boxes, see!'

He scrawls a few lines, missing the boxes completely.

'I would have agreed with you, Wayne, before last lesson,' I murmur. 'Come on, let's go and see what's in the corridor.'

'I don't want…' But his coat and bag are already in mid-air, sailing out of the open door. I hold it open as he follows them, then close it behind him. Before I kick in the small metal wedge I always put under the door when I've chucked a kid out, I am treated to a couple of naughty words followed by a muffled threat: 'My dad's gonna batter you!'

This is a phrase I must have heard a hundred times during my career (OK, I struggle to say 'career' with a straight face). Often 'dad' (that is, the poor wretch the CSA caught) does turn up to school. They are usually runtish and simple and it always amazes me that the Head even gives them the time of day. It's probably in some code of conduct or something.

Struggling for motivation, I employ an imaginary hamster

IT'S JUNE, the exams start next week, and then it's all over, for me anyway.

I've not accepted any work after then and the holidays can't come soon enough; I've had enough of this. I need to make some changes in my life, or I'm going to go stark, staring mad.

Life at St Jude's is a life of recurring themes.

Today, covering again for Miss Keebles, who is already learning how to work the system, the theme, once again, is: The Wrong Work.

'But we did this last lesson!' is a plaintive cry I have heard so many times, always backed up by 'We did, Sir, look!' as an exercise book page filled with indecipherable scrawl and a crossed-out drawing of a spliff is thrust under my nose.

They may be telling the truth.

Miss Keebles has given up sending in any work for them to do. Now it falls to the Head of Department to set the lessons and it looks like it will not be long before she goes off, too.

The classroom is an absolute tip. Piles of exercise books are scattered everywhere. There are endless heaps of work done by different groups on A4 lined paper, all jumbled up. The mountain of notes, exercise books and labels on the teacher's desk has long since overflowed onto the floor. The cupboards where the kids' books are kept are all broken and even the text books are all mixed up.

It is utter chaos and I cannot make any sense of what they are supposed to be doing or where they are up to. Just working out which subject this is is difficult enough.

I am not looking forward to meeting Miss Keebles' Year 7 English group for two reasons. Firstly, their only mode of behaviour is screaming chaos and, secondly, it's the afternoon, which is always worse than the morning. However, I visited my friends the lab technicians at lunchtime in order to borrow two things which I believe will give me a fighting chance of getting a peaceful lesson.

On my desk, I have a shoe box, partly-filled with straw and with holes drilled in the lid. Next to it lies a small thermometer and a voltmeter. Outside the room, there's the usual, chaotic gaggle of kids. Disappointingly, I notice little Jenny is with two or three of the worst offenders. Her behaviour and work have deteriorated all year; I make a mental note to contact her parents and implore them to get her out of this school.

As I line them up, I explain about how we must keep silent in the classroom as the hamster is not well. I have to look after him, because I used to be a vet (taking care to keep a straight face). If we are very quiet indeed we might be able to have a look at him at the end of the lesson. They sit down like little angels and get on with their work quietly. Why, oh, why did I not think of bringing a furry friend to the lesson years ago?

From time to time, I very carefully poke the thermometer into the box to take poor Harvey's temperature, and then note it down carefully. A small sheet of graph paper, neatly Sellotaped to the side of the box, shows how it has varied today. Occasionally, I put the two leads from the voltmeter in to check his heartbeat. I explain in a hushed voice that we can't use a stethoscope because his heart is very small and I would not be able to hear it (lots of 'oohs' and 'aahs' and a fair few puzzled looks, too; they don't know what a stethoscope is, Chalk, you fool).

Unfortunately, because Chevaunne let us all down by shrieking (we all held our breath until I pronounced that Harvey had indeed survived the shock), we will not be able to see him this lesson, but I am a reasonable man and I may give them another chance when I have them next time.

Lots of nods.

At the end of the lesson, they all troop out saying a quiet goodbye to our little rodent, and I carry the box up the stairs back into the prep room and place it carefully on the bench along, with the 'heart monitor' and the little thermometer.

'You're such a plonker!' laughs Mrs Tomkins, the lab tech, throwing the box of straw into the bin.

'Oi! Save that! I'm going to use it again!' I reply.

But as the term, and the school year, draws to a close I know that I won't.

I really have had enough of this.

Chatting with Mrs Chalk

TEN YEARS is a long time in any job, these days.

It's not the 1930s and gold watches for 50 years' service any more, you know.

I've done my bit, I've put something back.

I can't take any more of Shazney, Coyne, Dwayne and Brett.

I can't take any more teachers off with stress, SMT initiatives and threats from parents.

I came into this job to teach kids how to add up and take away, and all I'm doing now is providing state-sponsored crowd control.

I'm not educating anyone, really. I'm not interesting any of the kids. I'm not achieving *anything* to be honest.

We crack open a bottle of Aussie Shiraz and I tell Mrs Chalk I've made up my mind. I'm out of teaching, reluctantly. I'm accepting no more supply jobs after the exams. I'm going to try my hand in the world of work outside the classroom. Maybe I'll be a raging success, maybe I'll be a crashing failure. Most likely, I'll be mediocre.

She puts her hand on my arm, supportively.

'Whatever you think,' she says.

I thank my lucky stars I married her, and not Dwayne's mum, say.

'What's the latest on Anthony from Year 10?' she asks.

'He got a conditional discharge from the juvenile court,' I say. 'He's actually bucked up his ideas since then, much to my surprise. Maybe he'll do OK.'

'Let's hope so,' she says, sipping her wine.

It's not my problem any more. Well, not directly. It is my problem, of course, but only in the same way as it's everyone's problem now.

Don't bring me problems, bring me solutions

I'VE BLATHERED on at length in this book about the problems education, and society in general, faces.

The tens, and perhaps hundreds, of thousands of parents who have absolved themselves of all responsibility for their child's behaviour, both in and outside of school.

The widespread disintegration in some sections of society of respect for oneself, for one's neighbours and for authority and law and order.

The desperate desire for material wealth and fame, with a concomitant collapse in the work ethic.

The rise in the reckless consumption of alcohol and drugs.

The destruction of the family, the foundation stone of our society (we all know that kids from decent backgrounds can rebel and turn out bad, too, but children from unstable backgrounds are far more likely to do so).

The cult of equality, which insists that children must be treated in an identical manner when common sense and all the evidence shows that this 'one size fits all' approach simply does not work.

The excuse culture: it wasn't me and, if it was, it isn't my fault.

These factors have had serious consequences for education.

Large numbers of children start school with no idea of how to behave in a civilised manner. They cannot sit still, cannot listen to instructions and cannot understand the concept of having to do what they are told.

Problems that were rare in the past, such as direct verbal and physical assaults on teachers, have become far more common. Parental support has dwindled; in days gone by, mothers and fathers were on the side of the school in a dispute with a child. Now, many of them – themselves the products of this twisted system – will themselves physically and verbally abuse teachers who try to discipline their children.

237

The refusal to follow instructions has become perfectly acceptable in many schools. Vandalism and graffiti have become commonplace. Simple things such as arriving for lessons on time, bringing a pen with you and doing your homework have become unimportant. As the status and respect that teachers once enjoyed has disappeared, many have simply lost confidence.

This lack of confidence has travelled up the chain and now infects the school's SMT, the LEA and government. Teachers are not supported. They are bombarded with initiatives, schemes, directives and action plans: most of this pointless paperwork simply acts to take them away from teaching (which itself can no longer be carried out properly, according to time-honoured and effective methods).

Finally, the range of children entering Comprehensive Schools has grown. Children who were once sent to Special Schools are now dumped into the Comprehensive system. (Sometimes this is at their parents' request, but partly due to the closing down of many Specialist Schools.) It is a simple fact that the larger the range of ability or behaviour the less the teacher is able to teach.

But these are the problems. It's no use just moaning about the difficulties we face in teaching; plenty of people do that already (just look at the Times Educational Supplement forums on the internet).

What about some solutions?

First, let's be positive; all problems can be solved with enough effort and 'resources'.

Firstly, let's get school taken seriously again. Parents (guardians, primary care-givers, call them what you like) should be made to sign a legally-binding contract with the school their offspring attends.

It would go something like this:

Parent: I will send my brat to school each day on time. I will make sure he does his homework. If my child is punished, I will accept the judgment of the school. I understand that the school cannot make a silk purse out of a sow's ear. (Or make an Einstein out of an Ashley).

School: We will educate the child as best we can.

Furthermore, let's have three main types of Secondary school: call them 'Academic Schools', 'Practical Schools' and 'Mixed Schools'.

(As you can see, I'm unlikely to get one of those jobs where you get £80,000 a year and a fat pension to sit round dreaming up new names for things).

In the academic schools, we would give the brightest third of the population the grounding to go on to University, where they would read proper subjects, properly taught. They would sit challenging exams that employers would respect – pretty much like kids once did, with the old-fashioned O and A Levels

In practical schools, we would teach the least academic third technical skills like car maintenance, plastering, electrics, plumbing and building, together with reading, writing and simple maths. These qualifications would be recognised as challenging and, therefore, of merit. That has to be better than wasting their time trying to teach them algebra, foreign languages and religion.

In 'mixed' schools, funnily enough, I think they should do a mixture of academic and practical stuff (this is certainly where I would have ended up).

Entry would be decided by an exam, or by allowing teachers to make the decision. Movement between the different types of schools would be allowed at the end of a year, but at the teachers' discretion and following testing and interviewing by the target school. Parents would have to respect the professional judgment of teachers in the same way that they do that of doctors.

There would be a small number of kids for whom none of the above would be suitable. Rather than pay someone vast amounts to think up new names for them, let's admit that they need special schools and send them there. These should be as challenging as possible, and they should mix with other kids as often as possible. I'm not advocating shutting handicapped people away; this is about giving them the best education possible, in an environment which is as relaxed and enjoyable as possible.

One thing I absolutely know: the present system of dumping them in a mainstream education system, which cannot cope with them, is crazy.

All four types of schools would need to become smaller as well. Kids in smaller schools feel more like individuals and the teachers can get to know everybody. In huge schools they just disappear.

Likewise, with large classes. The smaller the class, the more attention can be given per child. That's pretty obvious.

Discipline and basic human ethics would be taught in all four kinds of school. We all need to know where the boundaries are, because it is perfectly natural to push gently against them and see what happens. Nowadays these boundaries seem to have gone and we can push and push without ever finding a limit.

Additionally, kids should be required to do some community work so that they come to value society.

All children should have a report, which would start when the child begins school at five and would carry on until they leave the educational system.

All schools need a common set of rules, as discussed earlier. And let's abandon the ridiculous, behavioural psychobabble that has infected our schools and adopt one, simple, consistent approach that we can all understand: Obey The Rules Or Else. Children who break the rules must be punished. The unpleasantness of the punishment should match the severity of the crime; I would advocate such things as proper detentions, lines, copying out work or picking up litter.

Children who repeatedly break the rules should be expelled and educated in secure units, preferably underground.

Finally, teaching is arguably the most important profession we have (after all, we educate the scientists, doctors and policemen of tomorrow). Teachers literally hold the future of the population in their hands. It is a massive responsibility and it should only be given to the best, who can only be attracted with good salaries and working conditions. The training of teachers must be improved and trendy teaching methods dispensed with in favour of what really works.

We have to accept that all the above will cost lots of money. But how much does each uneducated petty criminal cost? How much does unemployment cost? What is the cost to the state of lost competitiveness in industry caused by an uneducated workforce?

And if these obvious savings aren't enough, let's sack a few experts and advisors or stick a couple of pence on income tax.

At least we will feel that it's doing some good, for once.

How would you feel if you were a number 5?

THE BIG day arrives. A hundred desks are perfectly laid out in rows and columns in the school hall.

The kids are waiting outside.

Now the months of preparation, study and hard work will be brought to bear.

Yeah, right. Back to reality, Chalk.

'What's that, Gordon? No, you don't need a dictionary, it's maths today.'

Oh, bloody hell, here we go.

Our school rules, like those of many schools, say that pupils must wear their proper uniform or they will not be allowed to sit the exam. Judging by the multicoloured throng in front of me, if we attempted to enforce this rule rigorously we would achieve a pass figure of zero. Not that we are realistically aiming much higher, I hasten to add.

'Right, come on in; coats and bags at the front, sit down and keep quiet. Yes, you do have to sit at the desk with your name on it, Bradley.'

'No, Tracey, you may not wear your coat for the exam. It is summertime and about 30 degrees in here.'

'No, Jade, you may not put yours on the back of your chair.'

Everyone sits down and the teachers go round the desks, giving out pencils and pens (why bother bringing one for your GCSE exam if you've never had to do so in the last twelve years?)

We also remove personal stereos ('Yes, I'm sure you do work better to the sounds of Gangsta rap, Keeley, but, nevertheless, your Walkman – OK, OK, your mp3 player – is staying at the front. No, don't worry, I'll tell Mr Rogers that he may not listen to it, either.')

Teachers at other schools – well, good ones, anyway – often complain of the tedium of exam cover. They should come here. It's non-stop entertainment.

There are five of us in the room; Mr Blunt is in charge and myself and Mr Duncan are giving out the exam papers.

Glancing at the cover, I briefly wonder why there are so many exam boards. It's funny, but nobody I've asked seems to know. It's just one of those things that is simply accepted when, in fact, it's quite bizarre. We have a national qualification – the GCSE – and yet not everybody faces the same question paper. It is widely known that some boards are easier than others for certain subjects, both at GCSE and A Level, which makes this even more unjust. Of course, we try our best to exploit the injustice in our favour: we change board every couple of years, in a desperate search for an ever easier syllabus. The incentive for the boards to make the papers easier, generating higher grades and more schools as customers, is clear. (Incidentally, while writing this book I spoke to a friend teaching a Modular GCSE [where the kids have an exam every few months in Years 10 and 11]. He sent one set of papers off to their exam board for marking and when they came back, he was rather surprised to see that every child bar one had scored 100%. His department knew perfectly well that this was impossible, but said nothing.) Why can't we just have one syllabus and one text book? It would save millions of pounds each year, which could be spent on more Gender Awareness Outreach Project Facilitators.

There is a sudden burst of laughter as Mr Duncan slips on the floor and steadies himself against a desk, blasting the pupil with his 100% proof breath.

Pongy Mr Rogers walks down the rows and, as he passes a desk, its occupant shifts away. The kids manage to do this quite impressively, in synchronisation, like some sort of Mexican wave, and I have to turn away as it is very funny to watch.

Mr Green is at the front, intently studying an exam paper. He looks absolutely fascinated by it and has already forgotten what he is supposed to be doing here.

Mr Blunt gives a quick briefing about exam rules, and off we go.

Almost immediately, a forest of hands reaches for the sky. There are enquiries about every possible topic, especially all the ones just covered 30 seconds ago in the briefing.

'How many questions do we have to answer?'

'The number that it says to answer on the front of the question paper, Sean.'

'How long do we have left?'

'There is a clock on the wall in front of you and the exam finishes at 10:30am, which is what Mr Jones has just written on the blackboard in large letters.'

'My pen's run out!'

'Here I am to the rescue, Dawn, with a new pen just for you. Yes, it is only a cheap Biro. No, you cannot go and borrow one off Miss Wade, she is teaching in her lab. I don't care if she always lets you borrow one. Look, just use that one OK?'

And so on, and so on.

Because most of the kids cannot even understand what the question says, let alone answer the damn thing, they soon start looking for more interesting diversions. Before long, the inevitable 'accidental' dropping of pencils, monkey noises, whistling and humming begins. There is more coughing going on than in a TB clinic.

'Yes, Liam, I will chuck you out if you kick the back of Cheryl's chair again. No, I know that you aren't bothered, just don't do it again.'

'No, Cheryl, you will not refer to Liam as a 'f*cking tw*t'. At least, not that loudly, please. Yes, I know he is, but get on with your exam. No, you aren't supposed to say *anything* – it's an exam. What do you mean, you can't do it? I know that, I've taught you for five years.'

In a school like ours, you have to drop your standards and then lower them some more until they are practically underground; the only alternative is insanity.

'I'm not going to tell Keeley off for chewing, Gordon, because at least she is getting on with the exam, which is more than can be said for you.'

Oh, actually, she's writing a letter. 'Keeley, get on with your exam!'

Up and down the rows of desks I wander, perfectly happy.

Occasionally, I give out another piece of A4 and pretend not to notice what is being drawn on it. I am being paid by the hour and this is an oasis of calm compared with what is going on in the rest of the school.

It's absolutely roasting, though, so I start to open a couple of windows as I pass them. Not spotting Mr Blunt's frantic gesturing, I open another and only realise my mistake when the wind blows half a dozen papers off desks and onto the floor.

Immediately there is pandemonium with kids scrabbling round on the floor snatching at any piece of paper.

Cries of 'Gerroff, that's mine!' and 'Give it us back, yer bastard!' fill the air, along with appeals to various staff to sort out the disappearance of Keeley's letter.

Mr Blunt gives me a furious look as we spend the next ten minutes trying to restore calm.

Glancing at the paper, I see once again how much exams have changed these days. For example.

Old Fashioned Question:

'What is 5x3?' (1 Mark)

Modern question:

'How would you feel if you were a number 5 and two new number 5s came to join you from somewhere else? Would you make friends with them, because they are the same as you, or would you feel that they were not as good as you because you had been here longer? Do you think other number 5s would treat them differently? Can you think of any similar situation in the world today?' (25 Marks).

The clock ticks around to the appointed moment and the kids are told to put down their pens. Only about three of them are still writing, so that doesn't confuse anyone.

Papers are collected in and they dash out, without being told to leave.

Off they go, then: some to McDonald's, some to the park with a bottle of vodka from Mr Koshushko's, others to an empty home on the Cherry Tree. A hurricane of ignorance has just been unleashed on the world.

Outside, the sun's behind clouds and rain clouds are gathering.

I walk across the playground to my car, mentally reviewing the day and thinking about the future.

A window opens on the top floor behind me and a kid shouts out: 'Oi, you!'

I glance back, to see a small face appearing, cherub like against the dirty red brick of St Jude's.

'F*ck off, Chalk, yer w*nker!'

He's ducked back inside now, and I can hear him chortling.

Off I go, to the welcoming arms of Mrs Chalk.

Never to return.

EPILOGUE

I HAVE left the world of education, and I'm not going back.

There was no dramatic tipping point; it was more like the coastal erosion the kids don't learn about in geography any more. The constant, low-level lapping of the waves, the rising tide of disillusionment, finally brought me to the realisation that I was wasting my time.

I am finished with spending my days dealing with kids who don't want to learn.

I've had enough of management incompetence, governmental interference and experts. The deep, deep feeling of frustration with the way our school is run (and education generally) have simply become too much for me.

So I'm off to concentrate on Chalk Enterprises. Somebody else can have my job as crowd controller – I'm afraid that's all that teaching is nowadays, in an ever-increasing number of schools.

I must add this, though: there are many superb children and young adults who are intelligent, articulate, honest and thoughtful of others. They will grow up to become equally good adults.

There are, obviously, many terrific parents who teach their children manners, honesty, and respect for others. They insist on good behaviour and are prepared to invest the huge amount of time and effort needed to bring up a child well. They encourage their child to read widely, to develop hobbies and to take an interest in those less fortunate.

There are many, many great teachers, whose abilities in the classroom put mine to shame (I won't be much missed, I'm afraid). Some spend time after school running revision classes or any number of activities. Others cheerfully give up weekends and holiday time to run Duke of Edinburgh Awards schemes and school trips. Many prop up weak departments, or work damned hard sorting out the mess that is left from long-term absences. They do all the above without extra pay, and even, often, without thanks, simply because they want to help the kids.

There are Senior Management Teams who do support their staff, regardless of any problems this might cause for their own advancement. They refuse to take the easy way out, of simply keeping a lid on things, pushing problems back down again and ignoring persistent offenders.

There are Heads who are not afraid to stand up to parents. There are Heads who will expel persistently naughty kids. There are those who bother to find out which teachers turn up every day for years without fail, who gives up her evening to come to school and watch the carol concert, who 'goes the extra mile' as the saying has it. They thank them and make them feel appreciated. These are Heads who are brave leaders, rather than time-servers and box-tickers.

There are school governors, too, who realise that their first duty should be to support the Staff, and there are LEAs who want to do the same.

The problem is that there simply aren't enough of all of these.

But insofar as I should attempt anything so grandiose as a dedication, this book is for those people.

Also from Monday Books

Generation F / Winston Smith

(ppbk, £8.99)

Youth worker Winston Smith - winner of
the Orwell Prize for his edgy, controversial
and passionate writing - opens a door on
the murky, tragic world of children's care
homes and supported housing schemes.
Frightening, revealing and sometimes very
funny, *Generation F* is his story.

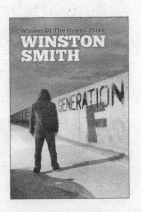

'**Winston Smith paints a terrifying picture**'
- *The Daily Mail*

'**What carried the day was his passion and conviction that
we should know what wrongs had been done in our names**'
- *Orwell Prize judges*

Sick Notes / Dr Tony Copperfield

(ppbk, £8.99)

Welcome to the bizarre world of Tony Copperfield, family doctor. He spends his days fending off anxious mums, elderly sex maniacs and hopeless hypochondriacs (with his eyes peeled for the odd serious symptom). The rest of his time is taken up sparring with colleagues, battling bureaucrats and banging his head against the brick walls of the NHS.

If you've ever wondered what your GP is really thinking - and what's actually going on behind the scenes at your surgery - *SICK NOTES* is for you.

'A wonderful book, funny and insightful in equal measure'
– Dr Phil Hammond (Private Eye's 'MD')

'Copperfield is simply fantastic, unbelievably funny and improbably wise... everything he writes is truer than fact'
– British Medical Journal

'Original, funny and an incredible read' *– The Sun*

Tony Copperfield is a Medical Journalist of the Year, has been shortlisted for UK Columnist of the Year many times and writes regularly for *The Times* and other media.

***Wasting Police Time* / PC David Copperfield** (ppbk, £7.99)

The fascinating, hilarious and best-selling inside story of the madness of modern policing. A serving officer - writing deep under cover - reveals everything the government wants hushed up about life on the beat.

'Very revealing' – *The Daily Telegraph*
'Passionate, important, interesting and genuinely revealing' – *The Sunday Times*
'Graphic, entertaining and sobering' – *The Observer*
'A huge hit... will make you laugh out loud'
– *The Daily Mail*
'Hilarious... should be compulsory reading for our political masters' – *The Mail on Sunday*
'More of a fiction than Dickens'
– *Tony McNulty MP, former Police Minister*
(On a BBC *Panorama* programme about PC Copperfield, McNulty was later forced to admit that this statement, made in the House of Commons, was itself inaccurate)

A Paramedic's Diary / Stuart Gray
(ppbk, £7.99)

STUART GRAY is a paramedic dealing with the worst life can throw at him. *A Paramedic's Diary* is his gripping, blow-by-blow account of a year on the streets – 12 rollercoaster months of enormous highs and tragic lows. One day he'll save a young mother's life as she gives birth, the next he might watch a young girl die on the tarmac in front of him after a hit-and-run. A gripping, entertaining and often amusing read by a talented new writer.

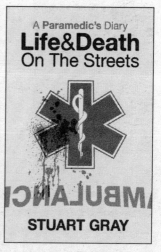

As heard on BBC Radio 4's Saturday Live and BBC Radio 5 Live's Donal McIntyre Show and Simon Mayo

In April 2010, Stuart Gray was named one of the country's 'best 40 bloggers' by *The Times*